An OPUS book

THE MEDIEVAL EXPANSION
OF EUROPE

THE
MEDIEVAL
EXPANSION
OF EUROPE

J. R. S. PHILLIPS

Oxford   New York

OXFORD UNIVERSITY PRESS

1988

Oxford University Press, Walton Street, Oxford OX2 6DP

Oxford New York Toronto
Delhi Bombay Calcutta Madras Karachi
Petaling Jaya Singapore Hong Kong Tokyo
Nairobi Dar es Salam Cape Town
Melbourne Auckland

and associated companies in
Berlin Ibadan

Oxford is a trade mark of Oxford University Press

© J. R. S. Phillips 1988

First published 1988 as an Oxford University Press paperback and
simultaneously in a hardback edition

British Library Cataloguing in Publication Data
Phillips, J. R. S.
The medieval expansion of Europe.——
(OPUS)
1. Geography, Medieval   2. Discoveries (in geography)——History
I. Title II. Series
910'.94 G89
ISBN 0–19–219232–9
ISBN 0–19–289123–5 Pbk

Library of Congress Cataloging in Publication Data
Phillips, J. R. S.
The medieval expansion of Europe.
(OPUS)
Bibliography: p.
Includes index.
1. Discoveries (in geography) I. Title.
II. Series.
G89.P48 1988 910'.9 87–31360
ISBN 0–19–219232–9
ISBN 0–19–289123–5 (pbk.)

Set by Colset Private Ltd,
Printed in Great Britain by
Biddles Ltd.
Guildford and King's Lynn

For Nuala

Preface

The term 'the expansion of Europe' has become familiar as a description of the period of western European overseas exploration, exploitation, and settlement which began in the fifteenth century, and has ended only with the extinction of the various European empires in the second half of the twentieth century. In the light of the enormous amount of popular and scholarly attention which has been given to the dramatic moments of this long period, such as the voyages of Columbus and Vasco da Gama, and the conquests by Cortés and Pizarro in Mexico and Peru, it may appear paradoxical to present a book with the title 'the medieval expansion of Europe', and concentrating on the period between about AD 1000 and 1500, as if these centuries are to be given equal importance with those that followed. Yet, with some qualification, this is what is being suggested.

This book has three separate but closely related objectives. First, it seeks to determine the extent and nature of the relations between western Europe and the three continents of Asia, Africa, and America between about 1000 and 1500. In the case of Asia the source material is abundant, and has been the subject of a great deal of scholarly study. The evidence for European knowledge of Africa and America is far less in quantity, and is frequently controversial and difficult to interpret. None the less it is often important and always interesting, and so repays closer examination. The second, and much more difficult, aim is to assess the degree to which new information gained about the outer world was absorbed into scholarly theory and popular conceptions. As will become apparent, there is no straightforward answer to this problem. Indeed, a great variety of ideas, which often owed more to classical Greek and Roman sources than to the fruits of contemporary discoveries, was in circulation in western Europe throughout this period. The final purpose is to discuss the relationship between the medieval expansion of Europe and the ideas about the world which were current in medieval

Europe, and the better known and more thoroughly documented expansion of Europe which took place in the fifteenth century. It will be argued that there was a very close relationship between these two periods, and that without the practical knowledge gained and recorded by medieval travellers, the techniques of ship design and navigation that had been developed by the beginning of the fifteenth century, and above all without many of the fantasies and false expectations which were an inherent part of European conceptions of the outer world, the discovery of the sea routes to America and India at the end of the fifteenth century would, both literally and metaphorically, have been inconceivable.

Some of the conclusions of this book will be controversial, and it is not expected that they will meet with general acceptance. On some occasions it has also been necessary to make a judgement on a difficult issue of fact or interpretation, and in these cases there will obviously be room for differences of opinion. The book has, however, been written in the belief that, with such exceptions as the exploits of Marco Polo or Giovanni di Piano Carpini, the extent of medieval European contacts with other continents was much greater and far more persistent than is generally realized, and also that the history of the fifteenth- and sixteenth-century expansion of Europe has usually been written with scant regard for its medieval antecedents. If some readers feel that in the process of redressing the balance too much emphasis has been given to those antecedents, it is hoped that this point will be remembered.

The Eurocentric view of the world which is present throughout this book has been adopted deliberately for the purpose of examining a particular set of problems, and is not meant to imply either that medieval, or indeed modern Europe, was the most important part of the world, or that in some sense the sole purpose of the existence of the rest of the world was to lie dormant until its turn came to be discovered. Two of the most striking features of the medieval expansion of Europe are the poverty of European understanding of what was discovered, and the minimal effect that Europeans had upon most of the regions of the world with which they had contact. Medieval Europe groped painfully towards a better comprehension of its neighbours, without ever making full use of the great stores of new information brought back by travellers, and without access to some of the best sources of knowledge such as the *Geography* of Claudius Ptolemy, or the *Book of Roger* by Idrisi. This was in sharp contrast with the Moslem world, which not only inherited the best of classical scholarship but then proceeded to add to it by scientific observation and travel. The opportunities for travel which were potentially available to Moslems are well illustrated in the fourteenth century by Ibn Battutah of Tangier, who visited India and China as Marco Polo and other Europeans had done, then crowned these achievements by crossing the Sahara to visit the African kingdom of Mali on the river Niger, a feat which no Christian European could hope to emulate. The fact that in 1498 Vasco da Gama completed his journey to India with the aid of Ibn Majid, who happened to be one of the leading Arab navigators of the day in the Indian Ocean, needs no further comment.

The navigational skills of the Chinese are nowhere better demonstrated than in the series of voyages in the Indian Ocean by large and well-equipped fleets of junks under the command of Cheng Ho which took place between 1405 and 1435. These reached as far afield as East Africa at a time when the Portuguese were painfully starting to explore the west coast of the continent, and were totally unknown in fifteenth-century Europe. The Chinese were far better equipped than Portugal or any other European nation to undertake a policy of overseas expansion, and yet, for reasons which need not be discussed here, they chose not to continue. Conversely, the European travellers who went to China in the thirteenth and fourteenth centuries were few in number. So far as can now be known, the merchants and missionaries came and departed, leaving hardly a ripple behind them. However, the Europeans who saw China in the thirteenth and fourteenth centuries were deeply impressed by the technical skills and the complexity of Chinese society. Even when it was again closed to foreigners after the fall of the Mongol ruling dynasty in 1368, Cathay remained a vivid memory in Europe, and helped to inspire the ambitions of fifteenth-century European explorers to an extent far beyond the economic value of any past trade between East and West.

The bibliography can provide only a general indication of the enormous and constantly growing literature on medieval European relations with the outside world. While it has been possible to introduce some revisions at an advanced stage of writing to take account of recently published work, such as Professor Bernard Hamilton's important paper on the origins of the *Letter of Prester John*, 'Prester John and the Three Kings of Cologne', in *Studies in Medieval History presented to R.H.C. Davis* (London, 1985), other publications are too new to be more than noted. The representation of medieval European geographical ideas and perspectives in the form of maps can now be studied in volume 1 of *The History of Cartography: Cartography in Prehistoric, Ancient and Medieval Europe and the Mediterranean*, eds. J.B. Harley and David Woodward (Chicago & London, 1987). It is to be hoped that volume 3 of this very important series, *Cartography in the Age of Renaissance and Discovery*, will not be long delayed. When I was writing Chapter 9 it seemed inappropriate to give detailed attention to the Vinland Map because of the strength of the scholarly and the scientific evidence that it is a twentieth-century forgery. The debate will no doubt continue, but the scientific arguments will certainly have to be reconsidered in the light of the recently published findings of a team of scientists and scholars at the University of California at Davis: T.A. Cahill, R.N. Schwab, B.H. Kusko, R.A. Eldred, G. Moller, D. Dutschke, and D.L. Wick, 'The Vinland Map revisited: new compositional evidence on its inks and parchment', *Analytical Chemistry*, 1987. (I should like to thank Professor Donald Logan for drawing this paper to my attention.) The history of the crusades is another area in which important new work is appearing. The forthcoming second edition of Professor Hans Eberhard Mayer's *The Crusades* (Oxford, 1988) and Professor Jonathan Riley-Smith's new book, *The Crusades* (London, 1987) should now be added to the bibliography.

I have incurred many debts in writing this book, but I should mention particularly my former colleague, the late Denis Bethell. The book may be added to the already long list of works inspired by him or influenced by the wide range of his knowledge and enthusiasm. My students at University College Dublin have also contributed more than they realize through their own enthusiasm and searching questions. For the errors that remain I must take full responsibility.

National Humanities Center   J.R.S. Phillips
North Carolina
December 1987

Contents

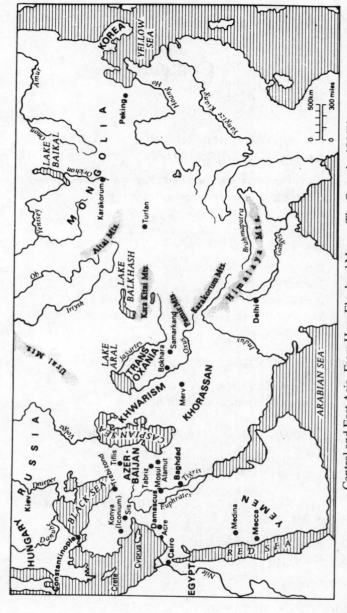

Central and East Asia. From Hans Eberhard Mayer, *The Crusades* (OUP).

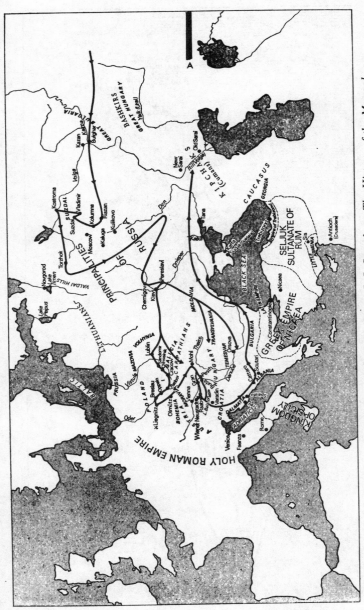

The Mongol invasion of Europe 1237–42. From J. J. Saunders, *The History of the Mongol Conquests* (Routledge & Kegan Paul).

Southern Syria and Palestine. From Hans Eberhard Mayer,
The Crusades (OUP).

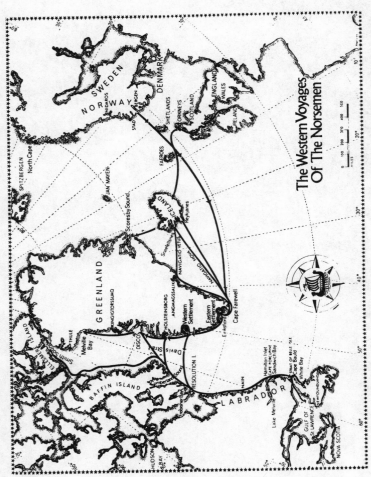

The Western Voyages of the Norsemen. From Gwyn Jones, *The Norse Atlantic Saga* (OUP).

I

The beginnings of the
medieval expansion of Europe

1

Classical discoveries and Dark Age transformations

By the middle of the second century A D the civilization which had grown up around the shores of the Mediterranean had reached the peak of its achievement and confidence. Under the rule of a series of highly competent emperors its most recent political expression, the Roman empire, had reached its maximum extent, stretching from the Atlantic Ocean to the Persian Gulf, and from the forests of Germany to the edge of the Sahara, and to contemporaries its demise must have seemed inconceivable. Contacts also existed with regions far beyond these administrative and military boundaries. Since the discovery of the monsoon winds by the Greek merchant Hippalus in the first century A D, trading voyages in the Red Sea and Indian Ocean had become commonplace. Roman merchants sold their wares from permanent trading stations like the one at Arikamedu on the Bay of Bengal, and Roman products and occasionally even Roman subjects could be found as far afield as South-East Asia and China. The east coast of Africa was known as far south as modern Zanzibar and Dar-es-Salaam. Carthaginian sailors are thought by some to have travelled down the west coast to the vicinity of Sierra Leone as early as 500 BC and attempts to circumnavigate the continent may even have been made, but in Roman times the limit of knowledge of the Atlantic margin of the continent was set at the Canary archipelago. In Europe the Romans had commercial relations with unconquered Germany and Scandinavia, with the far north of Britain beyond Hadrian's Wall, and also with Ireland.

For the ordinary inhabitant of this world the area of his conscious knowledge was much more circumscribed, but over the previous millennium intrepid travellers like Pytheas of

Marseilles, who made the first known circumnavigation of Britain in about 300 BC, or military adventurers such as Xenophon in Persia around 400 BC, and Alexander the Great in central Asia and India nearly a century later, as well as a host of unnamed merchants and mercenaries, had added piecemeal to the store of knowledge. This slow accumulation of information was enshrined in the descriptive and theoretical works of geographers, most of them Greek, of whom the last and certainly the greatest was a writer of the second century AD, Claudius Ptolemy of Alexandria, the author of two treatises, one on astronomy and the other on geography, which contained ideas of permanent importance for European civilization.

Since the time of Pythagoras in the sixth century BC it had gradually become accepted that the earth was a sphere, and his successors had supplied ingenious methods of demonstrating this by empirical observation. In turn this implied that the circumference of the earth could be measured, and in the fourth century BC Aristotle recorded a figure of 400,000 Greek stadia, later refined by Eratosthenes (276–196 BC), the head of the famous Ptolemaic library at Alexandria, who obtained a result of 250,000 stadia, only about one-seventh in excess of the true figure of 25,000 miles. Pythagoras had probably also been responsible for the concept by which the surface of the earth was divided into five distinct zones: a central zone on either side of the equator which was considered to be both uninhabitable and impassable on account of the intense heat; two temperate zones constituting the habitable areas of the globe; and two polar zones which were deserted because of cold. The division of the circumference of the earth into 60 degrees by Eratosthenes, afterwards modified to the still familar 360 degrees by Hipparchus (*fl. c.*162–125 BC), made it theoretically possible to calculate co-ordinates of latitude and longitude for individual places. Six of the eight books comprising Ptolemy's *Geography* contained this type of information, although it is uncertain whether it was he or some later scholar who took the logical next step of transforming the gazetteer into the series of maps which are still associated with Ptolemy's name.

The conclusions reached by Ptolemy and his predecessors suffered from a number of serious limitations. Very few of the calculations in Ptolemy's gazetteer were the product of direct observation: instead he depended on the often very vague information obtained from other geographers or from the reports of travellers, so that errors were probable even in well-known regions of the world. The Mediterranean, for example, was made to extend over 62 degrees of longitude, 20 degrees more than the reality, while Ptolemy's prime meridian, his equivalent of the modern Greenwich line, passed through both Cape St Vincent in Spain and the Canary Islands, which are in fact about 9 degrees of longitude apart. Ptolemy was aware of the deficiencies in his work, which derived from the near impossibility of making accurate measurements of distance and time. The problem of calculating longitude was not finally solved until the eighteenth century, when timekeepers sufficiently reliable for use in navigation first became available. Some of the errors of classical geography, such as the tendency to overestimate greatly the size of the island of Taprobane or Ceylon, were not peculiar to Ptolemy, but he added a few of his own which were to be of considerable importance to the sailors and scholars of Renaissance Europe. While retaining the traditional belief that the length of the land mass of the world was approximately twice its breadth, he greatly exaggerated its size by assuming the existence of large areas of unknown territory to the east and north. He also departed from the conclusion of Eratosthenes by accepting the much smaller figure of 180,000 stadia for the circumference of the earth which had been calculated by Posidonius (fl. 135–51 BC). This double error contributed to the belief of a much later generation that a sea voyage from the extreme west of Europe to the east coast of Asia would be shorter and more feasible than was actually the case. Ptolemy set another problem for the future when he contradicted the beliefs of earlier geographers and sailors by assuming that the southern part of Africa merged with a land mass which surrounded the Indian Ocean, thereby creating what amounted to a second Mediterranean Sea on a vastly greater scale, and, if correct, ruling out absolutely any circumnavigation of Africa.

All classical writers, however, accepted the existence of three continents, Europe, Asia, and Africa. Some considered that these were encompassed by a world ocean, but for all of them their world was centred securely on the shores of the Mediterranean, and Europe, the smallest of the three continents, was known in far more detail than the other two. Beyond what was certainly known lay other lands which were the subject of hearsay and rumour, such as the Ultima Thule of Pytheas in the far north, which may have been Iceland, or the territory to the south of the great wastes of the Sahara, or the land of the Seres in the furthest east from which silk came. Of knowledge of anything more remote, of an American continent for instance, there is not a hint, while the antipodes beyond the impassable equatorial zone existed only as a scholarly paradox.

For all their limitations, the achievements of geographical science by Ptolemy's day were still impressive when compared with what followed. During the third century AD the Roman empire, which had supplied security for men of learning as well as opportunities for travel, suffered a political and military crisis which almost brought it down. The division of the empire for administrative convenience into a western portion, based on Rome, and an eastern, based on the new capital of Constantinople, gradually led to a separation of interests and deprived the vulnerable western provinces of ready access to eastern resources for defence against outside attack. There was also a growing economic imbalance within the empire as the cities of the east prospered on the luxury trade of Asia, while those of the west declined in importance, the populations becoming increasingly concentrated in a pauperized countryside. The settlement within the empire of barbarian peoples from beyond the Rhine and the Danube, and their employment in the Roman army, blurred the distinction between Rome and the outside world, and prepared the way for the large-scale barbarian incursions of the fifth century, and for the subsequent collapse of the western Roman empire.

In the west Rome was succeeded by a collection of kingdoms and principalities, some of which, like Britain in the fifth century, were almost closed worlds in themselves. The narrowing of political horizons affected even highly educated men, such as the sixth-century historian and bishop Gregory of Tours, who was chiefly concerned with events in his own province of Gaul, and knew little or nothing about developments in the surviving eastern part of the Roman empire. In the eighth century the Anglo-Saxon scholar Bede, fully aware that he was living on the fringes of the known world in his own time, widely read in the classics, and taking great pains to verify and to add to his data from reliable sources, none the less never left his homeland of Northumbria.

Geographical learning in the former western provinces of the Roman empire was not affected simply by military and administrative collapse, and the consequent difficulties for the scholar or would-be traveller. Other more subtle factors had been at work even while the late classical world was still in being. Understanding of the Greek language, which had been the vehicle of most earlier scholarship, was in decline throughout the western empire during the fourth and fifth centuries. A scholar of the calibre of Augustine of Hippo never fully mastered it, and Jerome did not learn Greek until he went to live in the east. Translations of Greek works into Latin were common but not sufficient to make up for the loss of the original language. This meant, for example, that although the works of Ptolemy were known to the Roman historian Ammianus Marcellinus in the fourth century, and were recommended for study by Cassiodorus in the sixth, they did not form part of the mainstream of late antique learning, and were not passed on to western European scholars of the early medieval period. The loss of Greek was doubly important because it coincided with a tendency to rely on much inferior Latin authors, such as the first-century Pliny the Elder, and the third-century Solinus, and to use them in turn to produce abbreviated versions of the classics for a public which lacked both the linguistic skills and the willingness to read their Greek rivals in the original. These processes were already far advanced in the fifth century, when Martianus Capella produced his summary of all that the conventionally educated person needed to know about the seven liberal arts. Geography, lacking an independent status, was treated only under the heading of geometry, and suffered accordingly. Martianus was at least aware of the ideas of Ptolemy, but he did not regard him as a greater authority than other writers, and was ready to assert that his own knowledge of the world was every bit as great. The result was the revival of older notions, such as the supposed connection between the Caspian Sea and the northern ocean, and the location of the source of the Nile somewhere in West Africa, both of which Ptolemy had expressly contradicted in favour of the true descriptions.

Even more serious was Martianus' preservation of fabulous material of the kind related by Solinus, whose *Collectanea Rerum Memorabilium* won him the nickname 'Polyhistor' for the multitude of his tales, such as his accounts of Calabrian snakes which sucked milk direct from the cow, of men who could turn themselves into wolves, or of others who covered themselves with their ears while asleep. Both authors were themselves drawing on already ancient traditions going as far back as the Greek writer Ctesias in the fifth century BC, who was the source of many of the wonders associated with India, and both were to be widely read by later generations, along with the works of other writers like Pliny, or the anonymous author of the *Physiologus*, a collection of animal stories of about AD 200, or the fourth-century Pseudo-Callisthenes of Alexandria. From these in turn derived many of the strange expectations about the wider world which were to be so beloved of medieval Europeans. Just as important, the growing mystification surrounding geographical knowledge meant that, in the absence of any opportunity to verify accounts of the world at first hand, it was exceedingly difficult even for a scholar of great determination and curiosity to discriminate between them.

The appearance of Christianity as a widespread influence in the Roman empire was another factor contributing to the decline of classical learning. Some Christian intellectuals, like Tertullian in the early third century, Lactantius in the fourth, or Pope Gregory the Great in the sixth, saw the classics as a source of great danger for Christians, while others, like Augustine and Jerome in the late fourth and early fifth centuries, felt that they should be studied only as an intellectual exercise, and not as an end in themselves. An alternative approach was that of Augustine's master St Ambrose, who argued that 'to consider the nature and position of the earth does not help us in our hope of the life to come'. In the same century St Basil the Great remarked that if the Bible had nothing to say on a subject such as the shape of the earth, then a Christian was not bound to consider it either, a view shared by Cassiodorus two centuries later. Yet Ambrose, Basil, and men like them were not cultural Philistines. Christian writers of the fourth and fifth centuries were fully occupied in the task of presenting Christian doctrine to a world in which Christianity had only recently become the dominant faith, in countering the teachings of heretics, or in justifying Christianity to the remaining pagans who held it partly responsible for the disasters which were then befalling the empire.

None the less Christianity did make a contribution to the general store of notions which were available to the people of medieval Europe. Many of these arose naturally out of the central importance of the Holy Land in the history of Christianity, and out of the practice of pilgrimage which was stimulated, if not largely created, by the discovery at Jerusalem in AD 326 of the relics of the True Cross by the mother of Constantine, the first Christian emperor. The pillar of salt into which Lot's wife had been turned, and of which only the alleged site remained when Egeria, one of the early pilgrims, passed that way in the 380s, had been restored to existence a couple of centuries later. The pious believer could also be shown the very couch used by Christ at the wedding feast at Cana, and perhaps (like Antoninus of Placentia in about 570) be moved to carve his own or his parents' names upon it. Like the Welsh saints, David and Cadoc, who are both said to have visited Jerusalem in the sixth century, he might even hope for the gift of tongues to aid him on the journey. The idea that Jerusalem was at the centre of the world, which appears in some world maps of the twelfth century when the recent experience of the early crusades had made it topical, can be traced back to the account of the travels of the seventh-century Frankish pilgrim Arculf. Another peculiarity of Christian geography, this time resulting from the universal proselytizing mission of Christianity, was the portrayal, in a series of maps dating from the tenth to the thirteenth centuries, of the twelve apostles, each in the corner of the world in which he was supposed to have preached.

In the person of the sixth-century monk Cosmas, who was ironically a native of Ptolemy's home city of Alexandria, the new Christian culture threw up a thoroughgoing critique and complete rejection of classical geographical theories. Cosmas created in his *Christian Topography* a systematic world-view based chiefly on Biblical evidence and his own personal vision, but possibly also drawing on ideas from the fourth-century writer Theodore of Mopsuestia. The earth was depicted as an oblong rather than a sphere, with the heavens consisting of a vaulted canopy supported on walls enclosing the boundaries of the earth; the inhabited land was surrounded by water beyond which there was another earth in which Paradise was located, and which also encompassed the ocean. The extremities of this second earth, from which Noah had allegedly come at the time of the Flood, were connected to the extremities of heaven, while the rising and setting of the sun, which Cosmas claimed was much smaller than the earth, were achieved by its regular passage behind a large hill at the northern end of the world.

Another oddity is the work known as the *Cosmography*, which purports to be a translation of an earlier account of the travels of a certain Aethicus Ister who witnessed a great many marvels, including Amazons, dragons, ants as large and fierce as dogs, and an island peopled by dog-headed men; he failed to find Noah's Ark on the summit of Mount Ararat, or the Garden of Eden, but made up for this by circumnavigating the world via the encircling ocean. The *Cosmography* was a work of fiction, drawing on information in earlier writers and on the author's own vivid imagination, in much the same way as *Mandeville's Travels* in the fourteenth century. To judge from the number of surviving manuscripts of the ninth and tenth centuries it was well known in its day, and added yet more fantasies to the European imagination.

It was formerly thought that the *Cosmography* was written in the seventh century, possibly in Merovingian Gaul, but it has also been argued that it originated in Bavaria in the late eighth century, and that the name of its author, Aethicus Ister, or more properly Pseudo-Aethicus, conceals the identity of an Irish missionary named Ferghil or Virgil who was bishop of Salzburg.

This identification is hotly disputed, but Virgil of Salzburg is of interest in another connection, since he fell out with the English missionary St Boniface over the teaching of an unorthodox geographical doctrine which seems to have consisted of the belief that an entirely separate world existed beneath the known one, with its own inhabitants and its own sun and moon. Ireland was indeed prolific in original and fantastic views of the world, and developed a form of voyage literature known as the *imram* which incorporated pagan elements of a land of Elysium located in the west, as well as the Old Testament and Christian notion of a promised land which could be reached only by those of sufficient faith. There are many examples of such travels in Irish literature, such as the *Voyage of Mael Duin*, but the best-known is centred on the career of the sixth-century St Brendan, abbot of Clonfert, who was credited in the ninth-century *Vita Brendani* and the somewhat later *Navigatio Brendani* with voyaging in the western ocean from island to island, each more remarkable than the last. His supposed discoveries were to be of more than literary importance, since in the fourteenth and fifteenth centuries they had a considerable influence on the motivations and expectations of early European explorers of the Atlantic.

It should not, however, be thought that Christian writers in general indulged in eccentricity and fantasy, or that they were necessarily hostile or indifferent to the ideas of the classical past. The theories of Cosmas in relation to the motion of the sun were apparently adopted by a seventh-century writer known only as the Ravenna Geographer, but otherwise his work was little known, and in the ninth century the patriarch Photius of Constantinople dismissed him as an author of fables. Similarly, the representation of the world as divided up among the twelve apostles derived from a map which accompanied a commentary on the *Apocalypse* written by the Spanish monk Beatus in about 776, and was intended to provide a symbolic illustration of the spread of Christianity rather than a literal description of the world. It is also worth stressing that many of the marvels and fantastic tales which passed into the medieval European consciousness were ultimately of pagan classical origin. One such story, the famous legend ascribing the absence of snakes from Ireland to a curse placed upon them by St Patrick, can be traced back at least to Solinus in the third century. The use of allegory or deliberate fictional composition by Christian writers is another possibility to be borne in mind by the modern reader, who may otherwise misunderstand their purpose and significance.

The greater part of post-classical geographical writing was closely related to that of the past, despite the lack of any direct knowledge of Ptolemy's works, and the difficulties which certain classical theories created for Christians in an age which was very much aware of the dangers of heresy. The antipodes, for instance, gave concern to men of such differing outlook as Augustine and Cosmas because some classical authors had suggested that they might be inhabited, even though their supposed inaccessibility meant that no one could ever put this theory to the test. For Augustine, acceptance of the idea implied that mankind would have been created twice; it would also have denied the single incarnation of Christ, and was theologically unacceptable. For his part Cosmas argued that since the Gospel was preached to the whole world, and there was no evidence that it was taken to the people of the antipodes, these were therefore uninhabited, and indeed could not exist. Belief in the existence of the antipodes was never formally condemned by the Church, and it was not, as is sometimes stated, the cause of the dispute between St Boniface and Virgil of Salzburg, whose ideas seem more reminiscent of those of Cosmas. Instead the antipodes survived, usually without inhabitants, as a fascinating, if slightly dangerous, topic in geographical writings throughout the medieval period.

One of the post-classical geographers most widely known to later generations was the seventh-century Isidore of Seville, who made extensive use of his pagan predecessors Pliny and Solinus, as well as of the great fifth-century writer Orosius, whose *Historia adversus Paganos* had been an attempt to justify Christianity. Isidore is the closest one can get to a representative early medieval geographer, and many already familiar ideas appear in the two books he devoted to geography out of the twenty volumes of his *Etymologies*, in which he set out to encompass all human knowledge. The traditional three continents of Europe, Africa, and Asia were outlined, as was the division of the world into zones of heat and cold, and the antipodes were described as lying beyond the equator. At first sight it appears that Isidore also accepted the concept of a spherical earth. The pagan writers, Pliny, Macrobius, and Martianus Capella, all of whom Isidore used, made clear reference to the idea; Isidore even quoted the figure which Macrobius had given for the circumference of the earth. On the other hand, it is not at all certain that Isidore fully understood what he read in his sources. Although he described the heavens as a sphere in which the sun and moon revolved, his reference to the zones of climate as circles upon the surface of the earth seems to imply that he thought of the world as a flat disc rather than a sphere. He is therefore an ambiguous and unreliable authority on this important point, but his voice was to be heard down the centuries in the works of other scholars such as the ninth-century encyclopaedist Rabanus Maurus, archbishop of Mainz, who followed Isidore with only some refinements of scriptural quotation.

Fortunately the problem does not have to be abandoned on such an unsatisfactory note, since in the eighth century Bede referred to the spherical shape of the earth in a way that shows that he clearly understood what he was saying. He noted the differences in the length of day and night at various points on the earth's surface, as well as the fact that the constellations of stars visible from the northern hemisphere would not be visible from the southern; he even made allowance for irregularities in the shape of the earth caused by mountain ranges. Bede's writings were well known to later generations, so that it is reasonable to conclude that his accounts of sound geographical theories were available to those who were interested and capable of profiting from them. Since medieval scholars also had access to the works of classical writers such as Macrobius and Martianus Capella, and, from the early twelfth century, to works produced in Moslem Spain and Sicily, there is plenty of evidence to show that the true shape of the earth could still be known and understood.

The hallmarks of Bede's work were perhaps clarity of exposition and intellectual curiosity rather than any great originality, but in an age when the opportunities for gathering new information and criticizing that of the past were necessarily limited, these were qualities of great value. None the less there were some signs of a change in the intellectual climate. Bede himself made some interesting remarks about the variations in tides according to geographical location which may be the result of his own observations, and which again show that he understood the implications of the earth's shape. A century later, in about 825, the Irish scholar Dicuil wrote a treatise entitled *De Mensura Orbis Terrae* while he was at the court of the emperor Louis the Pious. In the time-honoured fashion he quoted the leading authorities of the past in order until he came to the subject of the mysterious island of Thule which, since classical times, had been regarded as the northernmost limit of the known world. Having referred to the descriptions of Thule given by Pliny, Solinus, Priscian, and Isidore, he then refuted their statements that Thule was surrounded by ice, and that permanent day and night alternated for six months each in the year, on the basis of first-hand information from a number of clerics who had been to the island thirty years earlier. These visitors had discovered that the ice began one day's sail to the north of Thule, and that at the summer solstice the sun disappeared only briefly, leaving a twilight sufficient for them to pick the lice from their shirts. Dicuil's testimony shows both that a critical faculty could exist alongside the most traditional of information, and also that, despite the confusion which had overtaken the western part of the Roman world since the fifth century, contact between widely separated areas was still possible.

In the remainder of the empire more of the classical patterns of travel were maintained. Direct trading links between the eastern empire and India were disrupted by the rise of Sassanian Persia and the Ethiopian kingdom of Axum, but a few individual travellers still got through. One of these was the fantasy geographer Cosmas whose earlier career as a merchant had won him the nickname of 'Indicopleustes', or 'the India traveller', which is perhaps also an indication that such journeys were becoming a rarity by the sixth century. In 552 the eggs of the silkworm were smuggled from China to Constantinople by two monks, and provided the foundation of one of the most important features of the Byzantine imperial economy. In about 628 the Egyptian writer

Theophylact Simocatta was able to produce an accurate account of China, and on four occasions between 643 and 719 Byzantine envoys were sent there to seek assistance against the conquering Arabs. Christian missions were also active, reaching India in the first century A D. Christians were noted on the Malabar coast and in Ceylon by Cosmas in the sixth century, and by the early seventh century at the latest Christianity had become established in the empire of China. In 543 the Byzantine emperor Justinian sent missionaries to Nubia where they founded a church which lasted until the fourteenth century, while farther south, in Ethiopia, Christianity has survived down to the present day. Moslem expansion in the seventh and eighth centuries severed most direct communications with the Christian communities in Africa and Asia, and so far as western Europeans were concerned their very existence was almost totally unknown until the widespread distribution of Christians in Asia in particular was discovered with some surprise by western travellers of the thirteenth and fourteenth centuries.

No western Europeans went as far afield as their Byzantine counterparts during the centuries of disruption, but some contacts did occur. Discoveries of Mediterranean pottery types on sixth-century sites of the darkest period of British history suggest that some trading connections were preserved, as does the apparent voyage of Byzantine ships early in the seventh century in search of British tin. The missions to England of St Augustine in 597, and in the seventh century of Theodore and Hadrian, the one from Tarsus in Asia Minor and the other from North Africa, again show that the world was not entirely dislocated. Pilgrim travel to the east continued even after the Arabs conquered the Holy Land in the 630s. Seventh-century visitors to Jerusalem included the Frankish pilgrim Arculf mentioned earlier, Vulphy of Rue in Picardy, and the Burgundians, Bercaire and Waimar. Between 722 and 729 the Anglo-Saxon missionary Willibald, a member of the royal house of Wessex and later bishop of Eichstadt in Germany, made the return journey from Rome to Jerusalem, and by the time of the emperor Charlemagne the number of pilgrims and increased sufficiently for him to seek permission from the Caliph Harun-al-Rashid for the establishment of a hostel to accommodate them in the city. Arculf's pilgrimage was to become especially well known in medieval Europe because of the strange chance that on his return in about 680 his ship was blown off course to the remote Scottish island of Iona, where he told his experiences to Adamnan, abbot of the famous Irish monastery there. In 701 Adamnan's account was given to King Aldfrith of Northumbria, and was later read by Bede who incorporated summaries of it in two of his own works, thereby ensuring its fame.

The Irish contributions to some of the more extravagant geographical notions have already been noted, but Adamnan on his lonely island is also an apt reminder of the contribution made by Ireland to the preparatory phases of the medieval expansion of Europe. The conversion of Ireland, begun in the fifth century by Palladius and Patrick, added to the spiritual empire of Rome a province that had been only dimly known to its secular predecessor, and in their turn Irish missionaries like Columba, the founder of Iona, and Columbanus, spread through Britain, Gaul, Germany, and Italy. But from the viewpoint of geographical discovery the real Irish achievement either lies concealed under the allegorical writing of the *imrama* or is preserved in the more sober prose of Dicuil. There is no proof of the skilfully presented and plausible modern assertions that St Brendan crossed the Atlantic to America, but it is certainly true that Irish monks sailed to many of the islands around the British Isles in search of solitude, while the evidence of Dicuil together with that from Scandinavian sources strongly suggests that Irish hermits, perhaps even as early as Brendan himself, had been in Iceland before the arrival of the Vikings in the middle of the ninth century.

Of all the activities of western European travellers during the so-called Dark Ages, the Scandinavian expansion which began at the end of the eighth century was to be the most extensive. The occupation of Iceland in the ninth and tenth centuries, the discovery of Greenland at the end of the tenth century, and of North America a few years later around the year 1000, and the creation of a network of international trade routes was a series of achievements of epic proportions, and must form an important part of any account of the medieval expansion of Europe. But these achievements are best examined separately (see chapters 2 and 9), since the Vikings operated either on the fringes of or far beyond Europe, and many of their exploits, especially those in the Atlantic, were scarcely known outside their own ranks, and had correspondingly little influence on Europe as a whole. To the Christian peoples of Europe and their rulers the Vikings were at first pagan intruders and plunderers rather than an integral part of their world. Alfred the Great of Wessex might find it of interest to include details of the recent voyage by the Norwegian Ohthere around the North Cape of Norway and into the White Sea when he was making his translation of Orosius, but taken as a whole the explorations of the Vikings were a prelude to the expansion of Europe, a demonstration of what might be possible, and not the first stage of that expansion. Other and more fundamental developments within western Europe were required before any general and sustained expansion could occur.

2
Europe in the eleventh century

There is sufficient evidence to show that knowledge of the most important classical geographical theories survived into the early medieval period, and that some Europeans continued to travel, especially as pilgrims and missionaries, and succeeded even in making some fresh discoveries. But it must also be emphasized that the evidence for these conclusions is variable both in quality and quantity, and is widely distributed both in location and time. A single pilgrim traveller of the seventh century does not prove any general awareness of the wider world on the part of his European contemporaries; nor does the existence of a perceptive and careful scholar such as Bede imply that similar perceptiveness and care were necessarily features of contemporary or later scholarship. The view of the world which was possessed by medieval Europeans, even educated ones, was a jumble of theories and information, some of it accurate but also containing a great deal of error and pure fantasy, a confusion which was perpetuated in part by the lack of opportunity for gaining experience of the world at first hand. The population of western Europe lived in an essentially local environment in which agriculture, which was the concern of the great majority of the people, was devoted to subsistence or to satisfying the needs of a very limited market, and in which 'the visitations of trade tended to be as unexpected as famines, plagues and invasions'. In many respects the subjects of Rome had lived similarly restricted lives, but they had also been conscious of somehow belonging to a much greater entity. For their descendants in the west the empire was no more, and Europe was merely a geographical expression with little political or emotional content.

In contrast, the surviving portion of the Roman empire in the east retained much of its cosmopolitan nature even after the loss of its Syrian, Egyptian, and North African provinces in the seventh century. It still had control of Asia Minor and the Balkans, and as late as the eleventh century continued to govern territory in the Italian peninsula, while the activity of missionaries extended its cultural influence to the peoples of Moravia, Bulgaria, and Russia. At its lowest ebb the Byzantine empire never lost its assurance of being a direct continuation of the Latin empire of Rome; neither did it abandon classical Greek culture, despite its own fundamentally Christian character.

If the contrast between western Europe and the eastern empire was sharp, that with the Moslem world, which had incorporated lands where Greek learning was still flourishing, and had translated much of this inheritance into Arabic, was even more marked. Arabic editions of many Greek scientific writings were made in the eighth and ninth centuries, including those of such key figures as Aristotle, Euclid, Galen, and Hippocrates, and also of Ptolemy. Ptolemy's treatise on astronomy, commonly known to the Arabs as *Almagest* or 'the greatest', and his *Geography* both became a staple part of Moslem knowledge, and were translated and commented upon many times at a period when they were both unknown in the west. The great extent of the Arab dominions, from Spain to Central Asia, and the even greater extent of their trading connections with eastern Asia, with east Africa as far south as Zanzibar and Madagascar, and with trans-Saharan Africa also made it possible to add a large amount of new geographical information from first-hand experience. Arab merchants were established in Ceylon and in the Chinese port of Canton by AD 700. From the port of Basra in Mesopotamia to China there was an unbroken chain of communication along which the luxury goods of the east flowed back to the west, in which Europeans took no part, and of which they had virtually no knowledge.

However, by the eleventh century major developments were taking place within western Europe which initially created a new internal stability and new institutions, but which ultimately were to lay the foundations for a renewal of expansion beyond its boundaries. For the first time since the fall of the empire in the fifth century, western Europe was relatively free from outside attack. The Moslem invaders who had conquered Spain and attacked France in the eighth century, and had ravaged Italy in the ninth, were now chiefly confined to the Iberian peninsula, to Sicily, and to the islands of the western Mediterranean. Elsewhere the Arabs remained a considerable nuisance: in 931 they raided Genoa, in 988 many of the population around Bari were taken off to Sicily as slaves, and as late as 1016 the town of Luni in Liguria was attacked. However, by about 1100 Moslem power in and around Europe was either held in check or was definitely on the wane.

The devastating raids of the Hungarian nomads which fell on Italy, Germany, and France from the late ninth century had been ended when Otto the Great defeated them at the Lechfeld in 955; while the more widespread raids of the Scandinavian peoples which had been in progress since the end of the eighth century were ceasing by the middle of the eleventh century. By this time Danish and Norwegian settlers had established themselves in northern France, England, and Ireland; the spectacular but unsuccessful invasion of England by King Harald Hardrada of Norway in September 1066 was virtually the end of an era in European history.

Security might still be precarious, but with hindsight it is evident that in the eleventh century the social and political institutions of western Europe were fast taking on the shape which was to be familiar for the rest of the medieval period. The feudal nobility were at one level a source of division and political disorder, but under the leadership of skilful rulers, like the tenth-century counts of Anjou or the eleventh-century dukes of Normandy, they also became a means of unity and strength. From their ranks came the steady supply of highly trained mounted warriors who helped to guarantee European freedom from outside attack, and who were to play a major part in successful European aggression and military superiority overseas, in much the same way as ships armed with cannon were to do in the fifteenth and sixteenth centuries. If feudal principalities were one basis for a new-found political stability, kings and kingship were another. At the highest level, the attempted revival of the empire of Charlemagne which began with the coronation of Otto the Great in 962 did at least remind people that large political units were conceivable, although it also doomed Germany to a conflict between pope, emperor, and princes. More successful than the empire were kingdoms such as England, already united in the eleventh century, and France, whose king was at first weaker than many of his vassals, but who was by the end of the thirteenth century to outstrip all his rivals. There were also the new kingdoms of Castile and Aragon which emerged out of the reconquest of Moslem territory in Spain, and in central Europe, those of Poland, Hungary, and Bohemia. For much of Europe national monarchies were to prove a means of concentrating political power in the hands of their rulers, and of focusing the loyalty of their subjects.

Another important feature of eleventh-century Europe was a general rise in the level of population. Exactly why this was taking place is difficult to explain: it was perhaps a combination of greater physical security, improved agricultural equipment and techniques, and the absence of major outbreaks of plague such as had devastated Europe in the seventh century. Whatever the explanation, there is little doubt that from about the middle of the tenth century the population of Europe was increasing, and that it continued to do so for some centuries to come. The consequences can be seen in the expansion of existing towns, the foundation of new ones, and in the clearing and working of forest and other waste land to accommodate and feed the extra mouths.

This latter process has aptly been described as one of internal colonization, but its most dramatic aspect was the movement of population into newly conquered lands. The settlement of the Frankish peoples of Germany in central and eastern Europe at the expense of the heathen Saxons and Slavs had begun in Carolingian times, but it gathered a new momentum during the eleventh and twelfth centuries in the regions beyond the Elbe and the Oder, to which colonists from Germany and the Low Countries were encouraged to take their agricultural and craft skills by the rulers of Brandenburg, Saxony, and Holstein. In the thirteenth century the military religious order of the Teutonic Knights, which had originally been founded in Palestine in about 1190, contributed to the war of conquest and settlement against the heathen tribes of Prussia and Lithuania which had begun in the mid-twelfth century. In a similar fashion settlers from Normandy made their way into Moslem-held Sicily and southern Italy from the early part of the eleventh century, turning their conquests into a kingdom in 1130, while men from various parts of France took part in forays against the Moslems of Spain.

Colonization was not limited to heathen or infidel lands. After 1066 the descendants of the Scandinavians who had founded Normandy a century and a half before established themselves in England with their supporters from Brittany and Flanders, and by 1200 had moved, with varying degrees of success, into the neighbouring lands of Wales, Scotland, and Ireland. A detailed treatment of all these conquests and transfers of population is beyond the scope of this book, but it is essential to emphasize that the expansion of Europe into other continents during the medieval period was preceded, and to some extent made possible, by a similar expansion within Europe itself. The enthusiastic European response to the preaching of the first crusade, for example, and the willingness of large numbers of people to travel great distances from their homelands did not occur in a vacuum. The objectives of the crusades to the Holy Land were perhaps less tangible and less certain of achievement than those of the expansion nearer to home, but parallels between the two movements did exist, and should not be forgotten, not least the fact that people from many of the same areas of Europe, from France, Germany, and the Low Countries, were involved in both.

The prolonged economic depression which had its roots in the late classical world was also coming to an end in the eleventh century, or more accurately this is the period when signs of economic growth are first generally apparent to the historian. There are, however, good reasons to think that the origins of this growth rested some time in the past on an agricultural base many of whose technological improvements, such as the heavy plough, had already been achieved by the ninth century, and which helped both to support and stimulate the increase in population and in internal settlement. Some of the greater production of food which resulted was absorbed simply by the needs of more people or in royal taxation, and did not in itself act as an incentive for trade, but on the shores of the Mediterranean in particular there were places where trade was already an important activity. In the eleventh century such places were few, and were the cause of disbelief and surprise to their neighbours when, like Venice, they did not 'plough, sow or gather vintage', but they were to be the starting-points of what has been termed a European commercial revolution which rested on a more secure foundation than the loose-knit network of trade routes created by the Vikings, and which was eventually to outstrip the commerce of both the Byzantine and the Moslem worlds.

No less important in any attempt to discover the sources of the medieval expansion of Europe are the slow but ultimately dramatic changes which were taking place in the institutions of the Church. One of the earliest of these occurred within the supposedly closed society of the monastic order, which was itself a product of the last generations of the antique world. The relative isolation of the monasteries had helped them to survive political upheavals, and preserve something of the earlier culture, this latter role having been positively encouraged during the rule of the Carolingian emperors. The foundation of the Burgundian abbey of Cluny in 910, and of other new religious houses such as Gorze in Lorraine, was initially intended to sever the monastic life from the ties of secular control, but it was also to become one of the inspirations for a wide-ranging reform of the entire western Church. The Cluniac houses were also involved in the colonization of Europe, appearing, for example, from the late eleventh century as outposts of Christian civilization in newly reconquered areas of Spain. Even more significant in this colonizing role was another new order, the Cistercians, founded in 1098, which spread within fifty years to regions as diverse as Germany, Spain, England, Poland, Ireland, and Wales. As well as stimulating economic growth in undeveloped areas the Cistercians were especially prominent in frontier regions of Europe, where they often helped to consolidate conquest.

In the course of the eleventh century the example of the Cluniac freedom from secular influence, and the public careers of a series of long-lived and influential abbots of Cluny, provided at least an indirect inspiration for the reform of the papacy, whose authority over the Church and in the world at large had hitherto been nominal. The schism of 1054 severed any remaining links between the churches of Rome and Constantinople, and the Lenten Decrees of 1059 demonstrated that in future the papacy was not to be filled by the decision of the emperor or by the machinations of the Roman nobility, while the pontificate of Gregory VII (1073–85) and the ensuing investiture contest served notice that the papacy intended to be supreme over both Church and State. The papacy was far from successful in all it undertook, but by 1100 its role in European affairs was well on the way to being transformed. The new aggressiveness on the part of the papacy in its international activities, which had lain to some degree behind the events of 1054, had also achieved a dramatic and seemingly miraculous conclusion in the fall of Jerusalem in 1099 to the crusading armies which had been set in motion by Urban II at Clermont in 1095.

None of the features of European society which have just been outlined were entirely new in the eleventh century. Just how far back in time it is necessary to go in order to trace their origins is a matter for argument, but the ninth and tenth centuries were probably the period in which many of them began. Western Europe could now fairly be described as a dynamic society, settling down to its own distinctive institutions, a society of which the intellectual vigour of individual scholars such as Gerbert of Aurillac was already a part, and to which the schools and universities would soon be added. The alleged fears of the millennium and of the impending Day of Judgement have been shown by modern scholars to have little substance outside the writings of the eleventh-century chronicler Ralph Glaber, but there is no doubt that Europe was still much disturbed and prone to great instability. Crop failures and famine, or an ambitious nobility indulging in the delights of private warfare, and with plenty of younger sons to provide for, were an assurance of social tensions. Not all the distressed peasantry could simply be absorbed by settlement in the Slav lands of the east, nor could a Norman conquest of England or Sicily be arranged in every generation to employ the surplus members of knightly families. The boundaries of Europe were becoming too straitened to hold back these pressures, but this did not in itself guarantee the overseas expansion of Europe which was about to take place. Something more was needed to direct energies into new channels, and it was provided in two distinct yet closely related ways: by the growth of international trade, and by the crusades.

3

Commerce and the crusades

Commercial links between western Europe and other regions had never entirely died out in the centuries after the fall of Rome. The wide distribution of the Jews throughout the Mediterranean basin, for example, allowed them to pass with greater ease than most others between the mutually uncomprehending and usually hostile worlds of Islam and Christendom, while between the ninth and the eleventh centuries the Scandinavian peoples had created a network of trade routes stretching from Ireland, via centres such as Birka in Sweden and Hedeby in Denmark, to Constantinople and Baghdad. However, the contribution of these latter activities to the revival of the commerce of Europe as a whole seems to have been relatively slight, perhaps because the era of Viking power was already coming to an end at the time when the international trade of other parts of Europe was showing the first consistent signs of a revival. The Vikings also lacked the expertise in the handling of money and in systems of credit which was to be a vital part of the commercial practices developed in the Italian cities from the twelfth century onwards. Indeed, the Viking trade routes were possibly as much an indication of those areas in which the Vikings were able to obtain plunder and tribute as of any ordered and regular patterns of trade.

The most important centres of trade lay in Italy: the survival of an urban tradition from Roman times, and the continuing links of certain parts of the peninsula with the eastern empire at Constantinople, as well as its geographical position in the centre of the Mediterranean basin, made it the natural place for any large-scale revival of commerce. The city of Venice on the Adriatic, for example, was well situated to take advantage of any opportunities for trade: indications of the existence of Venetian overseas trade with both Alexandria and Constantinople can already be found in the early ninth century. Bulky items such as salt, timber, and iron, together with the valuable commodity of slaves from the German and Slav lands, could be sold in Egypt, and the proceeds either spent there or used to help finance the purchase of spices and silk cloth at Constantinople. A three-way system of commerce grew up with Constantinople forming the most important element, partly because of Venice's political relations with the Byzantine empire. The already highly developed eastern economies were a vital market for the relatively few western products which they required. In turn this trade assisted in the accumulation of capital in the west, and by the end of the thirteenth century the western economy was able to eclipse its great rivals and mentors in the east.

As well as trading on its own account, Venice gradually became the major channel for the supply of eastern goods to other parts of western Europe. Venetian merchants were already active at the fairs of Champagne in northern France in 1074, and in 1082 were given extensive trading privileges in the Byzantine empire which consolidated their position in international commerce. The only major rival to Venice in the early centuries of its prosperity was the city of Amalfi to the south of Naples, which was also under Byzantine influence, but was in addition in close proximity to Moslem-controlled ports in Sicily and North Africa with which it traded freely. In the tenth century Amalfi was regarded in Moslem circles, even by merchants from as far away as Baghdad, as the most important city in Italy. A community of Amalfitans existed in Cairo well before the end of that century, and in 1048 a merchant from Amalfi, Costantino di Pantaleone di Mauro, was able to secure permission from the Fatimid ruler to found a hostel in Jerusalem for visitors from his home city. Merchants from Amalfi were to be found all over the eastern and the western Mediterranean, and their business continued to flourish until the capture of Amalfi in 1073 by the Norman Robert Guiscard abruptly ended both the city's independence and its privileged position at Constantinople.

By the eleventh century other Italian ports, notably Genoa and Pisa, were also emerging, initially through their successful counter-attacks against Moslem raiders and their bases. Corsica and Sardinia were taken in 1015–16; Bône in North Africa was attacked in 1034; in about 1063 the Arab arsenal in the harbour of Palermo in Sicily was destroyed; and in 1088 the two cities took part in the successful attack on Mahdiya in Tunisia. Trade followed close on naval operations, and in the course of the eleventh century Genoese commercial colonies were established in Constantinople, Antioch (then under Byzantine rule), and Jerusalem; while trade with Alexandria also developed with the active encouragement of the rulers of Egypt.

Italian involvement in the eastern Mediterranean was already very extensive and significant well before the preaching of the first crusade in 1095, and was steadily growing in importance, since the political stability of Fatimid Egypt compared with the weakness of the Abbasid caliphate at Baghdad had led to the diversion from the Persian Gulf to the Red Sea and Egypt of the traditional Moslem trade with India and the Far East. The trade of Egypt was therefore of great value to Moslems and Christians alike, and neither side had any interest in disturbing it, with the result that Italian merchants did not view the exploits of the late eleventh- and early twelfth-century crusaders as an unmixed blessing. At the same time the network of contacts which the Italians had created in the eastern Mediterranean, and their great resources in merchant and naval shipping, were to give them a major role in the crusades, and indeed were to be an important element in the initial success of the crusading movement and in the continued existence of the crusader colonies in the Holy Land.

Italian commercial operations were not the only form of western European contact with the eastern Mediterranean before the beginning of military expeditions at the end of the eleventh century. The practice of pilgrimage to Jerusalem, which had begun in the fourth century, grew in scale from the tenth century, partly as a form of penitential exercise on the part of westerners. But it was also a response to the easier travel which was now afforded by the land route via Constantinople, or by the alternative sea route which was opening from ports in southern Italy such as Bari. The Moslem rulers of Palestine were also not averse to making a profit out of Christian pilgrims, and gave them active encouragement.

Apart from a brief interruption during the reign of the mad

Fatimid caliph al-Hakim (died 1021), who persecuted both Christians and Jews and destroyed the church of the Holy Sepulchre at Jerusalem in 1009, pilgrimage became even easier and more extensive in the eleventh century. Pilgrims from the Low Countries and Germany could now travel via Hungary through the Balkans, which had been reconquered by the Byzantine emperor Basil II in 1019, and then overland through Byzantine territory in Asia Minor. Pilgrims from France and Italy had the option of an easy sea journey to Durazzo, and then on by road to Constantinople. Usually pilgrims had few difficulties in reaching Jerusalem, although their numbers sometimes caused problems with local officials or with food supplies. Duke Robert of Normandy took a large company with him in 1035; the notorious Fulk Nerra, count of Anjou, died in 1040 in the course of his third pilgrimage; and in 1064–5 the bishop of Bamberg led a party of about seven thousand.

The invasion of Palestine in 1071 by the Seljuk Turks and the confusion caused by their defeat of the Byzantines in Asia Minor did cause some disruption to the pilgrim traffic, although the Seljuks were not overtly hostile to it. A well-organized and well-armed expedition, like that of Robert I, count of Flanders, in 1089, could still get through to Jerusalem, but in the 1090s conditions in the Holy Land became more disturbed, and many pilgrims were turned back, including Peter the Hermit who was soon to play a major role as one of the leaders of the first crusade. Western European attention was therefore becoming increasingly focused on the Holy Land at the very time when opportunities to go there were, temporarily at least, restricted, and this in turn helps to explain some of the enthusiasm of the response to Urban II's preaching at Clermont in 1095.

While the pacific side of the crusades was foreshadowed by pilgrimages, their military aspect was also to be found in the eleventh century in the form of offensive wars against Moslem-held territory. The aggressive activities of the Italian cities of Genoa and Pisa have already been mentioned, but in the Iberian peninsula and in Sicily events were taking place on a far greater scale. The collapse of the Ummayad caliphate of Cordoba in 1031 was followed by the appearance in Moslem Spain of a number of separate and individually weak states, while at the same time new kingdoms were starting to emerge among the Christian population of the peninsula. King Sancho of Navarre, whose kingdom was the most important in the early eleventh century, died in 1035 leaving his possessions to be divided among his three sons, one succeeding in Navarre itself, and the other two becoming the founders of the new realms of Castile and Aragon which were destined to outstrip the parent kingdom in importance. The Moslem states were invaded, and in 1085 Alfonso VI of Castile captured the city of Toledo, one of the major political and cultural centres of Moslem Spain. The remaining Moslem rulers were now thoroughly alarmed, and invited the assistance of the Almoravids of Morocco who invaded Andalusia in 1086, and in 1090 conquered virtually all of Moslem Spain and a number of Christian-held border towns. Toledo, however, remained in Christian hands; Valencia was held by the Christian warrior Rodrigo di Bivar, better known as el Cid; and by 1095 the peninsula was roughly divided between the Spanish Christian kingdoms and the North African Moslems.

Although the *Reconquista* was primarily the concern of the Iberian peninsula itself, people from elsewhere in Europe, notably France, did become involved in it on occasions in the eleventh century. In 1064 a force led by the duke of Aquitaine and the count of Poitou took part in the capture of Barbastro; in 1073 Ebles de Roucy led an army to Spain; and in 1086 a number of French nobles, including the duke of Burgundy, went there in response to an appeal for help after the invasion of the Almoravids. Another interesting point of contact between Spain and France was produced by the marriage of the daughter of the king of Castile, one of the prime movers of the *Reconquista* on the Spanish side, to Raymond of St Gilles, count of Toulouse, who was shortly to be one of the leaders of the first crusade. Too much should not be read into these pieces of evidence, but they do at least indicate that men from the same social classes and regions as those who later took part in the military expeditions to the eastern Mediterranean were already conscious of the Moslems as a potential enemy.

In the meantime men from another part of France, led by the

sons of the minor Norman baron Tancred de Hauteville, had been busily conquering Moslem territory in Sicily. In 1061 Robert Guiscard and his brother Roger took Messina, followed by Palermo in 1072; in 1091 the seizure of the entire island, together with Malta, was completed; and in the following decades Sicily became the basis of a highly organized Norman state which achieved the dignity of a kingdom in 1130 under Roger II. As well as being a springboard for possible further conquests at Moslem expense, such as the capture of Mahdiya in 1088, Sicily was also the chief source of grain for the Moslems of North Africa, who were therefore compelled to acknowledge an important change in the local balance of power.

Moslem Sicily was, however, only one of several areas of Norman activity in the Mediterranean. According to legend, Norman pilgrims landing on the mainland of southern Italy in 1016 on their return from Jerusalem became involved as mercenaries in local politics. The region owed either direct allegiance to the Byzantine empire, in the cases of Apulia and Calabria, or a very doubtful loyalty in those of the Lombard principalities of Benevento, Capua, and Salerno. With the arrival of Robert Guiscard in the late 1040s to join three of his elder brothers, the Norman ambitions in Italy turned openly to conquest. In 1059 Guiscard was formally recognized by the pope as the ruler of Calabria and Apulia, having first defeated a papal army at Civitate in 1053, and by his death in 1085 he was the effective overlord of southern Italy.

The fall of the city of Bari, the last Byzantine outpost in Italy, in 1071, opened the way for direct Norman intervention in other territories closer to Constantinople. Unreliable Norman mercenaries, such as those who had taken part in an unsuccessful attempt to reconquer Sicily in 1038–40, or Hervé who had gone over to the Turks in 1057, Robert Crispin who rebelled in 1068, and Roussel of Bailleul who tried to create a principality for himself in Asia Minor after the Byzantine defeat at Manzikert in 1071, had given the Greeks some idea of what to expect. In 1081 Robert Guiscard took Durazzo on the Adriatic as a prelude to an invasion of the Balkans. Nothing further was achieved, and in 1083 the Normans withdrew to Italy. The latter stages of this campaign were led by Guiscard's son Bohemond, a man whose immense ambition was to make him one of the most successful leaders of the first crusade, as well as deeply suspect to the Byzantines whom he was then supposedly assisting.

Before the end of the eleventh century the interests of western European pilgrims, merchants, and military adventurers were turning significantly towards the eastern Mediterranean; not exclusively so, as the wars in Spain and Sicily and the trade relations with North Africa indicate, but the interest was none the less sufficient for a further development of it to appear likely. What form that development would take was not yet clear: in 1090 it might have seemed probable that the Normans or others would have made renewed attacks upon Byzantine territory, and that Italian merchants would continue to extend their trade with both the Byzantine empire and Egypt. The actual shape of events was rather different, and was to be determined by other factors within European society as well as by military and political upheavals within both the Byzantine and Moslem worlds.

The key to much of what followed, at least in so far as it helps to explain the large-scale European military expeditions to the east which began at the end of the eleventh century, lies in the revitalization of the western Church, and in particular of the institutions of the papacy, which was discussed earlier. If the concept of Europe had little more than a geographical significance, there was an alternative and very potent focus of loyalty for the peoples of Europe in the idea of Christendom. This idea embraced Christian western Europe, but was capable of extension to include Christians living elsewhere, in the lands of Greek allegiance or in other lands where Christians were perhaps only a tiny minority.

The notion of Christendom first appeared in the ninth century, partly as a way of expressing the contrast and the mutual hostility between Christians and the Moslems whose conquests were then still in progress. Around the beginning of the eleventh century the physical boundaries of Christendom within Europe itself were expanding rapidly with the successful conversion of many of the pagan peoples of the continent, and their formation into new political units. In 999 St Stephen, the first Christian ruler of the

Magyars, until recently the scourge of Europe, received a crown as king of Hungary, and in future years both pilgrims and crusaders were to find their journeys to Constantinople and the Holy Land greatly assisted by this new-found security along the Danube; in the year 1000 another Christian kingdom, also owing allegiance to the emperor in Germany, was created in Bohemia; and in 1018 Poland, long the scene of missionary activity, became a third new Christian realm under its former duke Boleslav the Mighty. A generation before, in 988, the Russian principality of Kiev under Vladimir I also appears to have accepted Christianity, although this time of the Greek rather than the Roman persuasion. A similar pattern was developing among the Scandinavian peoples. Around the year 1000 the Norse colony of Iceland on the outermost fringes of Europe adopted Christianity after an impassioned debate in its assembly, the Althing; at about the same time the home country of Norway, during the reigns of its kings Olaf Tryggvason and St Olaf, was undergoing conversion; Denmark had been converted during the latter part of the tenth century at the time of King Harald Bluetooth, and in 1027 his grandson, Cnut the Great, king of Denmark and England, and soon to be king of Norway, sealed the Scandinavian entry into Christendom by his pilgrimage to Rome. Only Sweden remained more resistant to Christianity, but here too it was well established by the early twelfth century.

Within Christian Europe there was another very significant development as religious leaders, first of all in Burgundy and Aquitaine, and apparently acting independently of the papacy, attempted to find ways of curbing the violent behaviour of the nobility. The movement known as the Peace of God, first proclaimed in the late tenth century at the Councils of Le Puy in 975, and of Charroux in 989–90, was intended to provide ecclesiastical protection for special categories of society who were otherwise defenceless, notably for monks, clergy, and the poor. An elaboration of this idea is first clearly seen in the proclamation at the Council of Toulouges in Roussillon in 1027 of the Truce of God, according to which no acts of violence were to take place on the Lord's Day. The prohibition was later extended to other religious festivals and seasons, such as Lent and Advent, and reached its

full development in 1054 when the Council of Narbonne decreed
that no Christian should kill another.

These actions were of essentially local significance, and the
sanctions available for their enforcement were obviously limited,
but like the idea of Christendom they contained within them a
germ which was capable of extension if the central authorities of
the Church were ever to replace simple prohibitions on violence
by an attempt to harness and direct the military capacities of the
nobility to their own ends. Such proved to be the case during the
eleventh century, and may be considered as another aspect of the
reformed papacy's assertion of its supremacy over both lay and
ecclesiastical society.

In 1059 Robert Guiscard became a papal vassal, and received
approval of his intended conquest of Sicily; in 1064 the Barbastro
campaign appears to have been given support by Pope Alexander
II; and two years later Duke William of Normandy began his
invasion of England with the propaganda advantage of a papal
banner. Direct papal involvement in military operations became
much clearer during the pontificate of Gregory VII, whose concept of Christendom was wider than that of any of his predecessors, and for whom the *militia Christi* was no longer to be professed religious fighting spiritual battles for spiritual ends, but
real knights fighting real battles under the leadership of the
Church. In 1073 he urged a campaign against the Moslems of
Spain where any conquered lands were to be held from the
papacy; in 1074 he asked a number of papal vassals, the counts of
Burgundy, Toulouse, and Savoy, to join Godfrey of Lorraine in
an expedition against the Normans in southern Italy, and then to
go to the aid of Constantinople against the Turks. It seems that
Gregory suggested that the emperor Henry IV might also go to
the east, and that if the army were to be led by the pope in person
it might even reach the Holy Sepulchre in Jerusalem. This grandiose design came to nothing, not least because the emperor had
other ideas about his relationship with Gregory VII, but it was no
more grandiose than the scheme which succeeded little more than
twenty years later, and should not be dismissed too lightly.
Gregory did not, however, give up altogether, and in 1080
gave encouragement to Robert Guiscard's planned attack on the

Byzantine Empire, probably with a reunion of the churches in mind. In 1088 his successor Victor II approved the attack on Mahdiya in Tunis, and in 1089 Urban II tried to organize assistance for the defenders of Tarragona in Spain.

The final link between the growing papal interest in and control over military expeditions was provided by events in the east, following the destruction by the Seljuk Turks of the Byzantine army at Manzikert in 1071, and the consequent loss of virtually the whole of Asia Minor. The Byzantine emperors had long made use of mercenaries from Europe, notably the Varangian guard recruited from Scandinavia, and more recently of small bands of Normans, so that it was no innovation for them to seek external help. It is possible that Gregory VII's plans of 1074–5 were formulated in answer to such an appeal, while in about 1090 Count Robert of Flanders was asked by the emperor Alexius Comnenus to send a force of mercenaries after his return from the pilgrimage to Jerusalem on which he was then engaged, and appears to have done so. What is certain is that in March 1095 Urban II received an appeal for further military assistance from Alexius, and that this appeal led directly to the preaching of the first crusade by Urban at the Council of Clermont the following November.

It is altogether too simple to see the first crusade as an inevitable consequence of existing traditions of holy war against the Moslems, of papal ambitions, pilgrimage, economic expansion, and of the needs of a warlike nobility. The wars in Spain, for example, which offer the closest analogy to the later crusade, were largely an internal affair which would have existed with or without signs of papal interest, or intervention from other parts of western Europe. What finally produced the first crusade was a combination of pleas for military assistance from the east, a conscious decision by the pope to put himself or his legate at the head of the western response, the taking of a vow by the participants, and their use of a cross as the visible symbol of their vow, together with the offer of an indulgence by the papacy to all who took part in the expedition. Within a very short time the spiritual privileges enjoyed by crusaders in the Holy Land were extended to those who fought the Moslems in Spain, and from the time of the second crusade in 1147, a further extension was made to include campaigns against the heathen of north-eastern Europe. But the full blend of all the elements which went to make up a crusade was not present before the Council of Clermont in 1095.

No official record exists of Urban II's precise words at Clermont, so that there has been much debate on whether the pope's primary intention was to sponsor a military expedition to Jerusalem, or whether he mentioned Jerusalem as a means of arousing the enthusiasm of his hearers, and of drawing on its attraction as a destination for pilgrims. In the light of recent research it seems probable that Jerusalem was central to papal intentions, and that there may have been some advance preparation of support among potential leaders of an expedition before the assembly at Clermont. Even so, Urban can only have been amazed at the scale of the reaction to his preaching, and at its attraction to all social classes. From the point of view of the Byzantine emperor, Alexius Comnenus, the response was something entirely different from what he had hoped for, and contained serious dangers to the security of his remaining dominions.

The armies of the first crusade, together with the non-combatants who accompanied them, represented a bigger movement of European people than even the largest of the pilgrim enterprises which had preceded them, and can fairly be described as the first really significant stage in the medieval expansion of Europe. It has been estimated that as many as 100,000 people may have made the journey to Constantinople in 1096 and 1097, although nothing like this number was to reach the ultimate goal of Jerusalem two years later.

The popular leaders, Peter the Hermit and Walter the Penniless, gathered followers from France, the Low Countries, and Germany, and reached Constantinople well ahead of any of the aristocratic leaders of the crusade with the true fighting contingents. The latter were commanded by some of the most prominent of the European nobility of the time: Godfrey de Bouillon, duke of Lower Lorraine, and his brothers Baldwin and Eustace, count of Boulogne; Robert, count of Flanders, the son of the Count Robert who had been to Jerusalem in the late 1080s; Duke

Robert of Normandy and his brother-in-law Stephen, count of Blois. From Norman Sicily there came Bohemond and his nephew Tancred; and from southern France Raymond, count of Toulouse, who had the largest army and was also accompanied by the papal legate, the bishop of Le Puy. No king took part, but Hugh of Vermandois and Robert of Normandy were the brothers of the kings of France and England respectively; nor was there any significant contingent from Norman England although Robert of Normandy, Eustace of Boulogne, and Stephen of Blois all had English connections; Anglo-Saxon England may have been represented by Edgar the Atheling, nephew of Edward the Confessor and last English claimant to the throne of Wessex, who was in Byzantine service, and is said to have joined the crusading armies during the siege of Antioch. Germany and Italy were not important contributors until the so-called crusade of 1101 which was designed to reinforce and defend the newly won territories in Syria and Palestine.

Military successes at Nicaea and Dorylaeum cleared the Turks from Asia Minor, and restored territory to the crusaders' Byzantine allies; but then began the foundation of Frankish principalities, and less and less attention was given to Byzantine claims and interests. In March 1098 Baldwin of Boulogne took Edessa, and founded the first of the crusader states; in June 1098 Antioch, which had been taken from the Byzantines by the Turks as recently as 1085, was captured and became the basis of another principality under the rule first of Bohemond, and then of his nephew Tancred and his successors; and finally in July 1099 the city of Jerusalem was captured from the Egyptians who had regained it from the Turks only the year before.

With this last great military victory, sustained by the defeat of the Egyptian army at Ascalon in August 1099, and with the election of Godfrey de Bouillon as advocate of the Holy Sepulchre, the aims of the first crusade seemed to have been achieved, and western control of the Holy Land secured for the future. However, the crusaders' early success had depended on the current antagonisms among the Moslem powers in Syria and Palestine, and on the Moslem failure to appreciate that the invaders had come to stay, just as much as on the crusaders' own military prowess and religious enthusiasm. Once the Moslems had recovered from the shock of their initial defeats, the situation was likely to change to the disadvantage of the crusaders.

The disruption of the crusade of 1101 as its armies passed through Anatolia, and the defeat of the survivors at Ramleh in May 1102, together with the destruction of the army of the county of Edessa in 1104, were portents of what was to come. Equally important was the lack of manpower on the side of the crusaders, since many of those who reached Jerusalem in 1099 returned home once they had fulfilled their crusading vow, and did not make any permanent contribution to the defences of Jerusalem or of any of the other crusader states. This same pattern was to be repeated over and over throughout the history of the crusades.

The immediate outcome of the first crusade was to leave the crusaders divided into three separate groups, the largest of which was at Antioch, with a slightly smaller one at Jerusalem 300 miles away across hostile territory, and the smallest at Edessa, east of the Euphrates and 160 miles from Antioch. Although no extensive further conquests were to take place, the crusader states did continue to expand, chiefly by the capture of seaports to secure their communications with the west, and to increase the opportunities for trade. Jaffa had fallen even before Jerusalem; Arsuf, Caesarea, and Haifa fell in 1101, Acre in 1104, and Beirut and Sidon in 1110. The capture of Tripoli in 1109 led to the formation of a fourth crusader state, the county of Tripoli, under the rule of Bertram, the son and successor of Raymond, count of Toulouse. On the other hand, the port of Ascalon, which gave the Egyptians a stronghold uncomfortably near Jerusalem, did not fall until 1153, despite repeated attempts at its capture.

At their greatest extent, in the middle of the twelfth century, the crusader states consisted of a narrow coastal strip about 500 miles long from Cilicia in Asia Minor to the Red Sea, and extending about 100 miles at the widest point. The kingdom of Jerusalem itself was about 300 miles in length, from Beirut to Aqaba, and also incorporated the inland region of Transjordan, dominated by great fortresses such as Belvoir and Beaufort. Baldwin I of Jerusalem reached the Nile in 1118, and one of his successors, Amalric I (1163–74), invaded Egypt on five occasions, even occupying Cairo in 1164.

But these were fleeting successes. The crusading armies of 1101 lost a good opportunity of consolidating the western conquests by not taking the great Moslem cities of Damascus and Aleppo in Syria, while another chance to capture Aleppo was let slip in 1126. Now fully alerted to the dangers from the western invaders, the Moslem powers were also recovering their former unity, first under Zengi, who united Mosul in Iraq with Aleppo between 1127 and 1128, and then under his son Nur ed-Din, who took Damascus in 1154. All of this was but preparation for the emergence of Nur ed-Din's successor, the Kurdish soldier Saladin, who overran Fatimid Egypt in 1169. From 1175 Saladin was *de facto* sultan of Egypt as well as ruler of Moslem Syria under the overall authority of the caliph of Baghdad. With this concentration of power Saladin was to be the greatest single threat faced in the twelfth century by the crusader states in Palestine and Syria. However, the decay of the Latin position in the east had already begun when Zengi took the city of Edessa in 1144. Within a few years the entire county, the first of the crusader states to be created, and now the first to be destroyed, was lost, and with it the defensive hinterland for Antioch and the other states of Syria.

The disaster at Edessa led to the preaching of another great military expedition to the Holy Land on the pattern of the first crusade, commanded this time by the king of France and the German emperor, with a large number of French and German nobles. The second crusade was to be an almost total failure. Both the French and German forces suffered disastrous defeats at the hands of the Seljuk Turks in Asia Minor, and only a small proportion reached the Holy Land in 1148. To make matters worse, there was ample evidence of the hostility between westerners and Byzantines which had been latent during the first crusade, and which was to turn the crusade of 1204 into a direct attack on Constantinople. After their arrival Louis VII and Conrad III displayed their ignorance of local conditions by insisting on an attack upon Damascus. This might have made sense earlier, but since 1139 Jerusalem and Damascus had been in close alliance against the common threat from Zengi's forces at Aleppo. The attack failed, and in future Damascus was to be yet another threat to the crusader states. By Easter 1149 the western leaders had departed, leaving many new problems but few reinforcements behind them.

The second crusade did, however, have some significant side effects in areas other than the Holy Land. A number of German nobles decided to divert their energies to an attack upon the heathen of the Baltic lands. This resulted in the Wendish crusade of 1147, which had little immediate military effect, but established the pattern of German crusading and conquest in the Baltic region which was to last until the early sixteenth century. Another diversion from the main purpose of the second crusade occurred in the Iberian Peninsula after the arrival of an expeditionary force consisting of men from England, Scotland, Normandy, and the Low Countries which had left Dartmouth in England. In October 1147 they took Lisbon from its Moslem rulers, and so helped to create the new kingdom of Portugal, with an Englishman, Gilbert of Hastings, as the first archbishop of Lisbon. At the same time other forces from within Christian Spain were engaged in capturing Almeria and Tortosa, and in expelling the Moslems from Catalonia. These were to be the only solid achievements resulting from the vast efforts and careful preparations which had gone into the crusade.

The superficial brilliance of the kingdom of Jerusalem at the time of Amalric I concealed both the real weakness of the kingdom in manpower, and also its growing isolation. Natural disasters, such as the earthquakes which destroyed Antioch and Tripoli in 1170, and the military catastrophe suffered by the Byzantine army at Myriocephalon in 1176, which placed Asia Minor in the hands of the Turks as the battle of Manzikert had done in 1071, left the kingdom temporarily without allies. But above all the career of Saladin, who took Gaza and Aqaba in 1170, and created a ring of hostile territories surrounding the kingdom, should have given warning of an impending crisis.

In July 1187 the largest army that had ever been mustered by the kingdom of Jerusalem was practically destroyed at Hattin in Galilee by a superior force under Saladin. In the entire history of the crusader states in the Holy Land, which was punctuated by spectacular and almost miraculous victories as well as by the most profound of disasters, no defeat was greater or seemingly more complete in its consequences than that of Hattin. Within a very short time Saladin had conquered all the major towns of Palestine and Syria; only Antioch, Tripoli, and Tyre on the coast, and a handful of fortresses inland remained under Christian control. Jerusalem itself fell on 2 October 1187; Saladin received the applause of the Moslem world and the congratulations of the Byzantine emperor, who asked for the restoration of the Holy Places to the Orthodox clergy. It appeared that the remarkable extension of western European influence to the lands of the eastern Mediterranean which had begun with the Council of Clermont less than a century before was now irrevocably over.

All the western states in Syria and Palestine had been encompassed by the disaster suffered by the kingdom of Jerusalem, yet by another seemingly miraculous turn of events a revival of sorts took place within a few years of Hattin, and permitted the preservation of the Latin enclaves for another century. As in the case of the first crusade, the key to events in the Holy Land lay once again among the inhabitants of western Europe whose enthusiasm for the crusade, though never sufficient to ensure a consistent contribution to the defence of the Holy Land, tended to be awakened at times of crisis, as in 1147 after the fall of Edessa, and now again in 1187.

Even before news of Hattin arrived in Europe, the emperor and the kings of France and England had long been considering a new crusade as an aid to their own reputations as much as an aid to the Holy Land itself. But it took the dramatic events in the east to bring these ambitions to the point of decision, and to allow these rulers to put aside international rivalries and the distractions of domestic politics. In 1189 Frederick Barbarossa and a large number of German nobles and prelates left for Palestine, to be followed a year later by Philip Augustus of France and Richard I, newly established on the English throne. The losses from disease, battle, and disillusion that were inseparable from a crusade reduced the German army's effectiveness very considerably, a reduction made worse by the death by drowning in 1190 of Frederick Barbarossa, and the remnant which reached the Holy

Land did not play an important part in the crusade. The arrival of the English and French armies gave new impetus to the siege of Acre, which was the focus of the attempt to recover the kingdom of Jerusalem, and the city at last fell in July 1191 after a siege of two years. The only further gain was Jaffa, the port for the city of Jerusalem; but Jerusalem itself, the object of the most elaborate expedition that had ever left western Europe, could not be retaken, although Saladin promised Christian pilgrims access to the Holy Places. When Richard I left for home at the end of 1192 the third crusade was effectively finished.

It also proved to be the last large-scale expedition sent directly to the Holy Land. From now on the crusading ideal tended to be diverted in other directions, either because of the appearance of new crusading motivations, such as the suppression of heresy, or through the dominance of older motivations which had previously been held in check. Accordingly there took place between 1209 and 1229 the crusade by men of northern France against their brethren of southern France in the name of the elimination of the Albigensian heretics in the county of Toulouse. The hostilities which had been developing between Latins and Greeks since the eleventh century came to a head in 1204, when practically the whole of the army which had ben gathered at the instigation of Pope Innocent III for a new attempt to relieve the Holy Land went instead to Constantinople, sacked the city, and established a new Latin empire on the ruins of the Byzantine dominions. On two occasions, in 1218–21 and 1248–50, unsuccessful attacks were to be made against Egypt. The enormous wealth which resulted from its control of the commercial routes to India was one attraction, as it had been for Baldwin I and Amalric I in the twelfth century, but the fact that, since the time of Saladin Egypt had become the most dangerous adversary of the crusader states in Syria and Palestine, and hence the key to their ultimate survival, made it a logical point of attack. This lesson was to be remembered by crusading propagandists of the late thirteenth and the fourteenth centuries after all European control in the Holy Land had ceased.

None the less a considerable amount of attention was still devoted to Palestine and Syria. In 1197 a force of German crusaders took the cities of Sidon and Beirut, and restored communications between the kingdom of Jerusalem and the county of Tripoli. In 1219 and 1221 the sultan of Egypt responded to the military pressure exerted by the crusaders who were then in the Nile Delta by offering to restore Jerusalem in return for their withdrawal. The offer was rejected, but only a few years later, in 1229, Jerusalem was recovered without a blow being struck after the excommunicate emperor, Frederick II of Hohenstaufen, arrived in the Holy Land and made a treaty with the sultan al-Kamil. The agreement was to last for ten years only, the city was not to be refortified, and the Moslems were to be allowed access to their own holy places. In this symbolic fashion the kingdom of Jerusalem was reconstituted. In 1241 Richard of Cornwall, the brother of Henry III of England, arrived in Palestine, and by another treaty with the sultan of Egypt secured control of Galilee and the territory around Jaffa, Ascalon, Tiberias, and Sidon. The frontier on the Jordan was thereby restored, and the kingdom of Jerusalem attained the greatest extent that it was ever to achieve after 1187.

However, the revival of western power in the Holy Land was illusory. In July 1244 the army of the former Khwarismian empire in central Asia, now in the service of Egypt, took Jerusalem almost without opposition; a few months later the western forces suffered a defeat near Gaza on almost the same scale as at Hattin. Much of the remaining territory of the kingdom of Jerusalem was lost, but even now the enemies of the crusader states were unable to complete their conquest. In the early 1250s an internal revolution in Egypt replaced the Ayubid dynasty with a new one from among its Mameluke slave soldiers, with the result that for the first time since the days of Saladin the western enclaves faced a ring of Moslem enemies united under one ruler. The threat became all the greater after the defeat in 1260 at Ain Jalud in Palestine of an invading Mongol army which was the only force which might have countered Egypt.

The accession of the Egyptian sultan Baibars in 1260 marked the beginning of the end. From 1265 the ports and fortresses of the kingdom of Jerusalem fell one by one; and in 1268 Antioch was captured. The appearance in the Holy Land of western reinforcements, such as the army led by Prince Edward of England in 1271, had no effect, and after another brief respite the process of reconquest was resumed under Baibar's successor, Qalawun, who took Tripoli in 1289, and was moving against Acre when he died in 1290. His son Khalil resumed the attack, and on 18 May 1291 Acre, one of the most important and splendid of the crusader cities, fell. Within a matter of weeks Tyre, Sidon, Beirut, and Haifa had also surrendered, and on 14 August Château Pèlerin, which was garrisoned by the Knights Templar, and was the last Christian stronghold in the Holy Land, was evacuated. Two centuries of western European control over territory in the lands of Syria and Palestine had come to an end.

To the modern observer the collapse of the Latin states in the east at the end of the thirteenth century is less surprising than is their survival for so long, since the small scale of their population, in particular of the western segment of that population, was a fundamental weakness from the very start. At their peak the crusader states are estimated to have had a population of about 250,000, of whom about 120,000 lived in the kingdom of Jerusalem. Acre was by far the largest city with about 60,000 people, followed by Tyre, and only then by Jerusalem with 20,000–30,000.

The great majority of the population was of local origin. On the eve of the first crusade Moslems formed the bulk of the inhabitants of Syria and Palestine, but there were also many Christians of various allegiances, Greek Orthodox in Antioch and Maronites in Lebanon, as well as Copts, Nestorians, and Georgians. There were large numbers of Christians in Jerusalem itself, in Nazareth, and Bethlehem, and many Christian villages in the surrounding countryside. Jews also formed a significant minority. In the wake of the conquests by the crusaders there were considerable internal movements of population. Some of the new inhabitants imported into Jerusalem to replace those massacred after its capture in 1099 came from Christian communities in the Transjordan. In the cities of Tripoli, Antioch, and Edessa native Christians were also to form a large part of the population.

Settlers from western Europe could be found both in the countryside and in the cities. In the mid-twelfth century a village close to the fortress of Beit-Jibrin between Jerusalem and Ascalon had about 150 inhabitants drawn from the Auvergne, Gascony, Lombardy, Burgundy, Limoges, Poitou, Flanders, and Catalonia, while the village of Mahomeria had about 500 people from many of the same areas. However, westerners of peasant origin from France, Germany, or Italy frequently lived in the towns rather than in the villages, and were probably lured there by the prospect of personal freedom, and by the privileged status of burgess. Burgesses formed the greater part of the inhabitants of Acre, Tyre, and Jerusalem, and were to be found in all kinds of trades and crafts. This general extension of burgess privilege contrasts with its restricted character in most parts of western Europe, with significant exceptions such as twelfth- and thirteenth-century Ireland where burgess tenure was also used as a way of attracting settlers from outside. Burgesses were, however, rarely to be found operating as substantial merchants. The latter were usually Italian, with a few representatives from southern France and Spain, but they did not add significant numbers to the communities in which they resided.

Some of the leading members of the colonial nobility in the early days of settlement, like Godfrey de Bouillon and his brother Baldwin, who succeeded one another as advocate of the Holy Sepulchre and then as king of Jerusalem, or Bohemond prince of Antioch, and his nephew and successor Tancred, came from families which were already prominent in Europe, but for one reason or another had been unable to satisfy their ambitions at home, and were prepared to stay on in Syria or Palestine. Many of the future tenants-in-chief in the east were men of humble origin, like the founders of the families of Toron and Ibelin; they and the knightly class of the new settlements were drawn from among the mounted warriors who had accompanied the leaders of the first crusade.

The character of the nobility varied considerably from one crusader state to another. Edessa remained predominantly Armenian; Antioch was at first Norman, in keeping with its control by Bohemond, but considerable influence still lay with the leaders of the Greek and Armenian population of the principality. However, the defeat of the army of Antioch in 1119 marked a permanent decline in Norman influence in the east. The county of Tripoli had a Provençal nobility because of its connections with the county of Toulouse, while the nobility of the kingdom of Jerusalem tended to be drawn from northern France. The majority of the overseas recruits to the crusader nobility were in some sense French, but there were a few exceptions, such as the Genoese family of Embriaco who became lords of Jebail in the county of Tripoli in 1109, and continued to hold it, with Egyptian toleration, until 1298, seven years after the fall of Acre; or Conrad, marquis of Montferrat in Piedmont, who achieved fame by his defence of Tyre in 1187, and was assassinated in 1192 when on the point of becoming king of Jerusalem.

By the middle of the twelfth century the character of the crusader nobility was becoming set, and it was more difficult for newcomers to break into their ranks. But there were conspicuous exceptions. Reynald of Châtillon, who had arrived in the east in the company of Louis VII of France at the time of the second crusade, made himself a permanent fixture by judicious marriages, first to the heiress of the principality of Antioch, and later, in 1176, after spending fifteen years in a Moslem prison, to the heiress of Transjordan. As late as 1271 or 1272 Hamo Le Strange, one of the followers of Prince Edward, married the heiress of Beirut, and controlled the city until his death in 1273.

The greatest opportunity for an outsider to establish himself was, paradoxically, at the very top, at the level of the kingdom of Jerusalem itself. When the male line of succession broke down the resident nobility often found it easier to marry the heiress to a newcomer rather than to agree on one of themselves. Thus Guy de Lusignan, a member of a great family in Poitou, became count of Jaffa and Ascalon in 1180 when he married Sybilla, the sister of Baldwin IV of Jerusalem, and king of Jerusalem in 1186 after the death of Baldwin V, Sybilla's son by an earlier marriage. Guy was consequently in command of the army of the kingdom at Hattin a year later. When Sybilla died in 1190 the claim to the crown passed to her half-sister Isabella, and so to her successive husbands: Conrad of Montferrat; Henry of Champagne, who was a nephew of the kings both of France and England; and finally to another member of the house of Lusignan, Amalric king of Cyprus. After the death of both Isabella and Amalric in 1205, the crown was again transmitted to outsiders by heiresses, first to John of Brienne, and then in 1225 to no less a figure than the emperor Frederick II.

This was not the end of the shifting tenancies of the kingdom of Jerusalem, but the difficulty in ensuring a stable descent of the crown is in one sense a reflection of the chronic shortage of military manpower experienced by the crusader states. In 1180 the greatest number of knights who could in theory be mobilized by the king of Jerusalem was in the region of six to seven hundred, many of whom were supported by grants of money rather than of land, and lived in the cities, not in the countryside where their services would have been more immediately available. In practice, however, these military resources were supplemented by the mercenary troops which the wealth of the kingdom permitted its rulers to hire, and by the forces brought to the East from time to time by western rulers and noblemen on crusade. They were also supplemented by the hybrid product of the knightly and monastic impulses, the military orders. The knights of St John, or Hospitallers, had orginated very soon after the capture of Jerusalem in the need to offer medical assistance to pilgrims, while the order of Templars began in about 1118 as an organization designed to offer armed protection to travellers. Both, however, took on a predominantly military character, and between them controlled a force of knights at least equal to the feudal levy of the kingdom of Jerusalem, as well as large numbers of foot soldiers. The religious dedication of the orders, and their wealth also enabled them to garrison and to maintain many of the great fortresses on which the security of the crusader states depended. The Hospitallers, for example, became responsible for Krak, the greatest of all these castles, in 1144 when the count of Tripoli was no longer able to afford its upkeep; in the early thirteenth century this castle was said to have a peacetime garrison of two thousand men. Within the kingdom of Jerusalem the Hospitallers held twenty-five castles in 1180, and controlled twenty-nine in 1244 when the kingdom was considerably smaller in size. In the thirteenth century the military orders were one of the few reliable sources of defence available to the crusader states. The Templars, for instance, took over the coastal cities of Beirut and Sidon in 1278, while the Hospitallers regularly transmitted a large part of their European revenues for the defence of the Holy Land.

One of the earliest forms of support of the crusader states, as well as one of the factors that had made the crusading movement possible in the first place, had been provided by the great Italian commercial cities of Genoa, Venice, and Pisa. Their fleets played a vital role in transporting men and supplies to the Holy Land, and also in capturing the seaports which ensured the future preservation of communications with western Europe. Most of the major ports, such as Acre, Tyre, Beirut, and Antioch, and many of the lesser ones like Jaffa, Haifa, Sidon, and Caesarea were taken with the assistance of the ships of one or other of the Italian cities. In return they received extensive privileges. After the Genoese had helped to take Caesarea in 1101 they were given one-third of the city, and were freed from all tolls; Genoese colonies were also to be found at Antioch, Beirut, and lesser places such as Laodicaea and Ghibelet. By the thirteenth century members of prominent Genoese families were often residents of their colonies in the east, leading a poet to remark: 'So many are the Genoese, so scattered world wide . . . that they build little Genoas wherever they reside'.

This was no exaggeration, since foreign merchants in the Holy Land and Syria usually lived in independent communes controlled by representatives of the city from which they came, essentially as citizens of states within a state. In 1287, at a time when Tripoli was in revolt against its ruler, the Genoese envoy Benedetto Zaccaria even suggested outright annexation of the county by his home republic. A position very like that of the Genoese was occupied by Venice in respect of Tyre, of which it acquired one-third in 1124, and by Pisa at Jaffa and Ascalon. When the kingdom of Jerusalem was being reconstituted after 1187 all three cities appointed consuls to look after the interests of their citizens in Syria and the Holy Land, and with direct responsibility to their home governments.

The crusader states were inevitably involved in the growth of international trade in the twelfth and thirteenth centuries in which the Italians took the lead. The special attraction of the Holy Places in Jerusalem, where the church of the Holy Sepulchre was rebuilt in 1149, or of Bethlehem, Nazareth, and the river Jordan ensured a steady stream of pilgrims. These made up the outgoing cargoes of many ships from Genoa, Pisa, and Venice, and from Marseilles, which were the usual ports of embarkation. The city of Acre was especially important as the arrival point for pilgrims. Western Europe was also able to export woollen cloth, furs, and timber, and in return imported silk and cotton cloth, olive oil, sugar, and also spices which had originated further east. Beirut, Antioch, Tripoli, and Tyre were all important centres of trade.

However, none of these items of import and none of these ports seems to have been vital to the European economy. The consequences of a strong religious attraction and a partial military conquest were the main reasons for the development of commercial relations between Europe and Syria and Palestine. Many of the eastern cities, including Jerusalem, were of little commercial value; few, if any, of the products of the European settlements in the east were not more readily available elsewhere; the Moslem cities of Damascus, Aleppo, and Cairo, all of which were in contact with the trade routes across the continent of Asia or the Indian Ocean, lay outside European control, and had few direct commercial dealings with the coastal cities of the Mediterranean.

Despite the extensive privileges which Italian merchants possessed in those cities, and the often luxurious houses in which they could rest between voyages, the major centres of European trade with the east continued to be Alexandria and Constantinople, just as they had been before the start of the crusades. In these two cities were the termini of the great trade routes of the east, the greatest concentrations of luxury goods for import into Europe, and the best overseas markets for European exports. Extensive European commercial settlements existed in both cities: in 1215–16 Alexandria was said to house a community of three thousand European merchants.

Until well into the twelfth century commerce in the Holy Land

and Syria was conducted with the aid of the coinages of these neighbouring economies, the Byzantine hyperperon and the Egyptian dinar, both of gold. Many crusader coins were simply copies of one or the other, and as late as 1250 the papal legate Eudes of Châteauroux protested at the use of coins with Arabic inscriptions. The crusader solution was to mint coins bearing the cross and with Arabic lettering in praise of the Trinity. It is not surprising that in the long run a western conquest of Constantinople and its empire seemed to be of greater importance than the defence or the reconquest of Jerusalem; nor that European trade with Egypt continued even at times when the Egyptians and the crusader states were at war, and that this trade included items such as timber, rope and pitch which were vital to Egyptian seapower, and whose export was nominally forbidden.

Considerations of this kind suggest a rather ambiguous attitude towards the idea of the crusade, and towards the crusader states which that idea had helped to bring about, on the part of westerners at home in Europe. On the positive side of the argument there is the famous passage from William of Malmesbury that 'there was no nation so remote, no people so retired as not to contribute its portion. . . . The Welshman left his hunting, the Scot his fellowship with lice, the Dane his drinking party, the Norwegian his warship. Lands were deserted of their husbandsmen, houses of their inhabitants, even whole cities migrated.' The arrival of a fleet from distant Norway in 1110 under the command of the Norwegian king Sigurd contributed to the capture of Sidon and Beirut; there was even a guidebook to the Holy Land written for visitors from Iceland. References of this kind at least help to indicate the widespread appeal of the crusades. No statistics are possible, but a great many Europeans visited the Holy Land during the two centuries between 1099 and 1291, as pilgrims, merchants, or soldiers. The movement of people to the east went on constantly, and was not restricted to the grandiose expeditions led by members of the higher European nobility or by kings and emperors which are so misleadingly described as if they alone were *the* crusades.

The steady flow of European travellers to the east cannot, however, alter the fact that the great majority of those who survived the rigours of the journey went home again. There was no substantial transfer of population from Europe to the east to form a permanent colonial settlement, and this at a time when the population of Europe was growing steadily. Instead the overflow of population served to fill the empty lands which still existed within western Europe itself, went to the lands newly conquered from the Slavs in eastern Europe and the Baltic area, or was used to strengthen control of conquered territory in Wales or Ireland.

There was also, during the course of the thirteenth century, a growing body of criticism of the crusading idea within Europe from both lay and ecclesiastical sources. This is too complex a phenomenon to examine in detail, but it stemmed from such factors as the direction of crusades against the Albigensian heretics or against the Greek empire at Constantinople; from clerical resentment against papal taxation of the Church in aid of the crusade; and from those who felt that rulers like Louis IX of France expended time and money which could have been better employed at home. There were also discordant voices like those of the Dominican William of Tripoli and the English Franciscan Roger Bacon, who questioned the very existence of the crusade on the grounds of the bloodshed it entailed, and also because they considered that force was not a justified means of converting the infidel to Christianity; and there were the more cynical views of those who felt that expeditions to the Holy Land were a mere diversion from the delights of making money in the most profitable markets, or of secular rulers like Philip IV of France who were not prepared to lend support to crusading enterprises which might be used by the papacy to enhance its own prestige and authority.

None the less, significant, if relatively small, numbers of Europeans did make their homes in the conquered lands in Syria and Palestine, and the question has consequently been asked whether these settlers came in time to constitute a Franco-Syrian nation, made up of cultural and racial elements drawn from both Europe and the east. In a well-known passage the twelfth-century chronicler Fulcher of Chartres commented: 'We who were Occidentals now have been made Orientals, he who was a Roman or a Frank is now a Galilean or an inhabitant of Palestine. One who was a citizen of Rheims or of Chartres has now been made a citizen of Tyre or of Antioch.' We may also point to the sympathetic attitude towards Moslems expressed by Archbishop William of Tyre, or to the knowledge of Arabic possessed both by himself and by so obviously secular a figure as the notorious Reynald of Châtillon. New arrivals in the Holy Land often met with resentment from Europeans who were already resident there, or expressed amazement at the luxurious standard of life of some of the colonists, and suspected that they were becoming effete and too much influenced by their adopted country.

Such examples tend to obscure the more sober fact of a lack of colonists in the East, and the general unwillingness of those who did settle there to try to understand the world of Islam, many of whose adherents lived either in their midst or in close proximity. Nor was any serious attempt made to understand the complex-ities of the various Christian communities who lived in the cru-sader states. The Latin Church exercised religious dominance through its patriarchs at Jerusalem and Antioch, and behind them stood the power of Rome itself. A union between the Maronite Christians and the Church of Rome was achieved in 1181; other such agreements were attempted but none succeeded. Politically the most important of the other religious groups were the Orthodox Christians, because of their relations with Con-stantinople, even though in most cases no administrative con-nection with the Byzantine empire had existed for centuries. The Greeks were not openly persecuted but little attention was given to them, all of which added to the hostility which grew during the twelfth century between the Byzantine empire and the crusader states.

The Holy Land also seems to have been curiously little affected by new movements in western Christianity. Although the Cister-cians, for example, were founded at about the same time as the first crusade was under way, and despite the fact that one of their number, Bernard of Clairvaux, was prominent in the preaching of the second crusade, very few houses of this otherwise very prolific order were founded in the crusader states. The same appears to have been true of other religious orders, although their houses might individually be of great importance, such as that of the Augustinian canons which formed the chapter of the church of the Holy Sepulchre in Jerusalem. The Holy Land was the scene of the foundation of the Carmelite order of friars in the thirteenth century, but this was to be of greater importance in Europe than in the land of its origin. The same was partly true of the order of the Teutonic knights which was founded late in the twelfth century, and proceeded to play a leading role in the crusades against the heathen Lithuanians of the Baltic lands. The knights did, however, retain an interest in the Holy Land through their control of the key fortress of Starkenburg (or Montfort) near Acre. The only religious orders to be of special importance in the Holy Land were the two other military orders, the Hospitallers and Templars, which may be regarded as the special contribution of the Holy Land to the development of Christianity.

The overall impression is that the crusader states of Syria and Palestine went their own way in matters religious and secular, and that the society established by the relatively small number of European colonists was one which embodied elements of both western and eastern culture but which resolutely refused to fit into either. A relevant analogy is perhaps to be found in Ireland where the Norman, French, English, and Welsh colonists had come by the early fourteenth century to form a 'middle nation'.

In the end the survival of the European colonies in Syria and Palestine depended not just on their own limited resources, but on the degree of practical interest displayed by their fellows at home in Europe in the form of colonists for permanent settlement and military assistance at all times, not just when it was most urgently needed, and on a strong commercial incentive for preserving these European footholds. But their survival also depended on the good will of their Moslem neighbours or, if that could not be ensured, on Moslem disunity. When none of these conditions was fulfilled the end of the crusader states could be predicted. However valiant the defence of Acre in the summer of 1291, there was no way of restoring the position of the crusaders even to that of fifty years before, let alone to that of 1099. European merchants found the attractions of trade with the Moslem world and the spoils of the dismembered Byzantine empire greater than those of the Holy Land. Much of the military power which could have gone there went instead to Cyprus, whose rulers retained the empty title of king of Jerusalem until the fifteenth century; or, less justifiably, it was expended in creating French states in Greece out of former Byzantine territory, until the French were in their turn expelled by the Catalan Great Company of mercenaries early in the fourteenth century.

Even the material influence of the crusades on Europe seems to have been much less than was once thought. The art of fortification, for instance, appears to have been little more advanced in the east than in Europe: one of the few eastern influences that can be shown in Europe is the design of the walls of Edward I's castle at Caernarvon in North Wales, and there it came from Constantinople and not the Holy Land. The spices and luxury goods of the east could be obtained much more readily from Constantinople or Alexandria than from Beirut or Tyre. The existence of a hostile Moslem-controlled hinterland meant that although the crusader states were situated on the edge of a vast and exciting continent, there was little prospect of penetrating it from that direction, while the elimination of those states in 1291 removed the possibility altogether.

In one sense, therefore, the crusades were a dead end. They were one example of the potential for expansion which existed in western Europe between the eleventh and thirteenth centuries, but they were not the prime cause of the expansion, nor were they the only form which it took. It might also be argued that the growth of international trade, wherever it took place, was of far greater and more general importance to the economy of western Europe as a whole than a movement which tended to involve only a relatively small number of religious enthusiasts and military adventurers.

On the other hand the crusades brought Europe into close proximity with other cultures. It is true that contacts with Moslem society already existed in Spain and Sicily, but these areas were only on the periphery of a much greater Moslem world centred on the major cities of Baghdad, Damascus, and Cairo, of which Europeans now became aware, even if they did not often visit or try to understand it. And beyond the centres of Moslem culture there lay other even stranger and more dimly known lands as yet unpenetrated, and perhaps impenetrable.

Yet the idea of the crusade was to survive the débâcle of 1291, and was to take on new forms alongside the old in the fourteenth and fifteenth centuries. However unrealistic its aims may have been, the crusade was never entirely lost sight of in the later middle ages. There was also a strong sense of Christian missionary zeal, which had been given some expression in the Holy Land by the Dominicans and Franciscans, but which had not yet had an opportunity to flourish; and there were still commercial ambitions to be fulfilled. Out of the blue, as it seemed, and at almost the same time that the crusades were beginning to falter, there came the chance to realize some of these ambitions. In the third and fourth decades of the thirteenth century the armies of the nomadic Mongol horsemen emerged from the unknown heart of the continent of Asia. One of the results was an expansion of Europe of a kind never before achieved.

II
Europe and Asia

4

Europe and the Mongol invasions

The experiences of trade, pilgrimage, and the crusades made the
westernmost parts of the continent of Asia familiar destinations
to many thousands of individuals from western Europe. The
small numbers of European colonists who put down permanent
roots there were equally familiar with the dangers from the
Moslem enemies who surrounded them and with the experience
of catastrophe. But if western Asia was a source of immediate
danger, the remoter regions of the continent had for centuries been
a source of mystery and of legend: many of the wondrous animals
and races of men that were so beloved of the writers of classical
antiquity and their successors in medieval Europe were located in
various parts of the continent. However, in the twelfth century
new causes of European interest in Asia began to appear.

From at least the third century there had been a tradition in
Europe that the apostle St Thomas had gone to India soon after
the Resurrection to preach the Gospel, and had been martyred
there. In 883 Alfred the Great had sent Athelstan and Sighelm, a
future bishop of Sherborne, with gifts for St Thomas's shrine at
Mailapur on the east coast of India, and in the early twelfth
century the Anglo-Norman chronicler Orderic Vitalis also showed
his familiarity with the legend. In 1122–3 the story gained added
prominence when a man claiming to be an Indian partriarch
named John visited Pope Calixtus II in Rome, and gave further
alleged details of St Thomas and the church he had founded in
India. On its own the St Thomas legend did no more than provide
Europeans with the thought that in the heart of Asia there existed
a community of their fellow Christians; and as yet the crusader
states in Syria and the Holy Land were not under any critical
pressure from their Moslem neighbours. Twenty years after the
patriarch John's visit to Rome the situation was dramatically
altered.

On Christmas Eve 1144 the city of Edessa fell to the forces of Zengi; shortly after news of this disaster reached Europe, Hugh, the French-born bishop of Gabala near Antioch, arrived at the papal curia. On 18 November 1145, at Viterbo, Bishop Hugh had an audience with Pope Eugenius III, and told him of a certain Prester John, who was descended from the Magi and was a Christian, and who ruled over a kingdom of great wealth somewhere in the east. This king had recently won a great victory over the brother kings of the Medes and the Persians, and had intended coming to the aid of Jerusalem, but had been prevented from doing so because his army was unable to cross the river Tigris.

Bishop Hugh's story was also heard by Otto of Freising who incorporated it into the chronicle he was then writing. However, this second-hand report of 1145 was soon overshadowed by the appearance in Europe of a seemingly authentic letter from Prester John himself. He described himself as the ruler of the Three Indias, which extended from the Tower of Babel to the rising of the sun; he gave an elaborate account of the marvels and riches of his kingdom, and declared his intention of visiting the Holy Sepulchre after defeating the enemies of Christ. According to the thirteenth-century chronicler Alberic des Trois Fontaines, the letter had arrived in 1165 and was addressed in the first instance to the Byzantine emperor Manuel Comnenus, but was soon circulated to rulers in western Europe as well. Coming at a time when Moslem pressure on the crusader states was increasing, the letter was a welcome promise of relief. In 1177 Pope Alexander III wrote what is generally understood to have been a reply to Prester John, and sent it off to the east in the care of his personal physician and envoy, Master Philip.

Nothing more was heard of Philip after his arrival in Palestine, and Alexander III received no answer to his letter for the very good reason that Prester John had no existence in reality. For the moment the origins of the Prester John legend, and the relationship between the details given in the letter and other medieval beliefs about the wonders of Asia must be left on one side. What is clear is that from about the 1160s western European interest in Asia was stimulated by the prospect that somewhere in its unknown recesses there existed a king whose aid might once and for all bring about the triumph of Christendom over its enemies. The mission of the physician Philip in 1177, and the pilgrimages to the tomb of St Thomas by St Bernard the Penitent of Languedoc, and by the German, Henry of Morungen in the closing decades of the twelfth century were to be only the first in a long series of western ventures into Asia in the thirteenth and fourteenth centuries. Many of these travellers, whose journeys in fact produced a great deal of authentic information about the continent and its peoples, sought either deliberately or incidentally to discover the whereabouts of Prester John. In this sense the fantasies woven around this figure were a spur to a great era of European travel and discovery.

The gradual revelation of the mysteries of Asia was taken a stage further between 1218 and 1221, at the time of the siege and occupation of the city of Damietta in the Nile Delta by the European forces of the fifth crusade. In order to restore the flagging enthusiasm of their followers, some of the religious leaders of the crusading army, notably Jacques de Vitry, bishop of Acre, and one of the papal legates, Cardinal Pelagius of Albano, began to circulate a collection of prophetic writings which held out the prospect of imminent outside assistance for their campaign. The Christian ruler of Ethiopia was particularly singled out for this purpose. This would lead to the destruction of Islam and the reconquest of Jerusalem, to be followed shortly afterwards by the Last Judgement.

Another report circulating in the crusading army claimed that a certain King David, who was either a descendant of Prester John or to be identified with him, was at that very time advancing into Persia. It was also suggested that David was in some way connected with the tribes of Gog and Magog who had, according to legend, been shut up behind the Caucasus mountains by Alexander the Great, and whose coming would herald the end of the world. So convinced were Jacques de Vitry and Pelagius of the truth of this story that they reported it to Pope Honorius III, who in 1221 passed on the news to the bishops of England and France, and claimed that the armies of King David had been sent by God to destroy the Moslems. The crusaders at Damietta did not receive any outside help, and in September 1222 they were thankful to be allowed to evacuate Egypt in peace. Yet there *were* dramatic events taking place in the heart of Asia at this time, great clashes of arms and the fall of empires. A devastating raid on southern Russia in 1222 by hitherto unknown attackers from the east was another sign that something untoward and deeply disturbing was occurring.

In one sense Jacques de Vitry and Honorius III were right in their descriptions of what was happening. The armies in question did believe in a divine mission, and they were certainly bent on exterminating Islam, at least as a political force. But there any analogy with Prester John or King David came to an end. It is possible that David was actually Küchlüg, the ruler of the central Asian empire of Kara Khitai, but his movements were those of a fugitive not of a conqueror. Close on his heels were the armies of the Mongols, from a region of Asia so remote as to be totally unknown to anyone in Europe, and prepared to destroy anyone who lay in their path, regardless of religion. The false rumours of the advance of King David which penetrated to Damietta were in fact the first hints of great events which were soon to threaten the very existence of Europe as a cultural and political entity, and which profoundly affected its relations with the continent of Asia for more than a century to come.

The Mongols were yet another of the nomadic peoples of Asia who have come into conflict with settled cultures throughout recorded history: the Chinese, for example, were long familiar with the dangers that lay in the steppes to their north and built the Great Wall to keep out nomad attackers in the third century BC; in the seventeenth century the Manchus, the last of the great nomad invaders, set up the Chinese imperial dynasty which ended in 1912. The western European experience of such threats includes the Huns who attacked the Roman empire in the fifth century, the Hungarian raiders of the ninth and tenth centuries, the Seljuk Turks whose conquests in Asia Minor and the Holy Land were one of the causes of the first crusade, and the Ottoman Turks who threatened to overrun Europe in the fifteenth and sixteenth centuries.

Only exceptionally did these nomadic upheavals in inner Asia have more than regional implications, but when this did occur the consequences were awesome. The first known example of this kind was the empire created by the Turks in the mid-sixth century which lasted until its fall at the hands of Arab armies in 751. At its peak this empire stretched from the Great Wall of China to the Black Sea, and was known to the civilizations of China and Constantinople, as well as to those of India and Persia. The Mongols of the thirteenth century were conquerors on this scale, and were to create an even vaster domain.

In modern usage the name Mongolia is applied to a large area of steppe country between the Soviet Union and China, and to a province of China itself. The original Mongols, however, were a single tribe living in the region of Lake Baikal, but were also closely related to a number of other tribes, who included the Tatars, the Naimans, and the Keraits. Each tribe had its own individual characteristics, arising from its history or from the extent to which it had been influenced by the culture of more advanced neighbours, such as the Uighur Turks who were to supply the thirteenth-century Mongol empire with a written language for use in administration and in diplomacy, or by new religious beliefs like Buddhism and Nestorian Christianity.

The historical traditions of the Mongol tribe suggest that at an earlier stage they had inhabited the forest or the borderlands between the forest and the steppe, but long before the thirteenth century they and their related tribes all came to have in common a nomadic way of life practised on the steppes of the high Mongolian plateau, where they had to endure the extremes of cold of the long and savage winters, and the burning heat and violent storms of the brief summer months. The nomads depended for their survival on vast herds of animals, especially sheep and horses. The sheep provided meat and also wool, which was used either to make felt cloth which was spread over a wooden frame to make a tent, or for clothing which was rarely if ever washed in order to preserve its natural grease as well as that of its wearer, and so supplied added insulation against the bitter cold of winter. The key to the whole nomadic way of life was to be found in their horses, hardy and capable of great endurance, and much smaller than their European counterparts. Mare's milk was used to make a strongly alcoholic drink called koumiss, or was preserved in the form of curd for use on long journeys. But above all horses provided the mobility essential for the peacetime existence of the Mongols, and in war allowed them to move with a speed entirely unknown elsewhere.

The Mongol prowess in war drew them very forcibly to the attention of nearly every corner of Europe and Asia, and the consequences were to be seen in massacres and devastation throughout central Asia and eastern Europe. These consequences all derived ultimately from the career and influence on posterity of a remarkable military leader, Genghis Khan. He was born, most probably in 1167, allegedly of divine descent from the sky-god Tengri, and clutching a clot of blood in his right hand as a portent of future greatness. The reality was, however, somewhat humbler than the later legend. At his birth he was named Temujin after a Tatar chieftain who had been captured by his father Yesugei, a member of the ruling family of the Mongol tribe. After Yesugei was murdered the young Temujin led a hunted life, gradually acquiring a reputation for enterprise and daring which gained him a following, until in 1206 his rule over the Mongols and their neighbours the Tatars, Keraits, Naimans, and Merkits, was undisputed, and he was proclaimed as Genghis Khan or 'universal ruler'. Already at a comparatively advanced age for someone who had lived so conspicuously in a violent society, and with many campaigns behind him, Genghis Khan set out in his remaining twenty years of life to make his new title a reality.

The sense of divinely appointed mission which attended his conquests and those of his successors can vividly be illustrated by the response in 1246 of Genghis's grandson, the Great Khan Küyük, to a letter he had received from Pope Innocent IV. To the Great Khan any letter from a ruler who was not yet one of his subjects could only be an offer of submission, and Küyük professed to be baffled by the papal request that he should accept baptism, and by the complaint about Mongol treatment of the Hungarians and other Christian peoples who had recently been attacked. In reply Küyük remarked that the Hungarians and others had disregarded God's order, transmitted by Genghis Khan and by his successor Ögedei Khan, that they should submit to the Mongols, and had also killed the Mongol envoys:

Thus the eternal God himself has killed and exterminated the people in these countries. How could anybody, without God's order, merely from his own strength, kill and rob? And when you go on to say, 'I am a Christian, I honour God', how do you think you know whom God will absolve and in whose favour he will exercise his mercy? How do you think you know, that you dare to express such an opinion? Through the power of God, all empires from sunrise to sunset have been given to us, and we own them. How could anybody achieve anything except on God's order? Now, however, you must say from a sincere heart: 'We shall be obedient, we too make our strength available.' You personally, at the head of the Kings, you shall come, one and all, to pay homage to me, and to serve me. Then, we shall take note of your submission. If, however, you do not accept God's order, we shall know that you are our enemies.

In 1211 Genghis began the conquest of China by attacking the territory of the Chin empire, which ruled the northern part of the country, and took its capital Peking in 1215. His energies were then diverted to central and western Asia, however, and the Chin empire was not to fall entirely under Mongol control until 1234, after his death. In 1218 he destroyed the empire of the Kara Khitai, in the vicinity of Lake Balkhash, which had recently come under the rule of Küchlüg, the former chief of the Naimans and an old enemy of Genghis Khan. The Khitai ceased to exist as a people but their name lived on as 'Cathay', the term applied by Europeans to China in the medieval period, and still used in the Russian language today.

These conquests brought the Mongols to the Khwarismian empire, in the region between the Sea of Aral and Afghanistan, which was conquered between 1219 and 1222. This gave the Mongols control of great central Asian cities such as Bukhara, Samarkand, and Merv. For the first time the Mongols had confronted and destroyed one of the Moslem states of Asia. Genghis Khan then turned his attention back towards the east in order to conquer the Tangut kingdom of Hsi-Hsia, which formed a buffer between Mongolia and China, and it was during the siege of the capital Ning-Hsia that he died in 1227.

The Mongol campaigns in Asia under Genghis Khan and his successor, Ögedei Khan, won control of vast territories and caused serious disruption and alarm in other areas such as Iran which had suffered devastating raids but not permanent occupation. By the 1250s the Great Khan Möngke was ready to resume the advance, and in 1253 a new Mongol army left Karakorum in Mongolia for the west. In 1256-7 the Assassins, a Moslem sect which had terrorized its neighbours from mountain fortresses in Iran, were destroyed; in 1258 it was the turn of Baghdad, the capital of the Abbasid caliphate, and the spiritual centre of much of Islam. Baghdad fell in February, the caliph was executed, and five centuries of Moslem rule and culture came to an end. With little more than Syria and Egypt remaining, it now seemed as if the Mongols would soon conquer the entire Moslem world. In 1260 they invaded Syria and took Damascus, but on 3 September were defeated by the Egyptian army at Ain Jalud near Nazareth. This was their first major defeat, and as it turned out, was a significant stage in the delimitation of their empire.

In the east important conquests were still to be made. In 1259 Möngke died, and was succeeded by his brother Kublai, who promptly abandoned the old Mongol capital of Karakorum, and established himself in Peking (renamed Khanbalik), which became the base for the conquest of the Sung empire ruling China to the south of the Yangtze. This was completed in 1276 with the fall of the Sung capital of Hangchow, and in 1279 Kublai Khan became the first emperor of a new dynasty, the Yuan, which was to rule all of China for almost a century.

The Mongol advances in Asia may appear to have little or nothing to do with Europe, a mere appendage at the far western end of the much vaster Asian continent, and an unattractive prospect for conquest when compared with the wealth of China, or with that of the great cities of central Asia and Syria. From this point of view there might seem to be little need for a Mongol conquest of Europe, save perhaps in the interest of avenging slights to their authority, or in forwarding the completion of their world domination. On the other hand it was to prove of the greatest importance to Europe that the Mongols should have taken control of China and the lands to the west, because of the unprecedented opportunities that were provided for European diplomats, missionaries, and merchants. But before any of this could come about Europe had to survive an onslaught of a ferocity for which even the attacks of the Vikings and Magyars in earlier centuries hardly provided a comparison, and for which it was almost totally unprepared.

The first European experience of the Mongols had been in 1221–2 during a devastating raid into the Caucasus and southern Russia, which had been an almost incidental detail of the Mongol conquests then taking place in central Asia. The horror of the occasion is described by the Novgorod chronicle (although Novgorod itself was not attacked) which recorded: 'For our sins, unknown tribes came, none knows who they are or whence they came . . . nor what their language is, nor of what race they are, nor what their faith is . . . God alone knows who they are and whence they came out.'

Although the Mongols then disappeared from European view for the next fifteen years, a channel of communication with Asia was maintained by the kingdom of Hungary, whose king, Bela IV (1235–70), sent out a number of Dominicans as envoys. Their function was to establish contact with the pagan Bashkirs of south-western Siberia, who were thought to be of the same stock as the ancestors of the Hungarians, but with the additional aim of discovering more about the Mongols. The Hungarians were apparently also trying to convert to Christianity another pagan people, the Cumans of southern Russia. The exact chronology of all these activities is unknown, with the significant exception of the last Hungarian mission, undertaken by a Dominican named Julian, who left early in 1236 and returned in December 1237, having failed to reach the Greater Hungary of the Bashkirs, but bringing with him definite information on the impending Mongol attack. The warning was then transmitted to the pope by Julian himself.

By this time indications of the Mongol intentions were starting to accumulate, had anyone been fully able to appreciate them. At some stage the emperor Frederick II appears to have received a demand for submission to which he is said to have replied by offering to put his skills as a falconer at the disposal of the Great Khan. King Bela of Hungary also received a demand, the severity of whose terms was compounded by the protection he had given to Cuman refugees fleeing the Mongol advance. There is also the strange episode recorded by Matthew Paris of the visit to the English court by an envoy from the 'Old Man of the Mountain', the head of the Assassins of Iran, whose Syrian branch was well known to, and feared by, the European colonists of the crusader states. The envoy is said to have pleaded for western help against the common enemy, and to have been interrupted by the bishop of Winchester, Peter des Roches, who had been in the Holy Land in the late 1220s, with the words:

Let us leave dogs to devour one another, that they may all be consumed, and perish; and we, when we proceed against the enemies of Christ who remain, will slay them, and cleanse the face of the earth, so the world will be subject to the one Catholic Church, and there will be one fold and one shepherd.

These signs and portents were the outcome of a carefully laid Mongol plan of attack on Russia and eastern Europe, which was already in motion long before Julian of Hungary heard of it in 1237. Because of the great distances involved, any Mongol attack against territories on their periphery had to be planned several years ahead, and carefully co-ordinated for maximum effect. The campaign which began in Europe in the late 1230s had been decided upon at a *kuriltai* or assembly held at Karakorum in 1235, and coincided with the opening of operations against the Sung empire in China, with the conquest of the kingdom of Korea, and with an attack on the Seljuk Turkish empire of Rum in Asia Minor. Within the limits of a single campaign the Mongol armies were frequently divided, partly to ease the pressure on the pasture land required by their enormous herds of horses, but also in order to destroy individual opponents before they could assist one another. Often it would be agreed in advance that the divided armies should reunite on a given date, which it was the duty of the army commander to observe, so creating the possibility of developing strategic movements of envelopment against an enemy. The operations of the Mongol forces in Poland and Hungary in 1241 seem to have been dictated by some plan of this kind, and in 1289, when the Il-khan of Iran was in correspondence with Philip IV of France about a proposed joint campaign in the Holy Land in the spring of 1291, he was very insistent that both armies should arrive on the appointed date.

The Mongol army was also highly organized within itself into units ranging from ten men at the smallest to the *tümen* of 10,000 at the largest. This allowed for a precise chain of command and for strict discipline, and made it possible to exercise effective control over the actions of large forces. Cavalry troops, either heavily armed with a sword and lance, or composed of more lightly armed archers who were capable of firing their powerful compound bow from horseback, were the major part of the Mongol army. Since each rider might own as many as twenty horses, an army could travel swiftly and with little need for prolonged halts. At one stage the army which invaded Hungary in 1241 is said to have covered a distance of 200 miles in three days, an achievement which was impossible for the far more cumbersome European cavalry forces of the time.

The Mongol armies were undoubtedly often very large, numbering about 150,000 in the case of the force commanded by Batu and Sübedei which set out for its European campaign early in 1236. But such numbers were not necessarily present on a battlefield all at one time, while the size of Mongol armies may often have appeared much larger to contemporaries on account of the large numbers of spare horses, and the speed of their advance. It is also worth noting that modern use of the word 'horde' to mean very large numbers has probably also introduced some exaggeration. The Turkish word *ordu*, from which 'horde' derives, originally meant 'camp': in this sense the Golden Horde, the title given to the branch of the Mongols who ruled southern Russia after the conquests of the 1230s, was simply the name of their encampment, and had nothing to do with their numbers.

At the end of 1237 Sübedei advanced into Russia, capturing and destroying the city of Ryazan with all its population; in February 1238 the same fate befell the two cities of Vladimir and Suzdal, while Novgorod was saved only by the spring floods which made the ground around it impassable. After a lull during 1239 the Mongols resumed their advance. In December 1240 Kiev was destroyed, and with it almost the last of the principalities of Russia. Meanwhile in the north the Mongols were preparing to invade Poland which they entered early in 1241. Duke Henry of Silesia hastily gathered a Polish and German army, together with some help from the Teutonic Order and the Knights Templar, and from Moravia, and faced the invaders near Liegnitz in Silesia. Here on 9 April 1241 the European army was practically wiped out, nine sacks of ears were collected by the Mongols from the slain, and despatched to Karakorum as evidence of their victory, and the surrounding area was thoroughly devastated. Two days later the same fate overtook the army of the kingdom of Hungary at Mohi, at the hands of the main Mongol force led by Sübedei and Batu. During the rest of 1241 Hungary was conquered, its king was pursued into Dalmatia from where he escaped to an island in the Adriatic, and a small Mongol force penetrated to the vicinity of Vienna in Austria. On the face of it the French Templar who wrote to Louis IX that the Mongols were likely to conquer the Germans and would soon be on the borders of France was not exaggerating. At the end of 1241 Europe seemed to be on the verge of the greatest catastrophe it had ever suffered, with consequences for its future development that were quite unpredictable.

The initial reaction in Europe to the attacks of the Mongols was one of unreasoning horror and despair, fuelled by firsthand experience of the onslaught, by the oral and written reports of those who had survived it, and by the rumours which travelled ahead of the enemy advance. Some thought that the Mongol armies must be the tribes of Gog and Magog, released from their captivity, and heralding the end of the world. A more sophisticated response was the pun attributed to Louis IX of France which equated the Tatars, one of the related tribes of the Mongols, with the classical Tartarus, and concluded that they must have come from Hell itself. The English chronicler Matthew Paris, who recorded both this story and the texts of letters which gave details of the Mongol onslaught on Russia, and of their advance into Austria, as well as much other information, gave his view of the Mongols and their character in an extremely lurid passage:

Swarming like locusts over the face of the earth, they have brought terrible devastation to the eastern parts [of Europe], laying them waste with fire and carnage. . . . For they are inhuman and beastly, rather monsters than men, thirsting for and drinking blood, tearing and devouring the flesh of dogs and men. . . . And so they come with the swiftness of lightning to the confines of Christendom, ravaging and slaughtering, striking everyone with terror and incomparable horror.

The capacity of the Mongols to terrify their victims, even without the supernatural powers ascribed to them by Matthew Paris, is well described in a much quoted passage from the Persian historian Ibn al-Athir, who wrote a few years before Matthew, in the wake of the initial devastation of Iran by the Mongols but before its final incorporation into their dominions. Although the author did not claim to be an eyewitness to the stories he recounted, it is likely that they do give a fair representation of the reaction of a people to the swift, merciless, and seemingly irresistible onslaught of the invaders:

Stories have been related to me which the hearer can scarcely credit as to the terror of them [the Mongols] which God Almighty cast into men's hearts; so that it is said that a single one of them would enter a village or a quarter wherein were many people, and would continue to slay them one after another, none daring to stretch forth his hand against this horseman. And I have heard that one of them took a man captive, but had not with him any weapon wherewith to kill him; and he said to his prisoner, 'Lay your head on the ground and do not move'; and he did so, and the Tartar went and fetched his sword and slew him forthwith.

There is no doubt that in battle the Mongol tactics of swift movement and envelopment, their ability to fire arrows accurately from horseback, and their ruthless pursuit of defeated enemies, were enough to demoralize the strongest opponent, even when these were not combined with unfamiliar weapons such as the form of smoke-screen that was apparently employed at the battle of Liegnitz in 1241. The belief among some historians that the Mongols also used an early form of gunpowder artillery in their European campaign has been discredited, and it seems that the Mongols were at their weakest in the practical arts necessary for such military operations as sieges. They were always careful to spare the lives of engineers and craftsmen whom they captured.

In the case of their advance into Europe, there is some evidence that a resolutely defended fortress such as Breslau and even

Liegnitz itself could resist an assault, especially if the Mongols' timetable would be too much upset by a prolonged siege. In Asia, however, there had been, and were still to be, many occasions on which the Mongols took great cities such as Bukhara and Samarkand. If resistance was prolonged, or if the inhabitants had killed Mongol ambassadors or had committed some other act of defiance, atrocious massacres might follow the fall of a city. Ibn al-Athir recorded that 700,000 people were killed systematically after the capture of Merv in 1221, and at Baghdad in 1258 there was another mass slaughter estimated at from 800,000 to as many as 2,000,000 people. The figures are certainly much exaggerated, but it is equally certain that the extent and the frequency of the massacres committed by the Mongols were profoundly shocking even to a thirteenth-century world which was not unfamiliar with violent death.

No cities of the size of those in Asia were captured or indeed existed in Europe, so that the scale of the slaughter was probably much smaller. None the less the evidence of wholesale killings could be found on the battlefields of Silesia and Hungary in 1241; in the massacre of Hungarian prisoners in 1242 after they had been released, and thought they were free to return home; and in the human bones still littering the ground around the ruins of Kiev when Carpini passed that way in 1246.

Faced with such dismal and appalling events any orderly and concerted European resistance of counter-attack was unlikely. It is true that in July 1241 the emperor Frederick II wrote to Henry III of England (and presumably to his fellow sovereigns elsewhere in Europe) recounting the Mongol attacks, and calling on all the nations of Europe to send troops against them. But, given the controversial personality of Frederick II, and the continuing enmity between himself and the papacy, such a call to arms was little more than an exercise in rhetoric, and nothing came of the plan.

Instead Europe was saved from a probably fatal continuation of the conquests of 1241 by the death of the Great Khan Ögedei in December of that year. When news of it reached the Mongol commanders in Europe they withdrew, ostensibly in order to attend a *kuriltai* in Mongolia to elect a new Great Khan. The election of Ögedei's brother, Küyük, who had led one of the armies in Europe, did not in the event take place until 1246, the delay being symptomatic of the dissensions which were already starting to appear in the Mongol ranks, and which were the underlying reason both for their withdrawal from Europe and also for the gradual breakup of their empire in the years which followed.

None of this was known in Europe. The disappearance of the Mongols, almost as suddenly as they had come, seemed like a miracle. But mixed with the feeling of relief was the fear that the Mongols might one day return, especially since they still controlled large areas of Russia. Küyük might well have renewed the attack, had he not died suddenly in 1248; in 1258–9 the Mongols in Russia made another devastating raid into Poland in pursuit of the disobedient ruler of Galicia; Poland was invaded again in 1288, and it was only from 1290 that both Poland and Hungary returned to permanent European control. For half a century the resumption of the Mongol conquests in Europe had therefore seemed imminent, a point which should be emphasized and placed alongside the unhindered activities of European merchants, missionaries, and diplomats in the Mongol dominions in Asia, as well as the attempts that were being made at the same period to bring the Mongol rulers of Iran into a joint military enterprise against the Moslem powers in Syria and Egypt.

The beginnings of a more reasoned response to the Mongol onslaught, in the form of a desire to discover more about the invaders, and if possible to persuade them to call off their attacks, existed even when the terror they had caused was still fresh. Just as Bela IV of Hungary had done in the 1230s, so Pope Innocent IV now took the lead. Having first summoned a general council to meet at Lyons in June 1245 to discuss the Mongol threat and the situation in the Holy Land following the loss of Jerusalem in 1244, the pope appointed two Franciscans, Giovanni di Piano Carpini from near Perugia in Italy, and Lawrence of Portugal, to visit the Great Khan himself.

Carpini was an excellent choice as an envoy. He was a man of mature experience who had been one of the early associates of Francis of Assisi, and since 1222 had taken a leading role in the establishment of the Franciscan order in Germany, Scandinavia, and eastern Europe. In the 1240s the two major orders of friars, the Franciscans and Dominicans, were of recent foundation, full of enthusiasm, and inured to hardship and danger, and both were to be of great importance in western European diplomatic and missionary activity in Asia during the rest of the thirteenth as well as the fourteenth century. In later years the Franciscan devotion to poverty was to cause dissension within their order, and threatened the Church itself with division, but for the time being this very quality made the Franciscans particularly well suited to the challenges of travel and evangelization in remote and totally alien lands.

Carpini and his companion left Lyons in April 1245, were joined at Breslau by another Franciscan, Benedict the Pole, and arrived at the ruins of Kiev early in 1246. After satisfying the Mongols in the vicinity that they were genuine envoys, they were then hastened on their journey and were allowed little opportunity for rest, in order that they might arrive at Karakorum in time for the election of the new Great Khan. They reached the Mongol camp a few miles from Karakorum (which they were destined never to see) on 22 July 1246, and on 24 August witnessed the enthronement of Genghis Khan's grandson Küyük as Great Khan of the Mongols and their allies, and as ruler of a great part of Asia.

In these early years of the Mongol expansion, before their conquests of Iran and China had been completed, all roads led to Karakorum, the Mongol capital south of Lake Baikal. Envoys, suppliants, craftsmen, engineers, slaves, kings, and princes from any part of the world with which the Mongols had contact could be found there. While Carpini was at their court he met Yaroslavl, Grand Duke of the Russian principality of Suzdal, who died there, and whose two sons, Andrew and the famous Alexander Nevsky, were to visit Karakorum a year later to do homage to the Great Khan; a son of the king of Georgia was also there, and a number of Russians and Hungarians, some of whom had been prisoners of the Mongols for many years and knew their language and customs. When William of Rubruck was at Karakorum in 1254 he found a variety of foreigners: envoys from

John Vatatzes, the Greek emperor of Nicaea; a certain Basil, the son of an Englishman, who had been born in Hungary; a woman named Paquette from Lorraine who had been in Hungary when the Mongols arrived; and a Parisian master goldsmith Guillaume Boucher, who had been captured at Belgrade, and whose most conspicuous work at Karakorum was a silver tree at the entrance to the Great Khan's palace from which flowed streams of koumiss, wine, mead, and a rice drink. Shortly after Rubruck's visit Hayton, the king of Cilician Armenia, was there, as his brother Sempad, the constable of Armenia, had been in 1247–8, in quest of Mongol protection against the Seljuk Turks of Asia Minor.

Carpini returned to his starting-point at Lyons in November 1248. The news he brought with him was not encouraging. The letter he bore from Küyük in response to those of Innocent IV, in which the Great Khan expressed his amazement that anyone should dare to question the will of God as expressed through his Mongol agents, has already been quoted; but Carpini was able to add from his own experience a stern warning to the pope, and to Europe at large, that the dissension within Europe was a permanent temptation for the Mongols to resume their attack, and for this reason, among others, he had not taken up the Mongol offer to send envoys of their own.

Within a short time of his return to Europe Carpini was engaged in writing his *Historia Mongolorum*, which fascinated his contemporaries and which still has an immediacy of interest today. Carpini was not, however, the only European to venture into Mongol territory at this time, nor was he the only one to produce a narrative of his travels, so that before assessing the value of his account it will be useful to outline one of these other journeys.

In 1253 two more Franciscans, William of Rubruck, whose home was probably in Flanders, and Bartholomew of Cremona, set out from Acre in Palestine to visit the new Great Khan, Möngke. They did so at the instigation and with the support of Louis IX of France, who was then at Acre after his release from captivity in Egypt, and with the aim of discovering how far Mongol hostility to the Moslem world might be turned into active support for Christendom at a critical time in its fortunes in the east. Rubruck himself was also intensely interested in the possibility of spreading Christianity in the Mongol dominions should conditions prove favourable.

Rubruck and his companions travelled via Constantinople to the Crimea, and from there to the camp on the Volga of Batu, one of the invaders of Hungary in 1241. There they were met by a Mongol nobleman who had been ordered to escort them to Möngke, and who warned them to expect a journey of four months through cold so intense that it would split the rocks and the trees. The hardships proved to be as promised, and after a gruelling journey Rubruck arrived at Karakorum on 27 December 1253. After an eventful stay he left in July 1254, and arrived at Tripoli in Palestine in time to attend a Chapter of his order in August 1255. Rubruck's Minister then ordered him to return to Acre to lecture, and forbade him to go in person to Louis IX who had by this time gone back to France. In consequence Rubruck wrote an account of his journey which he dedicated to the French king.

Rubruck's narrative was not widely known in the medieval period, but the modern reader of his work and of Carpini's narrative has access to two independent accounts of a hitherto unknown part of Asia produced as a result of journeys undertaken within a few years of each other. Both accounts are substantial, Rubruck's being the longer, and both are of the utmost importance to an understanding of medieval Europe's knowledge of, and response to, the Mongols.

The narrative produced by Carpini gives the impression of an experienced diplomat carrying out his duties to the letter. He was required to produce information on the Mongol way of life, on their military organization, and on their intentions, and he did so effectively, leaving his masters in Europe in no doubt as to the risks they would run if they attempted to trifle with the Mongols. He warned, for example, that the Mongols were planning for an unbroken campaign of eighteen years against Europe, should this prove necessary.

On the other hand, despite the terror which the Mongols had induced in Europe only a few years earlier, Carpini portrayed them as human beings, and was careful to present what he saw as their good qualities: obedience, honesty, lack of violence amongst themselves, and the chastity of their women. It may be significant that Carpini was one of the few contemporary observers to refer to the Mongols by that name rather than describing them by the emotive name of Tartars. Carpini's account of Genghis Khan and his dynasty is accepted as generally accurate; he was aware of such cultural details as the Mongol adoption of the Uighur alphabet to write their own language; and his reference to the Mongol conquests in China is, though brief, the first western account of that country. Carpini also had the unique opportunity of being present at the time of the election of the Great Khan, and of witnessing his enthronement; he had several audiences with Küyük, whom he described as 'of medium height, very intelligent and extremely shrewd, and most serious and grave in his manner'.

Carpini's account is remarkable enough, but that of William of Rubruck is, if anything, even more interesting. Rubruck was evidently a man of great curiosity who was capable of making detailed observations of unfamiliar situations. He provides a more substantial description of the Mongol way of life and of his journey to the court of the Great Khan than Carpini, but has little to say about the history of the Mongols. He was concerned to describe what he had seen as accurately as possible, and in referring to the specially decorated wagons which were provided for married women, he remarked that he did not know how to describe them except by a picture, and that he would have made drawings of everything he saw if he had only known how to paint. This knowledge of the limitations imposed by words is also reflected by his admission that his interpreter was sometimes drunk, and that he could not always be sure that his words were properly translated to the Great Khan.

In Carpini's narrative there is, intermingled with accurate observation, a certain amount of fantastic material of the kind which is commonplace in medieval European writings. He refers at one point to Prester John, and describes him as the king of Greater India who had defeated the Mongols by making figures of men out of copper, filling them with Greek fire, and placing them on horseback, so burning up the Mongol army; he also speaks of an area where there were monsters in the shape of women, and where men took the form of dogs.

William of Rubruck shows a more critical turn of mind. He refers to a story he had heard about a leader of the Naimans, a Nestorian Christian called King John, but he then adds that when he passed through the pasture lands of this king he found that no one had heard of him apart from a few Nestorians. He remarks that the Nestorians 'used to tell of him ten times more than the truth . . . out of nothing they make a great rumour'. Similarly he rejects a story that somewhere beyond China there was a land in which a man would remain forever at the age at which he entered it. While he was at Karakorum William 'made enquiries about the monsters or human monstrosities of which Isidore and Solinus speak. They told me that they had never seen such things, which makes me wonder very much if there is any truth in the story'. During his journey to Karakorum Rubruck had travelled around part of the coastline of the Caspian, and he concluded on the basis of his own experience, and on the report of the Dominican Andrew of Longjumeau who had been to the region in 1247, that the Caspian was landlocked: 'and it is not true what Isidore says, that it is a gulf from the ocean, for at no point does it touch the ocean.'

Rubruck's narrative has a freshness of approach, as well as a great deal of closely observed detail, which makes it one of the greatest accounts of medieval European travel, and of the highest importance to the modern reader. In some respects it might be claimed to surpass even the much more famous account of the travels of Marco Polo produced half a century later. Both Carpini and Rubruck were travelling among people who were not only deeply alien in culture and in habitation, but who were also a source of the most profound danger to themselves and to their homelands. Yet they maintained a certain sympathy towards their barbarian hosts which compares favourably with the more common western European attitude towards their own internal barbarians, such as the peoples of the Celtic lands or of the Baltic whose cultures were regarded as primitive on the grounds of way of life or of religion, and who were therefore suitable candidates for conquest. As a contribution towards the study of ethnography, Rubruck's narrative in particular deserves to be ranked alongside the twelfth-century treatises of Gerald of Wales on the Welsh and the Irish.

Neither the mission of Carpini nor that of Rubruck had the slightest effect upon Mongol policy and intentions. Whatever the Mongols chose to do or not to do, they did out of considerations of their own best advantage. But the two envoys did make available to their fellow Europeans a body of information on a great and unprecedented scale. Much of what they had to report was not particularly encouraging, but one aspect of their joint experience was of great significance in helping to form the attitudes of Christendom towards the continent of Asia.

Western Europeans had already been aware since the time of the first crusade of the presence of large numbers of Christians of a variety of doctrinal beliefs and traditions in the Moslem-controlled lands of the eastern Mediterranean and Egypt. In the 1240s and 1250s it became apparent from the journeys of men like Carpini, Rubruck, and others that, whether or not the elusive Prester John would ever be found, there were scattered throughout central Asia substantial numbers of Christians, mostly of the heretical Nestorian persuasion, and rarely forming a majority of the local population, but none the less Christians of a kind. The existence of Christians in India was already known to Europe through the legend of St Thomas, but when European travellers first reached China in the final decades of the thirteenth century they found Christians there as well.

Carpini's references to eastern Christians are sparse. At one point he speaks about the Naimans as pagans, whereas Rubruck was insistent, correctly, that many of them were Nestorians. However, when reporting on the people of Cathay or China, of whom he had no first-hand knowledge, Carpini said that they were pagans but that

it is said they also have an Old and New Testament, and they have lives of Fathers and hermits and buildings made like churches, in which they pray at stated times, and they say they have some saints. They worship one God, they honour Our Lord Jesus Christ, and they believe in eternal life, but they are not baptized.

It has been suggested that Carpini's description applies to Buddhism, which was then the dominant religion in northern China, but which had also become receptive to influences from other religions, while the two testaments were in reality the Hinayana and Mahayana Buddhist scriptures.

In his account of the Great Khan, Küyük, Carpini referred to the presence of Christians in his household who told him

that they firmly believed he [Küyük] was about to become a Christian, and they have clear evidence of this, for he maintains Christian clerics and provides them with supplies of Christian things; in addition he always has a chapel before his chief tent and they sing openly and in public.

Carpini did not comment directly on this rumour, but from other remarks it is clear that he understood that the Mongols were the enemies of Christendom, while in the reply which Carpini carried back to Innocent IV from Küyük, the Great Khan said that he had no intention of obeying the pope's injunction to 'become a trembling Nestorian Christian, worship God and become an ascetic'.

William of Rubruck's experiences of Christianity in the east were much more direct, and were recorded in greater detail than those of Carpini, partly because Rubruck always regarded himself as a missionary rather than an envoy. He had insisted when he preached in the church of Santa Sophia in Constantinople on Palm Sunday that he was not the ambassador of Louis IX or of any other ruler, and was going among the pagans in accordance with his Rule. While on his journey Rubruck met a number of western Christians. The Parisian goldsmith Guillaume Boucher, for example, made vestments and sacred vessels which Rubruck used to celebrate the Easter mass during his stay at Karakorum. William was also very concerned about the spiritual welfare of some German prisoners who were said to be mining gold and making arms for the Mongols, and was disappointed that he was unable to visit them at any stage on his journey.

The majority of Christians whom Rubruck encountered were, however, of various eastern rites. The Nestorians were particularly numerous. Rubruck's attitude towards them was influenced by his realization that they had greatly exaggerated the importance of the ruler of the Naimans as a candidate for the role of Prester John. Nestorian influence may also have been connected with the rumour that Sartak, the son of the Mongol ruler on the Volga, had become a Christian, which led Louis IX to entrust Rubruck with a letter to him. Such experiences made Rubruck very sceptical of any similar stories he heard on his travels. The most elaborate came not from a Nestorian source but from an Armenian monk named Sergius whom he met at Karakorum. Sergius told him that he was going to baptize the Great Khan himself on the feast of the Epiphany. On the day nothing happened, except that Sergius, the Nestorian priests, and Rubruck all attended Möngke's court. As a result of this and other episodes, Rubruck recorded in his narrative that Möngke was in the habit of holding court on days which his soothsayers declared were feast days or which the Nestorians described as sacred.

On these days the Christian priests come first with their paraphernalia, and they pray for him and bless his cup; when they retire the Saracen priests come and do likewise; they are followed by the pagan priests who do the same. The monk told me that the Chan believes only in the Christians; however, he wishes them all to come and pray for him. But he was lying, for he does not believe in any of them . . . yet they all follow his court like flies honey, and he gives to them all and they all think they enjoy his special favour and they all prophesy good fortune for him.

William of Rubruck's final experience of the religious diversity of the Mongol court came on the Vigil of Pentecost 1254, when he and the Nestorian, Moslem, and pagan priests were all summoned before the Great Khan and ordered to demonstrate by disputation which of their beliefs was the superior. Not surprisingly the result was inconclusive, with Rubruck discovering that he had as little in common with his supposed co-religionists, the Nestorians, as with his non-Christian opponents.

Rivalry and even open hostility between western and eastern Christians were to be a marked feature of the relations between western Europe and Asia over the following century and more, but they were only a small part of a much more complex relationship with the east which was one of the consequences of the

Mongol conquests. From abject fear of the Mongols, and the prospect of imminent destruction, Europe was now progressing, through the experiences of official and semi-official envoys such as Carpini and Rubruck, and of many other individuals, most of whom have left no record, to a degree of knowledge about the Asian continent. Fear of what the Mongols might do in the future still existed, and Asia was still invested with marvels and with the expectation of Prester John, but there was more to Asia than these fears and fantasies.

Through their conquests the Mongols had, by the middle of the thirteenth century, gained control over a vast area of Asia, and were soon to add the whole of China to their dominions. The result has sometimes been described rather misleadingly as the *Pax Mongolica*. In many regions the Mongols had, as in Tacitus's famous description of ancient Rome, created a desert and called it peace; the Mongol dominions were also in practice far from united. None the less, for Europeans the possibility now beckoned of travel to lands which had been closed to them since classical antiquity. European merchants, especially from Italy, whose activities were already widespread by the middle of the thirteenth century and who were serving an economy which was near the peak of its medieval growth, were quick to take advantage of the new opportunities, particularly in Iran but also in India and China. The revelation of the existence of large numbers of Christians in Asia, of their presence at the courts of various Mongol rulers, often in important positions, and of the lack of any open hostility towards Christianity on the part of the Great Khans themselves, raised the possibility of evangelization by missionaries from western Christendom on a scale undreamt of hitherto. And if the Mongols could also be secured as allies against the world of Islam, who could guess what might then be achieved. Perhaps after all the faltering progress of the crusading ideal in the eastern Mediterranean might be crowned with a success beyond anything imagined by Urban II, and by the leaders of the first crusade a century and a half before.

5

The eastern missions

The Mongol conquests of the thirteenth century created new and unexpected opportunities for missionary activity by the Western Church, but the evangelization of heathen lands was in itself far from new. In the remoter history of Europe there were the examples of the conversion of Anglo-Saxon England and Germany between about A D 600 and 800, as well as the more recent conversion of the Hungarians and Poles, and of Scandinavia. In the twelfth century there was the movement of crusaders and settlers into the Baltic lands of Prussia and Livonia which led gradually to the conversion of the native population, and to the creation of new dioceses, such as that of Riga founded in 1200, to look after their spiritual welfare. The kingdom of Lithuania nominally became Christian in 1251, but was not fully converted until as late as 1386. Throughout the period of the most intensive European missionary work in Asia there was, therefore, a parallel movement going on within certain parts of Europe itself.

In the early thirteenth century missionary activity was encouraged by such events as the Fourth Lateran Council of 1215, and in particular by the foundation of the two orders of mendicant friars, the Franciscans and Dominicans. St Dominic's main concern was with the Albigensian heretics in southern France, but one of his earlier ambitions had been to convert the heathen Prussians. From 1221 the Dominicans of the newly formed Hungarian province were engaged in the conversion of the Cumans, a nomadic people living in the regions of southern Russia bordering on Hungary, a process which foreshadowed the later European involvement with more distant regions to the east. The even more ambitious hope that the Moslem world might be the object of missionary work was cherished in the 1220s by such men as Jacques de Vitry, bishop of Acre, and by Francis of Assisi: the latter even succeeded in 1219 in preaching before the Sultan

of Egypt, al-Kamil. In 1233 Gregory IX sent a number of
Franciscans, each supplied with a written exposition of the Christian faith and an injunction to listen to it, to the Moslem rulers of
Konya, Damascus, Aleppo, and Egypt, and also to the caliph at
Baghdad. In 1245 the envoys whom Innocent IV sent to the Mongols also bore recommendations to the rulers of any Moslem
lands through which they were to pass, in the hope that these
princes might accept Christianity.

Although areas such as the steppes of Russia, the Crimean
peninsula, Armenia, and the Caucasus were all zones of missionary activity by the mid 1240s, there does not seem to have been
any great missionary effort in western Asia until the mid 1260s,
by which time the Mongol Il-khans, owing allegiance to the Great
Khan, had established themselves in Iran and Mesopotamia upon
the ruins of the Abbasid caliphate.

Despite the predominantly Moslem population in these regions
there were many Christians, mostly Nestorians, among the subjects of the Mongols: these were favoured to such an extent that
the period between 1258 and 1295 has been described as a golden
age of the Nestorian Church. Christians were also to be found in
positions of political and military importance. The Mongol army
which invaded Syria in 1260 was commanded by a Christian
general named Kitbuka, a member of the Naiman tribe, while the
Il-khan Abaka (1265–82) was married to a Byzantine princess
who established a Greek bishopric at Tabriz. Abaka's predecessor Hülegü (1255–65), the conqueror of Baghdad in 1258, was
believed in Europe to have been on the point of receiving baptism
when he died in 1265, while in 1284 the Great Khan Kublai
thought it appropriate, when Arghun became Il-khan, to send a
Christian councillor, the Syrian Isa, from Peking to Iran with a
diploma of investiture.

From time to time favourable reports on the conditions in Iran,
and on the sympathy of the local rulers towards Christianity,
filtered back to Europe by such channels as the Armenian monk
Vartan, and the Dominican David of Ashby who lived at the
Mongol court between about 1260 and 1274. The chances of the
Il-khans actually adopting Christianity were greatly exaggerated,
but their toleration of Christianity and their military weakness

after their defeat at Ain Jalud in Palestine in 1260 made them especially anxious for good relations with western Europe, and so provided an opportunity for missionaries.

In 1278 an imposing embassy was sent by the pope to Tabriz, the
Mongol capital in Iran. It was composed entirely of Franciscans,
Gerard of Prato, Anthony of Parma, John of St Agatha, Andrew
of Florence, and Matthew of Arezzo, and was charged with deliver-
ing a statement of faith and an offer of baptism to Abaka, as had
been done to his predecessor in 1264, and was to happen again in
1288. What, if anything, the embassy achieved, is unknown, but
both the Dominicans and the Franciscans had long been established
in Tabriz by this date, as well as in other parts of the Il-khans'
dominions, and in adjoining regions of central Asia and Asia
Minor. Their religious houses tended to cluster along the trade
routes, from Trebizond to Tabriz, via Tiflis or Selmas, and from
Ayas (Lajazzo) on the Mediterranean coast of Cilician Armenia to
Tabriz, via eastern Anatolian cities such as Kayseri, Sivas,
Erzincan, and Erzerum.

The friars included remarkable men like the Franciscan John of
Monte Corvino, who was active in Armenia and Iran from the late
1270s, and who left the area in 1289 only to begin an even greater
task which took him to China. The Dominican Ricold of Montecroce, who came originally from Florence, was another outstanding figure. He was in Tabriz in about 1288, and preached there
for some months with the aid of an Arabic interpreter before going
on to Baghdad, where he met with other Dominican missionaries,
and preached to such effect that the local Nestorian patriarch seems
to have given the Latin missionaries freedom to deliver their message. Baghdad was still largely a Moslem city, however, and Ricold
instructed himself in the tenets of Islam in order to attempt the
conversion of the local population. In this he had no success, in
common with most such efforts. He also witnessed the sale in the
slave markets of Baghdad of Latin captives taken at Acre and
Tripoli in 1291, and he was present in 1295 when the adoption of
Islam by the Il-khan Ghazan (1295–1304), led to a violent reaction
against Christians and their church buildings. Ricold escaped only
with great difficulty, and eventually returned to Florence in 1301,
after which he wrote an account of his wanderings.

Although Ricold of Montecroce was ultimately unsuccessful in his preaching of Christianity in a hostile environment, his views on the qualifications and attitudes required by missionaries are very significant. He emphasized that a missionary should preach in the language of his audience, since an interpreter was usually incapable of rendering arguments accurately; he should have a thorough knowledge of the scriptures, and should make himself familiar with the doctrinal positions of every local Christian sect, without being over ready to condemn them as heretical; he should not allow himself to be side-tracked by arguments over details of liturgy and ritual, which were not matters of faith; and he should offer his hearers an example of genuine personal humility, and not act as if he were their superior. In his emphasis on the need to have a knowledge of languages and local beliefs Ricold had much in common with his contemporary the Spanish Franciscan Raymond Lull, whose main field of activity was North Africa, and who founded a Franciscan convent at Miramar on Majorca in 1274 to teach Arabic to his fellow missionaries.

This understanding of the requirements of missionary work bore fruit in the decree of the Council of Vienne in 1311 that chairs in Hebrew, Arabic, Greek, and Syriac should be founded in the universities, and also in the *Codex Cumanicus*, a glossary in Latin, Persian, and Cuman, which was produced by a Genoese in 1303 for use by missionaries and merchants in southern Russia and Iran. To what extent such efforts at encouraging the learning of new, and often very alien, languages succeeded is hard to assess. The comment by a Hungarian Dominican named John, who was active on the fringes of Siberia in the 1320s, that Englishmen, Germans, and Hungarians found it easier to master Turkish than French or Italian missionaries is one indication of a very practical approach to the problems of language. Alongside this, however, it is disappointing to note that the Franciscan missionaries who were active in China in the first half of the fourteenth century appear to have made little effort to acquaint themselves with Chinese, and were as dependent on interpreters as William of Rubruck had been at the Mongol court in the 1250s, when the eastern missions were just beginning.

The interest of western missionaries in the farther reaches of

Asia and in China was stimulated, as was that of their counterparts in the dominions of the Il-khans, by the knowledge of the
existence of local communities of Christians, and by persistent,
but invariably ill-founded, rumours that one or another Great
Khan was on the point of receiving baptism. Both Carpini and
Rubruck rejected such rumours when they were in Mongolia; so
too did the English chronicler Matthew Paris, who recorded in
1249 that news had come from the east of the baptism of the
Great Khan Küyük on the feast of the Epiphany in 1248 by
a Nestorian bishop named Malachy. Matthew described the
reports as shadowy rumours invented as a consolation for Christians, and perhaps to encourage the efforts of crusaders.

The return to Acre in 1269 of Niccolo and Maffeo Polo with
the news that the Great Khan Kublai wished to be fully informed
about western society played a part in reviving such tales, and the
two Dominicans, Nicholas of Vicenza and William of Tripoli,
who were to have accompanied the Polos when they went back to
Peking in 1271, were probably meant to test their truth. In
1276-7 a spate of rumours that Kublai Khan had actually been
converted swept Iran and Georgia, and it is possible, though not
provable, that the papal embassy which went to Tabriz in the
following year was also intended to go on to visit the Khan in
Peking.

The first definite papal interest in China was shown in 1289
when John of Monte Corvino arrived in Italy as an envoy of the
king of Armenia, only to find that he was swiftly appointed,
along with five other Franciscans, to go to China. He travelled
via Iran, where he spent some time preaching in Tabriz, and
where several of his companions appear to have remained, and in
1291 left for China by the long sea route from Ormuz on the
Persian Gulf. He arrived in Peking in late 1293 or early 1294 at
about the time that Kublai Khan died.

John of Monte Corvino's initial efforts were directed to the
region known as Öngut or Tenduc, whose inhabitants were
Turkish and included many Nestorian Christians. One of the
latter was the local ruler, Körgis or George, who was also the
Great Khan's son-in-law. John preached here so effectively that
George adopted Roman Christianity, allowed the construction of

a church, and had his son baptized John in honour of the missionary.

This hopeful phase in the spread of Western Christianity in the Far East ended in 1298 when George died during a conflict with the Mongol Khan of Chagatai, after which John of Monte Corvino transferred his activities to Peking. From there he wrote a letter dated 8 January 1305 in which he detailed his experiences since arriving in China. He wrote of his physical and spiritual isolation, of the great length of the journey to China, of his lack of a confessor until the arrival of a certain brother Arnold of the Cologne province a year earlier, of his need for books for use in worship and for copying by his converts, and also of his anxiety for news about the papacy, his order, and the west in general, about which he had heard disturbing rumours. He also described the hostility of the Nestorian Christians who had accused him of being a spy, magician, and deceiver, as well as of murdering another friar while on the way to China, and stealing presents intended for the Great Khan. There were, however, positive achievements to record: the conversion of George of Tenduc, the construction in Peking of a church with a tower and three bells, and the baptism of six thousand persons; he was also able to report that he had an adequate knowledge of the Mongol language and script, and had translated the whole of the New Testament and Psalms into it.

In a further letter written in February 1306 John added that he had now finished building a second church, close to the gate of the palace of the Great Khan who 'can hear our voices in his chamber, and this is told as a wonder far and wide among the nations, and will count for much according to the disposition and fulfillment of God's mercy'. Like many other European visitors to China at this period, he also remarked on the friendly treatment accorded him by the Great Khan: 'I have a place in his court and the right of access to it as legate of the Lord Pope, and he honours me above the other prelates, whatever their titles. And though the Lord Chaan has heard much of the Roman Curia and the state of the Latins, yet he greatly desires to see envoys come from those parts.'

John's two letters had been intended for his fellow Franciscans working among the Khazars to the north of the Black Sea, but they eventually reached the papal curia, with the effect that in 1307 Clement V appointed John the first Catholic archbishop of Peking. At the same time six other Franciscans were appointed to be his suffragans, and to provide him with consecration as archbishop. The six friars were themselves consecrated as bishops before their departure, but in the event only three of them, Andrew of Perugia, Gerard Albuini, and Peregrine de Castello, were to reach Peking, and that not until 1313. In the meantime Clement V had consecrated three more bishops for the archdiocese of Peking, Jerome of Catalonia, Peter of Florence, and a certain brother Thomas, but of these only Peter appears to have reached China.

The three bishops who arrived in 1313 found that since he wrote in 1306 John of Monte Corvino had begun to minister to a community of western Christians in the seaport of Zayton (Ch'uan Chow), which was the major centre for international trade on the southern coast of China, and was at the start of the highway which led to Peking via the important cities of Hangchow and Yangchow. Gerard Albuini was appointed bishop of Zayton on his arrival, to be succeeded by Peregrine de Castello in about 1317, and by Andrew of Perugia in 1323. John of Monte Corvino probably died between 1328 and 1330, and if a fragmentary tombstone found in Ch'uan Chow during the Second World War has been correctly identified, Andrew of Perugia followed him in 1332. The last of the friars who had set out for China so long before was now dead, and no provision appears to have been made for their replacement. News of John's death did not reach the papal curia at Avignon until late in 1333; a year later the newly appointed archbishop of Peking, a Franciscan named Nicholas, was only just setting out for the east.

Despite this inauspicious state of affairs, a considerable amount is known about the missions in China in the time of John of Monte Corvino. Apart from John's own letters, letters also survive from two of the Franciscan bishops of Zayton, Peregrine and Andrew, written in 1318 and 1326. As personal accounts of the hardships and dangers faced by their authors these letters are among the most moving documents in the history of the medieval expansion of Europe.

Both writers spoke of the wonders of the empire of the Great Khan:

If I were to write an account of the state of this mighty empire—the greatness of its power, the size of its armies, the extent of its territory, the amount of its revenue and its expenditure of charitable relief—it would not be believed. The Latins here have compared it in these respects to all the other kingdoms of the world, but do not write how it surpasses them (Peregrine).

And:

I forbear to speak of the wealth and magnificence and glory of their great Emperor, of the vastness of the empire and the number of its cities and their size; and of the government of the empire, in which no man dares to draw sword against another; for it would be long to write and would seen unbelievable to my hearers. For even I who am on the spot hear such things that I can hardly believe them (Andrew).

Peregrine in particular gave evidence of the work and achievements of John of Monte Corvino, the hostility he had faced from the Nestorians, and the success he had experienced in uniting various other Christian communities under the banner of Latin Christianity. There were Armenians in Peking, where they were building another church which they intended to leave to John, and in Zayton a church and a house had been given to the Franciscans by an Armenian lady. According to Andrew of Perugia, it was at the suggestion of this lady that Zayton had been created as a separate diocese. Another Christian community was formed by the Alans, allegedly thirty thousand strong, who served the Great Khan as soldiers, and who came to John of Monte Corvino with their families for spiritual guidance. Neither writer said much about other Europeans in China, although it is evident that Genoese merchants at least were to be found at Zayton; Peregrine also revealed that by 1318 he and his fellows had been joined by three more Franciscans, John of Grimaldi, Emmanuel of Monticulo and Ventura of Sarezana, the last of whom had entered the order while in China.

However, the true situation of the Franciscan missionaries is revealed by Peregrine's remark that, although many people rushed to hear them preach, they were unable to communicate because of their ignorance of the local language:

truly the harvest is great and the labourers are few and they have no sickle. For we brethren are few and quite aged and unskilled in the learning of languages. . . . We stand in need of nothing so much as brethren, whom we long for. For Brother Gerard the Bishop is dead, and we other friars cannot live long, and no others have come. The church will be left without baptism and without inhabitants.

The practical difficulties of lack of manpower and of the necessary skills were real enough barriers to any extensive success by the eastern mission, but the real problem for the Franciscans seems to have been their almost total isolation, with no hope of ever returning home. No amount of good treatment by the Great Khan, who supplied Andrew of Perugia with a bounty to the value of 100 gold florins, and of relative physical comfort could make up for this. At the end of his letter, which was addressed to the prior of his home convent in Perugia, Andrew remarked:

I have taken care to send a brief account of all these things to your Paternity that through you they may be brought to the notice of others. I do not write to my spiritual brethren and my chief friends because I know not who has died and who still live. So I pray that they hold me excused. But I greet them all and commend myself to them all as closely as I can . . . All the suffragan bishops appointed by the Lord Pope Clement for the see of Kambalik have departed to the Lord in peace. I alone remain.

There is one further Franciscan witness to the Chinese missions of the 1320s. This was Odoric of Pordenone who left Europe sometime before 1320, travelled to Iran, and went by sea to India and Ceylon, then through Sumatra, Java, and Borneo, and on to Canton in China. He reached Peking in 1325, and stayed there for about three years before returning to Europe by a land route through northern China and central Asia. Odoric was accompanied by another Franciscan, James of Hibernia, presumably from Ireland, who is the only native of Ireland or Britain who is known to have travelled so far afield in the medieval period. Neither he nor Odoric had any intention of staying in the Far East, and they do not appear to have been missionaries in the

ordinary sense. The account of his travels which Odoric dictated
to William of Solanga in 1330 reads far more like a collection of
travellers' tales than a report of missionary activity, and this
certainly helps to account for the popularity of the work in the
later middle ages.

What little Odoric did say about the Franciscan missionaries in
China raises as many problems as it solves. He mentioned that
there were two Franciscan convents in Zayton, and that he depos-
ited there the bones of a number of other friars who had recently
been martyred in India; he recorded the existence of a Franciscan
house in Kinsai (Hangchow), and said that he stayed in this city
with an important and wealthy man who had been converted by
four friars. There was another Franciscan house at Yangchow,
and in Peking the friars had a special abode in the emperor's
court. But nowhere did Odoric mention any of his fellows by
name. The existence of John of Monte Corvino as archbishop of
Peking was unremarked, although John had by that time been in
the city for more than a quarter of a century. Conversely there is
no reference in any of the other Franciscan writings of the time to
the arrival of Odoric and his companion in China. It has been
suggested, though it cannot be proved, that Odoric and the other
friars in China were on opposite sides in the controversy between
the Spirituals and the Conventuals which so bitterly divided the
order in the early fourteenth century. In this way a European
dispute may have had echoes in the Far East, just as John of
Monte Corvino appears to have been shocked by the tales of the
dispute between Boniface VIII and Philip IV, and of the troubles
in his own order which he heard from the mouth of the Lombard
physician who arrived in Peking in 1303.

By the time that Ordoric was embarking on his tour of the
sights of the Far East there had been many developments in
the work of the missions in other parts of Asia. As noted earlier,
the Franciscans and Dominicans had been active in central Asia
since the middle of the thirteenth century. The foundation of the
Genoese trading port of Caffa in the Crimea in about 1266 also
gave an impetus to the missions. In 1278 the provincial of the
Franciscans in Hungary was able to tell the pope of numerous
conversions among the Tartars; in the 1280s the existence of

Franciscan convents was recorded at such places as Soldaia, Caffa, and probably also at Sarai, the capital of the Kipchak khanate on the Volga. The Franciscans were also placed under the special protection of the khan by decrees which were renewed at intervals up to at least 1314. Like their counterparts in Asia Minor and Armenia, the Franciscan convents or simple residences spread along the trade routes into central Asia and to China: by about 1320 they were to be found as far afield as Astrakhan, Aksarai, Urgenj, and Almaligh. Evidence about the activities of the Dominicans is scarcer, apart from convents that are known at Caffa and at Tana, but it should be remembered that they had played an important role in the very earliest missions in western Asia in the 1230s, on the eve of the Mongol invasions of Europe. In 1320 a Hungarian Dominican wrote from the land of the Bashkirs to report the successes that he, two other Hungarians, and an English friar had achieved, and recommending that missionaries should adopt the nomadic way of life of the tribes to whom they were ministering. A Mongol governor of the region of Sibir (Siberia), 'a fertile and cold land', had also asked for missionaries to be sent.

In the early days of the missions individual friars were simply detached from their home houses or provinces for special duties elsewhere. But by the late thirteenth century the Franciscans, for example, had established two new vicariates, one for the custodies of Sarai and Khazaria, and the other for the custodies of Constantinople, Trebizond, and Tabriz; somewhere between 1320 and 1330 a third vicariate was set up to cover Cathay and the Far East generally. The Dominicans achieved the same purpose in 1312 when they formally created the *Societas fratrum perigrinantium propter Christum inter gentes*.

Throughout these proceedings a keen interest was taken by the papacy. Boniface VIII, for example, despite his other preoccupations nearer home, took time in 1296 to address a letter of encouragement to the Franciscans who were living among the Tartars of the Orient, and in 1299 he sent a group of nineteen Dominicans in the same direction. Men such as John of Monte Corvino, Odoric of Pordenone, and John of Marignolli were given authority as papal legates in the areas they were to visit. In

1291 Nicholas IV appointed two Franciscans, William of Chieri and Matthew of Chieti, to enquire into the way of life and manners of the friars working in the East, and it was probably a similar commission, this time from John XXII, which prompted the Dominican John of Cori in about 1330 to write the *Livre de l'estat du Grant Caan*, in which he gave the first report to the West of the recent death of John of Monte Corvino in Peking. Fears of unorthodox religious opinions among the faithful themselves, which appear to have arisen from troubles in the Roman Church in Iran during the pontificate of John XXII, probably explain the appointment in 1359 of a Dominican named Philip as inquisitor for Tartary, Iran, and Comania.

In 1253 Innocent IV issued a bull which envisaged the appointment of Franciscans and Dominicans to vacant sees in both Mongol- and Moslem-held territory. Ten years later an English Dominican William Freney was appointed as archbishop of Edessa (a city which had been back in Moslem hands for over a century), but his nomination appears to have been designed only to give him status as a papal envoy to Armenia, and within a year or two he was back in England. In the event no Latin bishop seems to have been consecrated to a diocese outside those ruled by the Christian princes of the eastern Mediterranean during the entire period from 1253 to 1307. The establishment of the archdiocese of Peking/Khanbalik by Clement V, the appointment of John of Monte Corvino as its first incumbent, and the consecration of suffragan bishops for the new province were therefore more than just a recognition of the value of John's labours in the Far East, but were also the first stage in a major reorganization of the Roman Church throughout Asia.

The initial area of responsibility of the new archdiocese was nothing less than the entire Mongol empire, including China and its neighbouring regions, but also Mongol Iran, and the khanates of Kipchak and Chagatai. This fact, combined with the hazards of the journey, helps to explain why the bishops consecrated for the province did not necessarily all reach China. The territory of the Il-khans was later to receive special treatment from the papacy, but gradually the other two khanates developed an episcopate nominally dependent on Peking. The dioceses included Caffa founded in 1321, Tana founded in about 1343, and Sarai on the Volga, where a Latin bishop is first known with certainty in 1352, all of which lay within the Kipchak khanate in the Crimea and southern Russia, and whose associations were really with the Black Sea and ultimately with the west; in the khanate of Chagatai in central Asia there was a bishop at Almaligh south of Lake Balkash by 1328, and one at Urgenj, on the river Oxus to the south of the Sea of Aral, before 1340. Of all these dioceses only Almaligh seems to have been far enough to the east to have any possibility of a real working relationship with Peking. For the rest the province of Peking was simply too large, and, even more important, its existence did not take adequate note of the very deep political divisions which had been present in the Mongol dominions since the death of the Great Khan Möngke in 1259, and which grew ever deeper after the death of Kublai in 1294.

The papacy was, however, very conscious of the importance to its scheme of evangelization of the dominions of the Il-khans. In 1318 this was recognized by the establishment of a new province centred on the city of Sultaniyeh which had, since 1307, replaced Tabriz as the Mongol capital in Iran. The first archbishop was Francis of Perugia, a Dominican who was then in charge of the *Societas Perigrinantium*; in 1323 he was succeeded by another Dominican William Adam, whose missionary journeys in Iran and the Indian Ocean between 1312 and 1317 had helped draw papal attention to the size of the task that lay ahead. In the report he had sent to the pope at that time, William had estimated that true Christians did not form one-tenth or even one-twentieth of all mankind. William's own successor in 1329 was to be the John of Cori who was mentioned earlier as a valuable source of information on the Mongol empire.

One important consequence of the foundation of the new province was the formal division of responsibility in Asia between the two orders of mendicant friars. The Franciscans were now to have exclusive control over all the Mongol territories included within the province of Peking/Khanbalik, while the Dominicans were to have authority in Iran, central Asia, and India. This even meant that convents of one order came under the overall control of the other.

Six prelates were consecrated for Sultaniyeh when it was first set up in 1318, as had been done for Peking in 1307. Four dioceses were established at points along the route between Ayas on the Mediterranean and Sultaniyeh, at Sivas in Cappadocia, and at Dehikerkan, Maragha, and Tabriz, the latter three being grouped closely together in the vicinity of the Caspian. The other dioceses were at Sevastopolis on the Black Sea, and apparently at Smyrna on the Aegean. In 1329 John XXII reorganized the province, transferring the see of Smyrna to Tiflis in Georgia, and creating two more new dioceses, one at Samarkand, and the other at a place named Quilon in India.

India had long been known to Europe as the location of a Christian community because of the widespread circulation of the legend of St Thomas (see Chapter 4), and there had been a number of European pilgrimages to the shrine of St Thomas at Mailapur on the east coast of India, the most recent of them in the late twelfth century. Nothing further is heard of India until 1267, when Clement IV wrote to Humbert de Romans, the head of the Dominican order, asking that a certain Brother Vazinpace, who had recently visited the lands of the Tartars, Ethiopians, and Indians, and of the Saracens of the east and the south, should be sent back to these regions with companions. Precisely what Vazinpace had achieved in the past is far from clear, but it seems likely that he had been one of the first Europeans to take advantage of the new opportunities created by the Mongol conquest of Iran and Iraq in 1258, and that if he had not actually travelled some distance by the sea route which began in the Persian Gulf, he had at least acquired some knowledge of India and of other lands bordering the Persian Gulf and the Indian Ocean.

The first western missionary who is known to have visited India was John of Monte Corvino who went there *en route* to China. He had left Tabriz in 1291 with a companion, Nicholas of Pistoia, and took the sea route to India where he spent thirteen months and made a hundred converts, and where Nicholas died and was buried in the church of St Thomas in the vicinity of Madras. In a letter which he wrote from Maabar, probably on the Coromandel coast opposite Ceylon, John gave the first general description of India to be provided by a medieval European. His purpose did not, however, involve any prolonged stay in India, and it was left for later visitors to initiate a more organized mission. In the meantime a number of other missionaries appear to have passed through India on their way to other destinations, such as the prelates who were sent by Clement V to join John in Peking, two of whom died in India.

In 1321 a party of five friars, four Franciscans, and a Dominican, landed at Thana on the island of Salsette near Bombay. It is not certain whether they intended to stay in India, or whether they too were on their way to China. In April 1321 the four Franciscans became involved in a disputation with local Moslems, were unwise enough to commit blasphemy against Mohammed, and were condemned to death by burning. Thomas of Tolentino (a famous figure in the Armenian mission who had been responsible for bringing the second of John of Monte Corvino's letters from Peking to the notice of Clement V, so precipitating the development of the Chinese mission), James of Padua, Peter of Siena, and a lay brother Demetrius from Tiflis in Georgia all died. Their bones were shortly afterwards buried by their Dominican companion, Jordan Cathala of Séverac in France; a little later these were exhumed by Odoric of Pordenone, and taken to Zayton in China where they were reburied in the local Franciscan convent.

Jordan of Séverac was to become famous in his own right, both as the author of a short treatise describing the marvels of India, and as the virtual founder of the Latin Church in fourteenth-century India. In October 1321 he wrote to the Franciscans and Dominicans of Tabriz, Dehikerkan, and Maragha in Iran, describing the martyrdom of his fellows, and how he had baptized a number of people in Thana, Sofala, and Broach. He appealed for more missionaries to be sent to India, and suggested places where they might work.

In 1324 Jordan wrote again, and spoke of the hardships he had suffered through the climate, poverty, and illness, and from the attitude of the local population which, he said, changed almost daily from friendship to hostility. But he was glad to endure this and begged for help: 'Let the holy friars come then, let them come with souls established in patience, that the harvest of baptized souls may be kept from the evil one.' Jordan's mission at this time appears to have been offered both to native Christians and to the pagan population, but his preaching was probably not conducted in public because of the enmity of the Moslems, and because of the rule of the sultan of Delhi who had recently conquered the region of Gujerat in which he was living.

After some years Jordan appears to have moved to the south of India, and to have based himself at Malabar in the kingdom of Quilon. Here there were many native Christians, and Jordan worked to such effect that in 1328 he returned to Europe to obtain further support. In August 1329 John XXII appointed him to be bishop of the newly created diocese of Quilon, with responsibility for the whole of India.

By the time of Jordan's appointment the chain of western religious houses and dioceses was almost complete from one end of Asia to the other. The only substantial addition to the organization of the Latin Church was the establishment in 1333 of another new archdiocese, based at Vospro (the modern Kertch) in the Crimea, whose area of authority appears to have overlapped confusingly with those of Sultaniyeh, Peking, and the Latin patriarchate of Constantinople.

The apparently flourishing state of the Church in Asia was, however, somewhat illusory, since the threat to its existence from the revival of Islam was now becoming evident. The martyrdom of Jordan's companions was a portent of what was to come. In 1339 the missions in central Asia came under threat when a fanatical Moslem ruler seized power at Almaligh, and executed the bishop, Richard of Burgundy, together with three other Franciscans, one of whom, Pascal of Vittoria, is well known to modern scholarship through a letter he wrote in 1338 in which he described his missionary experiences at Sarai, Urgenj, and Almaligh, and in which he prophesied his own death when he recalled the persecution to which he had been subjected, and expressed his expectation of greater sufferings in the future. He also reported the martyrdom three years before at Sarai of the Hungarian friar Stephen of Peterwardein, who had become a Moslem but had then been hacked to pieces after publicly recanting his apostasy.

The last detailed picture of the Asian missions was provided by the Franciscan John of Marignolli, who left Avignon as a papal legate in 1338. His mission was prompted by an embassy from Peking which had reached Avignon in 1336. Although the embassy's purpose was partly diplomatic, it also bore a plea from the leaders of the Christian Alans asking when a successor to John of Monte Corvino would be appointed. Since John's successor, Nicholas, had left Avignon in 1334, this indicated that he had probably died on the journey to China, and John of Marignolli was accordingly sent to investigate.

On his way to China John passed through Almaligh, where another political upheaval had occurred since the death of Pascal, and he spent some time refounding the western Church there, although it is unknown whether this included the appointment of a new bishop. He was well received when he arrived in Peking, and stayed there for several years. In his later account of the journey he mentioned the existence of a cathedral church belonging to the Franciscans adjoining the imperial palace, which was presumably the one built by John of Monte Corvino at the beginning of the century, as well as of several other Franciscan churches in the city. He also recorded the continued existence of three Franciscan houses at Zayton, which he visited at the beginning of his journey home in about 1346. When John reached India he found that a Dominican community was still in Quilon, where Jordan of Séverac had earlier been bishop, and he also visited the shrine of St Thomas at Mailapur.

It is very difficult to trace the later history of the missions in Asia after the return of John of Marignolli to Avignon in 1353. The death of the Franciscan James of Florence, bishop of Zayton, at the hands of Moslems in central Asia in 1362 seems to indicate that the papacy tried to re-establish a hierarchy in China. In 1370 a new archbishop of Peking, William of Prato, a former professor of theology at Paris and Oxford, was appointed, and it is likely that he reached his new post. In the meantime, in 1368, the Mongols had finally been expelled from China by a new native dynasty, the Ming, but even this did not bring about the immediate demise of the western Church in China. William of Prato may have been succeeded by a certain Charles of France, who had probably been long dead by 1410 when John XXIII replaced him with John, archbishop of Sultaniyeh, who was to act as administrator of the province but who died himself in 1412. A bishop named William was at Urgenj in 1393, but with such vague details the history of the missions in the Far East fades into complete oblivion. When western missionaries again entered China in the sixteenth century they knew nothing of the work of their predecessors. Except for a medieval Bible found in China, misleadingly known as the Bible of Marco Polo, and a few tombstones, there are few physical relics of this remarkable phase in the medieval expansion of Europe.

The province of Sultaniyeh also had a chequered history. John of Cori was succeeded by a certain William, who had possibly been elected by his suffragans without the knowledge of the papacy, but in 1349 the English Dominican, John of Leominster, informed Clement VI of the death of the archbishop and of most of the other bishops from plague and other causes, and reported that only three religious remained in the fifteen houses of the province. New archbishops were appointed to Sultaniyeh by the papacy in 1349 and 1368, while in 1375 the bishops of Maragha, Tabriz, and Nakhidjevan were authorized to elect a successor. The final appearance in the records of the appointment of an archbishop of Sultaniyeh was in 1398 when Boniface IX translated to the post the bishop of Nakhidjevan, an Italian named John. There were still occasional references to the presence in western Asia of western Christians and Dominican missionaries in the early fifteenth century, but Sultaniyeh itself was said in 1431 to be inaccessible to Christians and inhabited only by infidels. The diocese of Quilon in India had a bishop named James in the early 1360s, but disappears from the records thereafter, although Indian Christians visited Rome in 1403 and 1404 and Bologna in 1407.

In 1392 two Franciscans, Roger of England and Ambrose of Siena, appealed to the pope to help them to cater for the great number of converts they had made in the area of the Volga. Their work was probably severely disrupted by the devastation caused by the conquests of Tamerlane in the 1390s, but even then there were still some signs of missionary activity in western Asia and around the Black Sea. Sarai on the Volga disappeared as the seat of a bishop, but western bishops of Tana were appointed in succession until 1464. Astrakhan seems to have been a centre of western Christianity until well into the fifteenth century, a fact which may have had some bearing on its reappearance as one of the first of a new generation of missionary centres when the missions were resumed in the seventeenth century.

By the end of the fifteenth century the only known places of activity by western Christians were at Caffa, where the liturgy was maintained after 1475 by the expedient of purchasing priests in the slave markets of Constantinople, and at Tana, where Franciscans were still present in 1486. The religious links between western Europe and Asia were by this time extremely tenuous, but they helped to preserve some European awareness of the continent and its complexities, and so contributed, if only on a small scale, to the new phase of expansion in the fifteenth century.

6

European merchants and the East

The stages by which the frontiers of medieval Europe's international commerce were extended have been aptly and succinctly described by R. S. Lopez: from the tenth century when a Venetian merchant could meet with surprises even on the road to Pavia; to the eleventh when journeys to Constantinople had become routine; to the twelfth when Jerusalem had become a familiar destination; to the thirteenth when there existed a beaten path to Trebizond and Tabriz, Astrakhan and Tana; and finally to the fourteenth century when, in about 1340, the Florentine merchant and banker Francesco Balducci di Pegolotti could write that the route from Tana on the Sea of Azov to Peking, via Turkestan and Mongolia, was safe by day and night, and could give detailed instructions on how to reach China, together with information on local currencies and customs duties.

Apart from illustrating the vast geographical range of medieval European trade, this summary also indicates that the activities of European merchants in central Asia and the Far East were not simply the result of the opportunities created by the Mongol conquests in the thirteenth century, but grew directly out of the expansion of the European economy which had been in progress since the ninth or tenth century, and out of the resulting demand in western Europe for high-value eastern products. Given the chance to travel and the possibility of a profit at the end of the journey, European merchants were likely to go anywhere in the known world, and a few, like the Polos of Venice in the 1260s and 1270s, or the Vivaldi brothers of Genoa in 1291, were prepared to take the risks of a venture into the unknown. The result was that throughout Asia the establishments of European merchants matched those of European missionaries.

Economic growth was a general European phenomenon, as much a feature of the life of England and the Low Countries, and of the Baltic lands and Scandinavia, as it was of the countries of southern Europe. But in the middle of the thirteenth century it was Italy, where international commerce had first revived, which lay at the geographical centre of a network of trade routes radiating out from the Mediterranean, and also at the focal point of a system of currency and credit, and of business organization. All of Europe benefited from the enterprise of Italian merchants, but it was cities like Genoa, Venice, and Florence which held together the international trade of their time. The same motives which led the Genoese to sail through the straits of Gibraltar in the late 1270s to trade directly with the ports of England and the Low Countries, and which in about 1317 caused the Venetians to begin the regular annual sailings of the Flanders galleys, were also responsible for the appearance of Genoese vessels on the Caspian Sea before the end of the thirteenth century, for the construction of galleys by Genoese sailors on the Tigris in 1290, and possibly also for Genoese navigation on the Indian Ocean itself.

Less dramatic, but of equal significance for the growth of international trade, was the appearance between 1252 and 1284 of gold coinages in Genoa, Florence, and Venice, the first effective gold currency in western Europe since the days of Charlemagne: of the three coins now introduced, the Florentine *florin* and the Venetian *ducat* were to become international standards of value. For the purposes of trade with the Mongol dominions in Asia silver was required, so that there was an extensive exchange from gold into silver, which then flowed steadily eastwards. The new gold currencies were therefore of practical utility only in trading within the Mediterranean basin and in northern Europe, but their very existence was in itself a mark of European economic success, since much of the gold had been acquired through commercial links with the Byzantine empire and Egypt, and was the consequence of a fundamental change in the terms of international trade which had turned the historic western European deficit into a substantial surplus.

The actual volume of the eastern trade was surprisingly small. It has been said that in the fourteenth century the total amount of goods imported to Venice could normally be carried by three state convoys travelling once a year to Constantinople, Beirut, and Alexandria, representing in all only about 1,000–2,000 tons of merchandise. The significance of these imports was that, although they were generally small in volume, they were high in value and much in demand, so that the eastern trade assumed an importance out of all proportion to its material quantity. For an ambitious European merchant there was, therefore, considerable point in venturing as near to the source of the most valuable eastern products as he was able.

Many of the goods of the highest value and most in demand in Europe, such as pepper and other true spices, and to a lesser extent silk, orginated of necessity in regions of Asia to which Europeans did not have direct access. Until the closing decades of the thirteenth century the major source of eastern spices for the European market was the port of Alexandria in Egypt. From Alexandria there existed a land route to the Red Sea, and from there a regular sea passage to the west coast of India from which it was possible to proceed to China in Chinese vessels. This route was predictable and cheap but was also slow, the journey to China lasting as long as two years because of the seasonal nature of the monsoon winds, and the need to accumulate a sufficient cargo before setting out.

As a means of travel to the Far East the route through Egypt was closed to Europeans at all times, but there were some European attempts to gain access from other directions to the sea route in the Red Sea and the Indian Ocean. As early as 1182 the notorious Reynald of Châtillon, lord of Transjordan in the kingdom of Jerusalem, constructed five galleys on the Gulf of Aqaba with which he captured the port of Eilat, and also attacked Egyptian ports, and merchant and pilgrim shipping. The threat to Mecca and to Egyptian trade, possibly even in the Indian Ocean itself, was judged so great by Saladin that in 1183 he took very strong action to exterminate this Frankish operation.

The Genoese who sailed on the Tigris in 1290 were part of a contingent of nine hundred sailors who had been enlisted by the Il-khan Arghun with the apparent purpose of constructing two galleys which would then be employed on the Indian Ocean against Egyptian trade. Nothing came of this scheme since one of the Genoese caused an anti-Christian riot in Baghdad by desecrating a mosque, after which the sailors went downriver to the port of Basra where they divided into Guelph and Ghibelline parties, and attacked one another, so submerging an interesting project in an outburst of European politics.

Shortly before 1318 the Dominican William Adam, who was later to become the second archbishop of Sultaniyeh, suggested that a blockading squadron of three or four galleys, manned by twelve hundred Genoese, whom he described as both the best and most greedy of sailors, should be stationed in the Red Sea and the Gulf of Aden. Adam assumed that the Mongols of Iran would supply the Genoese with bases for the construction and the repair of ships, that other bases could be found on the coast of India, and that it would be possible to capture some of the islands around the Arabian peninsula as part of a general blockade of Egyptian commerce. This ambitious scheme came to nothing but there were echoes of it in 1324 when Jordan of Séverac noted in his second letter from India the great effect that might be achieved if the pope were to authorize the stationing of even two galleys in the Indian Ocean.

European naval power was not to become a reality in the Indian Ocean until the conquests of the Portuguese in the early sixteenth century, but from the time of the Dominican Vazinpace in the 1260s many eastward-bound Europeans travelled these waters. John of Monte Corvino did so in 1291, as did Jordan of Séverac and his companions, and Odoric of Pordenone and James of Hibernia in the early 1320s, while Marco Polo made the return journey from India to Iran in the 1290s. William Adam's proposals for a blockade were derived partly from his experience of voyaging in the Indian Ocean, with a companion Raymond Etienne, for a total of twenty months, nine of which were spent on the Christian island of Socotra awaiting a ship. In all these cases it appears that Europeans sailed in local ships, but there is also a small amount of evidence, derived from William Adam and from the fifteenth-century Arab navigator Ibn-Majid, that the Genoese may have had ships of their own on the Indian Ocean in the early fourteenth century. Unfortunately it is not known if these were vessels of Genoese design and construction, and if they were used for trading ventures between India and Iran.

An alternative route to the East existed from the shores of the Black Sea. A common starting-point was the Greek city of Trebizond on its southern coast, from where the road led to Tabriz in Iran, and then along the ancient caravan route through Bukhara, Samarkand, and Kashgar until it eventually reached China. A more northerly route also existed, from the area of the Crimea through central Asia, and was used especially by the missionaries, envoys, and suppliants who were required to head eastwards to the Mongol court at Karakorum in the 1240s and 1250s. It was also possible to reach Tabriz from various points on the coast of the Mediterranean, such as Ayas (Lajazzo) in Cilician Armenia, Beirut, or Antioch, and then onwards by the land route.

Once in Iran, the journey to the east could also be completed by sea using the port of Ormuz on the Persian Gulf, and it was from here that any Europeans who sailed the Indian Ocean were likely to depart. Ormuz had replaced Basra, which had been the chief port for trade with the East during the great days of the Abbasid caliphate at Baghdad, and had then been eclipsed in the tenth and the eleventh centuries when troubles in Iraq and the foundation of the Fatimid caliphate in Cairo had produced a major shift in political and economic power from Mesopotamia to Egypt.

There were, however, many variations on these routes both in their starting-points and in their course within Asia, the details often depending on local conditions. Until the coming of the Mongols all these routes were, like that from Egypt, closed to European merchants, except where the western termini happened to be in Frankish or other Christian hands. From the middle of the thirteenth century the Mongol control of much of Asia made it possible for Europeans to engage in direct commercial dealings with the East, and to reduce the cost of the luxury goods they wished to import. Even so, a journey to the East was a long and tedious affair. To reach Karakorum, when that was still the centre of the Mongol world, took over six months after leaving Kiev in southern Russia; eight to eleven months had to be allowed to travel to China either from the Crimea or Iran; while, as already noted, the sea voyage from Iran to China, via India, lasted about two years. Travel to the East was never a matter to be undertaken lightly, however well organized the Mongol dominions might appear to be, or however eloquently a merchant like Pegolotti might speak of the routine of eastern commerce.

Among the earliest signs that a new stage in the development of European international commerce had begun are the appearance of Chinese silk in the market of Genoa in 1257, and the journey to China between 1262 and 1269 undertaken by Niccolo and Maffeo Polo of Venice, the first westerners to go there since classical antiquity. Both these phenomena were direct results of the recent Mongol conquests which had opened routes free of Moslem control to the port of Ayas and to the Crimea respectively. But European merchants had begun to be active on the fringes of Asia even before this. When Carpini and his companions reached Kiev on their return from Mongolia in 1247 they encountered a number of Italian merchants who had come to Russia from Constantinople. On his way to Karakorum in 1253 William of Rubruck met merchants from Constantinople at Soldaia in the Crimea, though without indicating whether they were westerners or Greeks, and during his return journey in 1255 he visited Konya (Iconium) in Turkish-controlled Asia Minor, where he came across a Genoese merchant from Acre named Nicholas of Santo Siro who, with his partner Boniface of Molendino from Venice, had been granted the monopoly of the export of alum by the Turkish sultan.

Since the eleventh century the lands of the Byzantine empire and the city of Constantinople itself had been objects of great interest on the part of western merchants. The privileges which Venice had enjoyed in the empire since 1082 were confirmed in 1187 after the setbacks suffered by the large Venetian community in Constantinople in 1171, when ten thousand of them were imprisoned, and the attacks made on them in 1182. The conquest of the empire in 1204 by the armies of the fourth crusade, with Venetian naval support, gave Venice a dominant commercial position throughout the former Byzantine territories which enabled them to create permanent trading posts in the area of the Black Sea. When the Polo brothers went to Sudak on the Crimean peninsula in 1260, at the start of the journey which led them to China, they were visiting an already well-established Venetian colony where a third Polo brother owned a house.

The restoration of Byzantine authority at Constantinople in 1261, which harmed but did not destroy Venetian influence, did much to assist the Genoese who played an important part in the Byzantine victory. In the early 1260s the Genoese founded the colony of Pera immediately opposite Constantinople, and gained what became the base for the rest of their eastern trade. Their acquisition in about 1266 of a colony at Caffa in the Crimea, with the permission of the Kipchak khan Barka, added another important link, and by the end of the thirteenth century they were also established at Tana, at the mouth of the River Don on the Sea of Azov, and at Trebizond.

Despite such disturbances as the destruction of Caffa in 1296 and 1306, these Black Sea trading posts were to remain a key element in European commercial interest in the East for many years to come. But, important as they were, Caffa and its fellows were only the beginning of a much more extensive network of European commerce. Genoese merchants were at Sarai on the Volga in 1307, and probably long before that, but the focus of European activity in western Asia was at Tabriz in Iran. As the capital of the Mongol rulers of Iran, Tabriz was a major trading city in its own right, but it had the additional advantages of being not too far removed from other European bases nearer home, and also of being a natural starting-point for trading ventures deeper in to Asia, whether following the traditional land routes or the sea passage from Ormuz.

One of the first Europeans whose presence is known in Tabriz was the Venetian merchant Pietro Vilioni, who made his will there in 1264. Marco Polo also visited the city in 1295 on his way home from China. On that occasion he noted the activities of Genoese merchants, but they had certainly been established there since at least 1280, if not earlier. When the Il-khan Abaka sent his envoy, the monk Rabban Sauma, to visit the pope and the kings of France and England in 1287, the ambassador was accompanied by Tomasso de Anfussis, a member of a famous Genoese banking company, and spent the winter of 1287–8 in Genoa itself. Another Genoese with a commercial background, Buscarel de Giuzulfis, also entered the service of the Il-khans, and took part in embassies on their behalf to a number of European capitals between 1289 and 1302.

The relationship between the Italians and the Mongol rulers of Iran became more than just a business or a diplomatic one. Zolus Bofeti, better known as Isol the Pisan, stood as godfather at the baptism of Öljeitu, the brother of Ghazan Khan; Buscarel de Giuzulfis named his son Argone in honour of Arghun Khan; while some of the male offspring of the Doria family, one of the leading patrician families in the government of Genoa, bore such names as Tartaro (Tartar), Alaone, Abaga, and Casano (after the Il-khans Hülegü, Abaka and Ghazan), and Aitone (after Hayton, the king of Cilician Armenia). This easy intimacy between the two cultures was also reflected dramatically in 1300 when the Florentine Guiscard Bastari appeared at St John Lateran in Rome at the head of an embassy of one hundred, all dressed in Tartar clothing.

By the early years of the fourteenth century Tabriz had become a familiar and routine part of the activities of Italian merchants. But this was not enough to satisfy their ambitions. In 1295 Marco Polo was told of Genoese merchants who had launched small vessels on the Caspian Sea in order to carry their goods to the eastern shore. Beyond the Caspian the city of Urgenj, south of the Sea of Aral, was an important centre of European trade, and gave its name to organdi, a fine light cloth which was imported into Europe. A few bold merchants also penetrated into India. In 1315 Benedetto Vivaldi and Percivalle Stancone left Genoa for India after pretending that they were going only as far as Constantinople; Vivaldi died in India before 1322. The notarial instrument which the partners drew up before leaving Genoa was witnessed by members of the three families of de Anfussis, de Giuzulfis, and de Camilla, all of which were also prominent in the eastern trade. In 1321 Jordan of Séverac was assisted in recovering the relics of his dead colleagues by a young Genoese named Jacopo who may have been a merchant, and who afterwards carried Jordan's correspondence to Tabriz *en route* for Europe. A few years later, when Jordan had moved to Malabar in the kingdom of Quilon, he noted that European merchants regularly passed through there. Detailed information on the activities of European merchants in India is rare, but one striking exception was the journey made in 1338 from Urgenj to Delhi by a party of six Venetians, three of them from the family of Loredano. Although two of their number died on the journey, and part of the sum of 200,000 bezants for which they sold their goods in Delhi was swallowed up in bribes to local officials, the merchants seem to have made a satisfactory profit when they returned to Urgenj and liquidated their partnership. While there they met yet another Venetian merchant named Francesco Barbarigo.

For some European merchants the challenges and opportunities of central Asia and India were not enough, and they went as far afield as China. The commercial motives for such ventures are not as clear-cut as might be expected. Because of the cost of transport it was uneconomic to carry goods of European manufacture much farther east than Urgenj, with the exception of such items as high quality linens. Since classical times China had been known as the home of both raw silk and silk cloth, but the Chinese monopoly of these products had ended long before the thirteenth century, and silk could be obtained at many points between China and Constantinople. In the thirteenth century a flourishing silk industry was also established in northern Italy. The only incentives to import silk directly from China arose either from the particular attractions of Chinese woven silk, or from the very low price of Chinese raw silk. Lacking the desire to spread the Gospel or for a life of exile among the heathen which impelled the missionaries who went to China, one suspects that European merchants often went there as a virtuoso exercise in travel, as the highest peak of enterprise which there was to scale. It is not surprising that some of them, like Marco Polo, found other non-commercial roles to play after their arrival in China.

John of Monte Corvino was accompanied to China in 1291 by a merchant named Peter of Lucalongo, who is generally thought to have been from Genoa but who may have been a Venetian, and it was he who bought the land in Peking on which John began to build his cathedral in 1305. In his letter of 1318 Peregrine de Castello, bishop of Zayton, referred to a certain Ventura of

Sarezana who had become a Franciscan since arriving in China, and who might conceivably have been a merchant previously. Peregrine's successor, Andrew of Perugia, referred in 1326 quite unambiguously to the present of Genoese merchants in the city.

The Genoese appear to have been as prominent in the trade with China as they were in Iran. The fact that Pegolotti in his account of the route to China gave all the weights and measures in Genoese terms has been taken as especially significant, as has a casual reference in Boccaccio's *Decameron* which seems to assume a particular Genoese acquaintance with the Far East. As in Iran, individual Genoese whose initial presence was concerned with commerce were employed on diplomatic duties by the Mongol rulers. Andalo da Savignone, who had made a return journey to China in the early 1330s as a merchant, was sent to Europe by the Great Khan in 1336 to establish closer relations between China and the lands of the Franks 'beyond the seven seas and the setting sun' and also to procure horses and other marvels. Horses from the west, often described in China as 'blood-sweating horses' or as 'heavenly steeds', were much larger and stronger than local breeds, and were especially prized gifts. Andalo returned to China in about 1340 with at least one horse, which was duly celebrated in verses written in its honour by the imperial court poets, and commemorated in a portrait which survived until the early nineteenth century.

There are, however, a number of examples of Venetians who also went to China, apart from the most famous of them all, Marco Polo. Venetian merchants, such as Luchetto Duodo, Pietro Zulian, and Franceschino Loredano of the same family whose Indian exploits were mentioned earlier, were there in the 1330s and early 1340s. Most of this evidence is very matter-of-fact, and totally lacking in any detail which can involve the sympathies of the modern observer, but one striking exception exists in the form of the tombstone of Catherine Vilioni, who died at Yangchow in June 1342, and which was found in 1951 during the demolition of the city walls. According to the inscription she was the daughter of Domenico Vilioni, whose tombstone was discovered at the same time, of a family well known in Venice since the twelfth century, and was probably related to the Pietro Vilioni who made his will at Tabriz in 1264. Here we apparently have a family which had been involved in the commerce of Asia for the better part of a century, as well as evidence for the existence of a European community in China which was well enough established and sufficiently secure to have unmarried women in its midst.

Modern scholars have noted the coincidence that Yangchow was the city in which Marco Polo is traditionally believed to have held an appointment as an imperial Chinese official half a century before the death of Catherine Vilioni. It has also been suggested that the name Milione, which is usually thought to have been attached to Marco Polo and other members of his family in order to refer to the reputed wealth they had brought back from the East, was in fact derived from a connection with the family of Vilioni. If true, such a relationship would make Marco Polo's own travels in Asia more readily intelligible; but even if the suggestion is incorrect there is enough evidence about the activities of other European merchants in central Asia and China to show that his experiences, extensive as they were, and vividly as they were later retold, were not in themselves unique.

Marco Polo's journey to China was made as a direct consequence of the earlier stay there by his father Niccolo and uncle Maffeo, who had set out from Constantinople in 1260 on a routine trading venture to Sudak in the Crimea, after which they accompanied a caravan going to the capital on the Volga of Barka Khan, the lord of the western Mongols. When war broke out in 1262 between Barka and Hülegü, the Mongol ruler of Iran, the Polos were unable to retrace their route, and travelled farther east to Bukhara, which was controlled by the Mongols of the khanate of Chagatai; and from there they joined an embassy to Kublai, the Great Khan, and so reached China.

The elder Polos returned to Acre in Palestine in 1269, and according to the account of Marco Polo's adventures which was written about thirty years later, passed on a request from the Great Khan that the pope should send

up to a hundred men learned in the Christian religion, well versed in the seven arts, and skilled to argue and to demonstrate plainly to idolators and those of other persuasions that their religion is utterly mistaken and that all the idols which they keep in their houses and worship are things of the Devil—men able to show by clear reasoning that the Christian religion is better than theirs.

Allowing for the hyperbole of Marco Polo's ghost writer, Rustichello of Pisa, and for an over-emphasis on the Great Khan's interest in Christianity, it is likely enough that Niccolo and Maffeo did return to Europe bearing diplomatic messages from Kublai.

The newly elected pope, Gregory X, whom the Polos had met earlier when as Tedaldo Visconti he had been papal legate in the Holy Land, chose not one hundred holy men but only two Dominicans, Nicholas of Vicenza and William of Tripoli, to accompany the Polos back to China. Both friars flatly refused to go, leaving only Niccolo's young son Marco to join his father and uncle. It was an inauspicious start to a journey which was to be one of the great adventures of the middle ages, and which produced a famous work of literature.

From Ayas on the Mediterranean coast of Cilician Armenia the Polos travelled via Asia Minor and greater Armenia to Tabriz in Iran. Their first intention appears to have been to complete their journey by sea from the port of Ormuz, but they allegedly changed their minds after discovering that 'their ships are very bad, and many of them founder, because they are not fastened with iron nails but stitched together with thread made of coconut husks'.

Instead the party continued by land, crossing through a region of central Iran where 'what water there is is brackish and green as meadow grass, and so bitter that no one could bear to drink it. Drink one drop of it and you void your bowels ten times over.' The exact course of their journey after this is very hard to follow since the later account of it is full of digressions which may reflect actual travel by Marco and his companions, or simply be the result of information collected *en route*. They seem to have passed in the vicinity of the famous 'Dry Tree' which was 'of great size and girth', and stood in an immense plain: 'And there are no trees near it for more than one hundred miles, except in one direction where there are trees ten miles away. It is here, according to the people of the country, that the battle was fought between Alexander and Darius.'

Their journey also took them past the ancient city of Balkh, then largely in ruins following its destruction by Genghis Khan in 1220, to the province of Badakhshan in the Pamir mountains. Here Marco remarked with awe on the immense height of the mountains, 'so that for a man to climb from the bottom to the top is a full day's journey, from dawn till dusk', and was struck by the beauty of the high plateaux:

with a lush growth of grass and trees and copious springs of the purest water, which pour down like rivers over the crags into the valley below. . . . On the mountain tops the air is so pure and salubrious that if a man living in the cities and houses in the adjoining valleys falls sick of a fever, . . . he has only to go up into the mountains, and a few days' rest will banish the malady and restore him to health.

Whether Marco actually crossed the Pamir range after leaving Badakhshan is uncertain, but his next stop appears to have been the city of Kashgar where 'the inhabitants live by trade and industry. They have very fine orchards and vineyards and flourishing estates. Cotton grows here in plenty, besides flax and hemp . . . This country is the starting-point from which many merchants set out to market their wares all over the world.'

Then for thirty days they journeyed across the great Gobi desert where travellers were exposed not only to the usual hazards of a desert but to other fears as well:

When a man is riding by night through this desert and something happens to make him loiter and lose touch with his companions, by dropping asleep or for some other reason, and afterwards he wants to rejoin them, then he hears spirits talking in such a way that they seem to be his companions. . . . And sometimes in the night they are conscious of a noise like the clatter of a great cavalcade of riders away from the road; and, believing that these are some of their own company, they go where they hear the noise and, when day breaks, find they are victims of an illusion and in an awkward plight.

Finally, after a journey of about three and a half years, the Polos arrived in either 1274 or 1275 at Shangtu (Xanadu), the summer place of the Great Khan Kublai, 200 miles north of Peking. For the next sixteen or seventeen years Marco was to remain in China and its vicinity. Modern scholarship has tended to diminish the claims made in the account of his travels for his role in the service of the Great Khan. It is most unlikely, on chronological grounds, that Marco and his father and uncle had anything to do with the successful siege by the Mongols of the city of Siang-yang; nor is it likely that he was ever governor of the great city of Yangchow, as is implied in the narrative, although he may have held some subordinate office, possibly in the administration of the salt trade. It is also improbable that a certain Po-Lo who is recorded in the Chinese annals for 1277 as being appointed as a second-class commissioner to the Privy Council, was in fact Marco.

Whatever the truth about Marco Polo's position in China, it is clear that, in common with many other foreigners who could perhaps be trusted more than the native Chinese, he was well treated by the Great Khan, allowed freedom of movement, and was probably sometimes employed on official business. In this way he was later able to provide his European readers with detailed descriptions of the splendours of Kublai Khan's summer palace at Shangtu, and of the great palace in the imperial capital of Khanbalik (Peking).

He was to devote considerable attention to an account of the city of Kinsai (Hangchow), which was 'without doubt the finest and most splendid city in the world', a city of canals and of twelve thousand bridges, mostly of stone, very like his native Venice in general appearance but on a vastly greater scale. In describing the seaport of Zayton (Ch'uan Chow) on the coast opposite the island of Formosa, Marco's commercial sense led him to express himself in superlatives: this was

the port for all the ships that arrive from India laden with costly wares and precious stones of great price and pearls of fine quality. . . . And I assure you that for one spice ship that goes to Alexandria or elsewhere to pick up pepper for export to Christendom, Zayton is visited by a hundred. For you must know that it is one of the two ports in the world with the biggest flow of merchandise.

Marco was certainly in a position to compare Zayton and its commerce with the greatest ports of the western world, such as Constantinople and Venice, though it is not known whether he had actually been to Alexandria.

Marco Polo finally left China in either 1290 or 1292, together with his father and uncle, to escort a Mongol princess to Iran where she was to marry the recently widowed Il-khan Arghun. The convoy of fourteen Chinese junks sailed via the islands of Java and Sumatra to Ceylon, and then to the mainland of India where Marco made a pilgrimage to the shrine of St Thomas. He also visited the kingdom of Quilon in southern India, where he observed the production of pepper and indigo dye, and remarked that 'the heat here is so intense and the sun so powerful that it is scarcely tolerable. For I assure you that if you put an egg into one of the rivers you would not have long to wait before it boiled.' After a very long journey, in the course of which many of the travellers appear to have died, the Polos arrived at the port of Ormuz in Iran. They were delayed for several months at the Mongol capital of Tabriz, before resuming their journey overland to Trebizond on the Black Sea, from where they sailed to Constantinople, and then on to Venice where they arrived in 1295.

The account of Marco Polo's travels is difficult to interpret. One major reason for this is the fact that it was not written by Marco himself but by a professional writer, Rustichello of Pisa, with whom he was apparently imprisoned at Genoa in 1298. In order to reach the widest possible international audience Rustichello wrote his account in French. However, as one nineteenth-century commentator remarked:

'Its style is about as like that of good French authors of the age, as in our day the natural accent of a German, an Englishman, or an Italian, is like that of a citizen of Paris or Blois. . . . The author is at war with all the practice of French grammar; subject and object, numbers, moods and tenses are in consummate confusion.'

None the less the language was still recognizable as French, if not always readily understood.

A second characteristic which was presumably also imposed by Rustichello is the rambling, discursive style of the work, which is one reason for the modern reader's difficulty in imposing a clear chronology on the events described. As an experienced author, anxious not to waste good material, Rustichello also re-used appropriate passages from his other works. The opening address to 'emperors and kings, dukes and marquises, counts, knights and townsfolk' is very similar to the beginning of an earlier Arthurian romance; his description of the arrival of Marco Polo at the court of Kublai Khan and the splendour of his reception there has a parallel in Rustichello's account of Tristan's arrival at the court of King Arthur; while the war between the two Mongol khans, Hülegü and Barka, which broke out in 1262, has its parallel in the story of the conflict between the kings of Ireland and north Wales. The battle scenes which occur at intervals in the narrative, and which Marco Polo makes no claim to have witnessed, are probably also literary flourishes, as are the references to the kingdom of Prester John, or to the various wondrous races, such as the dog-headed men of the Andaman islands. We cannot of course rule out a contribution by Marco himself to some of the marvels told on his behalf, since he appears to have been a conventional man of his time who would have known what he expected to find on a journey through Asia.

Leaving aside the distractions of its literary form, there is no doubt that the work does essentially preserve a record of genuine travels, without dependence on material from the narratives of earlier European travellers in Asia. Marco Polo's accounts of his journey to the East, of his time in China and in India, his descriptions of the Great Khan's palace at Peking, of the seaport of Zayton, and of Chinese sea-going junks all bear the marks of firsthand experience. He was usually careful to say when he had not actually seen for himself something which he described. He did not claim, for example, to have visited Japan, but his account of the country, and of Kublai Khan's unsuccessful attempts at its conquest in 1274 and 1281, are the only European references to it before the sixteenth century. Sometimes it is left for scholars to deduce that he had not been to certain places, such as the islands of Socotra and Zanzibar, which seem to be referred to, and about which he may have heard from Moslem sources while on his way back to Europe in the 1290s.

A number of the things described by Marco Polo, which would have appeared as marvels to a medieval European reader, can readily be identified. Coal, asbestos, and the fine clay used for manufacturing porcelain are all evident behind his stories of a black stone that could be made to burn, of a kind of cloth which was cleaned by being thrown into the fire, and of the crumbly earth which was left to weather for thirty years before being made into vessels 'of an azure tint with a very brilliant sheen', and yet 'so plentiful and cheap that for a Venetian groat you might buy three bowls of such beauty that nothing lovelier could be imagined'.

It has, however, often been noticed that there are some surprising omissions from what purports to be an account of a long stay in China. There is no mention of tea, which was a familiar drink in China but totally unknown in Europe; no reference to be peculiarities of the Chinese script (which were referred to half a century before by William of Rubruck), even though it is claimed on his behalf that 'before he had been very long at the Great Khan's court he had mastered four languages with their modes of writings'; nor is there any mention of the Great Wall which should have been familiar to anyone who had spent time in Peking. It is not possible to eliminate these problems altogether, but one explanation may lie in the variations in detail between the surviving manuscripts of Marco's travels. The nature of the literary collaboration between Marco and Rustichello may be another part of the answer. There is no way of knowing, for example, whether Rustichello utilized all the material that Marco supplied to him orally or in the form of notes, or whether, as Marco's contemporary the Dominican Jacopo of Acqui is said to have remarked, Marco recounted much less of his true experience than he might have done, for fear of being branded a liar.

There may also be other explanations of the specific difficulties just noted. At the time of his arrival in China, Mongol control had only very recently been established, and there was a strong tendency for the new rulers to despise local customs and to exclude native Chinese from their administration. The imbibing of tea, for example, was most certainly not a feature of Mongol life on the great plains of their homeland, where their customary drink was koumiss, a powerful concoction which frequently led to death from alcoholism. At a more serious level it is very likely that Marco Polo, if he really were proficient at languages, could have learned Turkish, Persian and Mongol and their associated scripts. The language of administration in China at the time of Marco Polo's stay was Mongol, for which there were two different scripts, the one taken over from the Uighurs during the reign of Genghis Khan, while the second was devised by the Tibetan monk 'Phags-pa and introduced by a decree of Kublai Khan in 1269. It is possible that Marco learned both written forms of the Mongol language, making it seem that he knew four languages rather than three and at the same time helping to explain his ignorance of Chinese and its characters. In the case of the Great Wall of China, there is no adequate explanation, but one suggestion is that it became associated with the legend of the tribes of Gog and Magog who had been enclosed by Alexander the Great behind a wall, from which they would emerge only at the end of history.

Within half a century of Marco Polo's return to Europe, and while Rustichello's book was still at an early stage of its circulation, the conditions which had enabled him to travel freely in Asia were coming to an end. They were already changing when Pegolotti wrote so confidently around 1340 about the ease of travel to China. In the 1320s and 1330s Venetian merchants at Tabriz in Iran clashed both among themselves and with the Mongol authorities, which were now becoming hostile to Christians and western merchants; and between 1336 and 1344 the Genoese abandoned Tabriz altogether, partly as a result of this local hostility but also in a deliberate boycott of trade with Iran. In 1339 a Genoese merchant, William of Modena, was killed at Almaligh at the same time as Pascal of Vittoria and his companions; in 1343 there was a massacre of western merchants at Caffa in the Crimea, which was swiftly followed in 1346 by the siege of both Caffa and Tana by the Mongols of the Golden Horde; on the same occasion the Black Death was, according to tradition, imported into both cities, and from there taken by fleeing survivors into Europe itself. In 1337 the port of Ayas (Lajazzo) in Cilician Armenia, which had been a vital point of contact between the sea routes of the Mediterranean and the land routes of Asia, was captured by the sultan of Egypt. The collapse in 1335 of the Mongol ruling dynasty in Iran, and its replacement by native Moslem regimes was matched in China, where the last descendant of the once mighty Great Khans was succeeded in 1368 by a new Chinese dynasty, the Ming, which expelled both the Mongols and all other foreigners.

These political upheavals within both western and far-eastern Asia severely disturbed, but did not bring an immediate end to, European commercial ventures in Asia, despite the additional disincentives brought about by the onset of the Black Death in Europe in 1348, and by the decline in the fourteenth-century European economy. In 1371, for example, the new Ming emperor in China commissioned a European merchant named Niccolo, who had apparently been stranded in China by the change in regime, to go to Europe to announce the change in dynasty. This contact does not, however, seem to have been the precursor of any renewal of trade. In western and central Asia, on the other hand, some commercial activity may have continued for a time. Between 1344 and 1369 the successors of the Il-khans in Iran tried, with unknown results, to encourage Italian merchants to return to their dominions; in 1363 it was still possible to go as far east as Urgenj, according to the Venetian, Andreolo Dandolo, who had met another Venetian, Franceschino Noder, coming from Urgenj while he was on the way there himself; and in 1374 some Genoese sailed on the Caspian, though apparently as raiders rather than merchants.

The only region in which western commerce survived to any significant extent was on the very margins of Europe and Asia, in the area of the Crimea on the Black Sea, but it was trade at only a very localized level, not the beginning of much further flung activity. Caffa was rebuilt by the Genoese after the siege of 1346, and continued to flourish, despite numerous attacks, until it finally passed under Turkish rule as late as 1475. The Venetians' control of Tana underwent many vicissitudes, but they were apparently still in command in 1452, and in 1428 a raid had been made from there as far as the Caspian. In Trebizond, on the southern shore of the Black Sea, there was a Venetian merchant colony until 1462. Another trace of western influence still existed in the city of Matrega on the Black Sea coast of the Kuban. At an unknown date this had been granted by the Mongols to the de

Giuzulfis family of Genoa, whose members had been active both as merchants in Iran, and as envoys between East and West in the late thirteenth and early fourteenth centuries.

Matrega remained in the hands of the de Giuzulfis until 1482. At one level it was merely a relic of the days when European commerce had permeated throughout Asia and its margins. But the survival of European control at Matrega may also be taken as symbolic in its significance, since there were in the fifteenth century a number of occasions of contact between Europe and parts of Asia. Some of these were diplomatic; others were undertaken by men like Nicolo Conti of Venice, who were wandering travellers rather than merchants in the traditional sense. Taken together these contacts amounted, as will appear later, to a continuing awareness by Europeans of the wealth and prosperity that might once again be derived from Asia. Within twenty years of the loss of Matrega the first voyage of Vasco da Gama to India was to mark the beginning of a revival of direct European commerce with Asia, but on a scale without precedent.

7

The lost alliance: European monarchs and Mongol 'crusaders'

Although the Mongols might have resumed their attacks on Europe at any time before the end of the thirteenth century, if they had so wished, the activities of the papal envoys to the Great Khans, of the Franciscan and Dominican missionaries, and of the merchants from the great commercial cities of northern Italy, all assumed in one way or another that the Mongols might be induced to end or moderate their hostility. In the event these assumptions proved to be justified, but there was one form of contact between Europe and the Mongol dominions in which all these other activities overlapped and supported one another, and through which it was hoped that the Mongols might become actual allies against the world of Islam. For their part, the Mongols of Iran in particular sought allies among the Christian powers of western Europe in their own conflict with Moslem Syria and Egypt, one of the few regions in which the Mongols tried and failed to make a conquest. This phase in the relations between the Mongols and Europe lasted from the middle of the thirteenth century until the early decades of the fourteenth. During it the Mongols were transformed from the mortal enemies of Europe into the unexpected role of the allies of Christendom, almost indeed into crusaders who were as anxious as the rulers of western Europe to conquer Syria and the Holy Land, and to free Jerusalem from Moslem control.

The possibility of an alliance, or at the very least of a *modus vivendi*, was implicit in the relations between Europe and the Mongols from a very early stage. The mission of Giovanni di Piano Carpini to the Great Khan in 1245 was only one of a number of embassies sent out by Pope Innocent IV at this time. Three others are known to have been dispatched, those of the

Dominican Andrew of Longjumeau, of the Dominicans Ascelin and Simon of St Quentin, and of the Franciscan Dominic of Aragon. Dominic seems to have intended to visit the Christian kingdom of Cilician Armenia, a territory which was to play an important intermediary role between Europe and the Mongols. He returned to Lyons in April 1247 but does not appear to have made any contact with the Mongols, and the outcome of his mission is unknown. Ascelin and Simon travelled via Palestine to Tiflis in Georgia, where they were joined by another Dominican, Guiscard of Cremona, who was already resident there, and who had some knowledge of the Mongols. Eventually the party reached the camp of the Mongol commander Baiju in May 1247, over two years after they had set out. Baiju was most unsympathetic, and considered either executing the friars or forcing them to travel onwards to the Mongol capital at Karakorum. The only reply they were able to obtain to the pope's letters was the customary Mongol assertion of supremacy, and a demand that the pope should recognize Mongol authority or face destruction. Bearing this negative result, Ascelin and Simon returned to Lyons in the summer of 1248.

Meanwhile, both Carpini and Andrew of Longjumeau had returned, the one in November 1247 and the other in the spring of the same year, at about the same time as Dominic of Aragon. Andrew's eventful journey had taken him through friendly areas of Moslem-held Syria to Mosul in northern Iraq, and finally to the vicinity of Tabriz in Iran, which was already under Mongol control. He delivered the papal letters to the commander of a Mongol army he encountered, and did not meet Baiju, the senior Mongol officer in the region. Consequently he did not receive the dismal replies given to most of the other envoys of this period.

By the end of 1248 the papacy was therefore provided with a great deal of firsthand information on the Mongols and their way of life from a variety of visitors to the East. Their reports, and especially that of Carpini, left no room for doubt as to the formidable nature of the Mongol threat, and showed that western Europe was most unlikely to be able to counter it by military means. There were, however, one or two rays of hope. One of these was the friendly reception given to Andrew of Longjumeau by Simeon Rabban Ata, a Nestorian priest who in 1235 had been given authority by the Mongols over the Nestorian Christians of western Asia, and whose appointment represented the beginning of a revival of the Nestorian church throughout Mongol Asia which was to last for almost the rest of the thirteenth century. Simeon even offered his allegiance to the papacy, an attitude very different from that encountered by most western Christians in Asia, and especially by John of Monte Corvino in his battles with the Nestorians of Peking, but which has its parallel in the remarkable mission of Rabban Sauma to Italy and France in 1287-8. Another significant development was that for the first time Mongol envoys came back to Europe, in the persons of a Turk named Aybeg and a Syrian Nestorian named Sergius, who accompanied Ascelin and Simon of St Quentin on behalf of Baiju. Their functions were officially to bear Baiju's answers to Innocent IV's letters, and unofficially to gather information about Europe, as Carpini had suspected when he refused to allow any Mongol envoys to return with him to Lyons. But with hindsight there is the first faint hint that something other than hostility might develop in the relations between the Mongols and the powers of western Europe whom they had come so close to annihilating a few years before.

These hopeful signs were given more substance by a series of other events in 1247-8. Among the clients and vassals of the Mongols who attended the enthronement of the Great Khan Küyük near Karakorum in 1247, the occasion at which Carpini was also present, was Sempad, the constable of the Christian kingdom of Cilician Armenia, who was there to represent his brother, King Hayton I. In 1248 Sempad wrote from Samarkand to his brother-in-law, the king of Cyprus, and reported on the good treatment given to the many Christians who were at the Mongol court. The story was repeated to Louis IX of France, who was in Cyprus *en route* for Egypt at the start of his first crusading expedition.

At the end of 1248 Louis IX was himself visited in Cyprus by two Mongol envoys, Nestorians named David and Mark, who had been sent by Eljigidei, the personal representative of the Great Khan in western Asia. The letter they bore spoke very warmly of Christians of all persuasions, and promised them protection, but more significantly the envoys added an oral message revealing that the Mongols were almost ready to attack Baghdad, the last bastion of Moslem power in Asia, and hoped that Louis IX's attack on Egypt might be concerted with their own. The envoys probably also embroidered their report with stories to the effect that the Great Khan and Eljigidei had become Christians, and intended to restore Christian control of the city of Jerusalem, which had fallen to the forces of the Egyptian sultan in 1244. However suspect the motives of the Mongols and their envoys may have been, 1248 may be taken as the year in which an alliance between the Mongols and Europe was first seriously considered by both parties. From then until the early fourteenth century some kind of alliance or co-operation was an almost constant feature of their relations.

Louis IX responded early in 1249 by sending off an embassy of his own. This was composed of three Dominicans, Andrew of Longjumeau, who happened to be in Cyprus at the time, Andrew's brother Guy, and Andrew of Carcassonne, and was accompanied by the two Mongol envoys. In his enthusiasm Louis IX sent with them, according to his biographer Jean de Joinville,

a chapel which he had caused to be fashioned all in scarlet; and in order to draw the Tartars to our faith, he had caused all our faith to be imaged in the chapel: the Annunciation of the angel, the Nativity, the baptism that God was baptized withal, and all the Passion, and the ascension, and the coming of the Holy Ghost; and with the chapel he sent also cups, books, and all things needful for the chanting of the mass.

By the time friars reached Eljigidei's camp near Tabriz the situation within the Mongol dominions had undergone a dramatic change. As in 1241, it was once again the unexpected death of the Great Khan that caused the upheaval. Küyük had died a year earlier in 1248, leaving his widow Oghul Ghaimish as the temporary regent of the empire. Eljigidei was therefore so unsure of his authority that he refused to receive the envoys, and sent them on to the regent, who treated their arrival and their lavish gifts merely as an offer of submission to Mongol supremacy. Andrew of Longjumeau had travelled further into Asia than any other western envoy apart from Carpini, but the failure of his mission was deeply wounding to Louis IX to whom Andrew reported in 1251. Meanwhile Louis had suffered a disastrous defeat at the hands of the Egyptians, and had only recently been released from captivity. For the moment the notion of a possible alliance with the Mongol was suspended. Although the mission of William of Rubruck to Karakorum in 1253 was supported by Louis, and William later reported to the king, his journey was undertaken primarily for religious reasons. When a new opportunity arose for diplomatic contact with the Mongols it came yet again in the wake of a change in the circumstances of the Mongols themselves.

In 1258 the Mongols, under the command of Hülegü, the first of the Il-khans, captured Baghdad and destroyed the Abbasid caliphate. With this event the dissolution of all Moslem rule in Syria and Egypt seemed imminent. Early in 1260 the Mongols invaded Syria, quickly took the cities of Damascus and Aleppo, and by the summer had reached Gaza, on the borders of Egyptian territory. Unfortunately the news of the death of the Great Khan Möngke then arrived, and Hülegü had to return to Iran, taking with him the greater part of his forces. Meanwhile the Egyptians had reacted swiftly, and assisted by the fears of the European settlers in Acre, were allowed to advance unhindered up the coast of Frankish Palestine. On 3 September 1260 the Mongols were totally defeated at Ain Jalud in Galilee, their commander Kitbuka was killed, and within a short time they were expelled from Syria.

This was the first major reverse suffered by the Mongols in their career of conquest, and for the rest of the thirteenth century it remained the policy of the Il-khans to avenge the defeat by conquering Syria and Egypt. The defeat also coincided with a sharp deterioration in the relations between the Mongols of Iran and those of the Golden Horde in southern Russia, which led to a growing *rapprochement* between the Golden Horde and Egypt, and also, in 1262, to open conflict between the two groups of Mongols. This was the war which prevented Niccolo and Maffeo Polo from returning home, and so initiated their historic journey to China.

The Mongols of Iran now had a very definite need of allies, and the obvious direction to turn was towards the Christian rulers of western Europe, and the western colonists in the Holy Land and in Syria. In 1260 itself Christian attitudes towards the Mongols were understandably still wary. When news of the Mongol invasion of Syria reached Europe a number of crusaders left, at the instigation of Pope Alexander IV, to defend it from them. Bohemond VI, prince of Antioch, who openly assisted the Mongol invasion in company with his father-in-law King Hayton of Cilician Armenia, was excommunicated for his pains.

However, even in 1260 there were signs of a different reaction to the Mongols. While they were still in the Holy Land Thomas Agno of Lentino, who was bishop of Bethlehem, papal legate, and a future patriarch of Jerusalem, and who was probably aware that Kitbuka, the commander of the Mongol army, was a Christian, sent an embassy to Hülegü to discover the invaders' intentions. It was led by a Dominican named David, probably the Englishman David of Ashby who spent the next fourteen years at the court of the Il-khans before returning to Europe in 1274 as one of the Mongol envoys to the Council of Lyons.

David was apparently well received by Hülegü, who decided that it was time to make a direct approach to some of the most important of the western rulers. A recently discovered letter has revealed that in 1262 Hülegü wrote to Louis IX of France. Following Mongol tradition, Hülegü reasserted the Mongols' divinely appointed mission as conquerors, but he also offered that when Jerusalem was recaptured it would be restored to western control through the agency of a Mongol aide, a certain John of Hungary. In 1263 John of Hungary himself was sent to Italy with a letter for Pope Urban IV. Although he was intercepted in Sicily by the pope's enemy, Manfred of Hohenstaufen, the letter eventually reached the pope who replied to it in 1264 in the bull *Exultavit cor nostrum*, the first direct communication between the papacy and the Il-khans of Iran. Its contents were a cautious acceptance of Hülegü's message, of whose authenticity the pope was not fully convinced, but it was destined to be the first of many such communications in later years.

Contacts between Iran and western Europe were intensified by the accession in 1265 of the Il-khan Abaka, whose wife was the daughter of the Byzantine emperor Michael VIII Palaeologus, and who was therefore very conscious of the advantages that might flow from good relations with Christian powers. The Mongols of the Golden Horde were at this time in process of adopting Islam, so that the Il-khans were in real danger of being faced by hostile Moslem powers in both southern Russia and Syria. In 1267 Abaka made a friendly overture to Pope Clement IV in a letter which could not immediately be understood in Rome, because Abaka's temporary lack of a Latin scribe had forced him to write in Mongolian, but which none the less produced replies from the pope and from James I of Aragon, who sent James Alaric of Perpignan on an embassy to Iran. In his reply of 1268 Abaka suggested that the pope and the king of Aragon should send a force to join up with Michael VIII, and present the Moslems with a threat both from themselves and from the Mongols. A small Aragonese force did land in Syria in 1269, but Abaka was unable to send support, and the expedition achieved nothing. Meanwhile, in 1268, the Egyptians had taken Antioch, one of the few remaining Frankish strongpoints in Syria and the Holy Land.

The early 1270s were another time of lost opportunities in Syria and Palestine. Louis IX's crusade of 1270, which might conceivably have intervened there, went instead to Tunis in North Africa, partly because Louis's earlier experiences led him to distrust the Mongols, but also because of the ambitions of his brother, Charles of Anjou, against the territory of the Byzantine emperor who was still in alliance with the Mongols. In May 1271, however, Prince Edward of England, the future Edward I, who had earlier accompanied Louis IX to Tunis, and was a man of considerable military experience, landed at Acre with a small army. Edward immediately sent off three envoys, Reginald Russell, Godfrey Welles, and John Parker, to arrange with Abaka for a joint campaign against the Egyptians. Abaka was then fighting a civil war in Turkestan, but he did send an army of ten thousand horsemen to Syria. The combined forces of the Mongols and the English crusaders were insufficient to achieve anything significant; the Mongols were soon forced to withdraw, and in September 1272 Edward himself left the Holy Land.

Despite the failure of this expedition, Edward was to retain the ambition to make a further crusade. For their part, the Mongols' contacts with Edward seem to have convinced them that he might be a useful ally in the future. Relations between Iran and England were to continue throughout Edward's reign, and there were echoes of them as late as the middle years of the reign of his successor, Edward II.

The assembling of the Council of Lyons in 1274 at the instigation of Pope Gregory X, who as Tedaldo Visconti, and in his capacity as papal legate in the Holy Land, had been instrumental in the return of the Polos of Venice to China in 1271, proved to be another important link in the chain of relations between Europe and the Il-khans. Although the council was chiefly concerned with calling a new crusade, and with the reunion of the Greek and Latin churches, the forming of an alliance with the Mongols could be made to fit easily enough into this business. The pope had already ordered a tithe in aid of the crusade, and an embargo on all Christian trade with the Moslem world, when an embassy from the Il-khan Abaka led by the Dominican David of Ashby unexpectedly arrived in Lyons, where it made a deep impression upon the council.

Abaka's letter to the pope rehearsed the previous history of the relations between the Mongols and Europe, and expressed his desire for an alliance against the Moslems. The envoys, of whom three were baptized by the Dominican cardinal Peter of Tarentaise, also made much of the Mongol tolerance of Christianity, while David of Ashby circulated his treatise on the Mongols, *Les Faits des Tartares*, among the members of the Council. The pope expressed his pleasure at Abaka's letter, and promised that any future crusading army would seek the active co-operation of the Mongols. Yet, despite the fact that a crusade was actively being planned, Gregory X's reply fell short of a definite commitment to an alliance.

After his dramatic appearance at Lyons David of Ashby also went on behalf of Abaka to see Edward I of England, who replied in January 1275. Disappointed by the reception his proposals had received at Lyons and in England, Abaka tried again in 1276, sending two Greek Christians, John and James Vassili Georgios, to the pope. These envoys probably also belonged to the embassy which visited London in 1277 and apologized to Edward I for the Mongols' lack of co-operation in the Holy Land in 1271. Because of the death of the sultan Baibars in 1277, and the long inter-regnum which followed, a joint enterprise against Egypt in the late 1270s might have stood a good chance of success, but once again an opportunity was lost.

In 1284, after Abaka's unsuccessful invasion of Syria in 1281, which had emphasized the Mongols' need of allies, and a short period of rule by an Il-khan who favoured Islam, Abaka's son Arghun resumed relations with Europe. This phase of east–west contacts was to contain some of the most tantalizing possibilities of large-scale co-operation which might, if fulfilled, have trans-formed the political situation in the lands of the eastern Mediter-ranean. It has also left behind firsthand evidence from the Mongol side which, in its own way, is just as remarkable as the narratives of the western envoys and missionaries who travelled in Asia, and which again emphasizes the extent to which the Mongol conquests had tied together vast and previously uncom-prehending areas of the world.

In May 1285 Arghun sent the first of a series of embassies to Europe. Omitting to mention that Arghun's personal leanings were towards Buddhism, the envoys bore the now familiar pro-testation of Mongol sympathy towards Christianity. The leader of this mission was a Christian named Isa or Ase, whose name was probably a form of Jesus, and who was a councillor of the Great Khan Kublai. Isa had just come from China bearing Arghun's diploma of investiture as Il-khan, and he was to die in Peking in 1320.

Arghun's next envoy was Bar Sauma, another Christian from China, whose journey appears even more extraordinary because of the survival of a detailed contemporary account. Bar Sauma ('Son of Fasting'), who is more commonly known as Rabban Sauma, was of Turkish origin, probably a member of the Öngut tribe among whom there were many Nestorian Christians, and had been born in Peking. He had come westwards with a younger companion Mark, in order to visit the Holy Places in Jerusalem, but had instead settled in Iran. In 1281 Mark was appointed as patriarch of the Nestorians at Baghdad under the title of Mar Yaballahah III ('God gave him'), with Rabban Sauma as his visitor-general. Between them Mark and Rabban Sauma occupied a position not unlike that of John of Monte Corvino after he was appointed as archbishop of Khanbalik/Peking in 1307 with responsibility for the entire Mongol dominions. Rabban Sauma was accordingly a man of great experience and very well suited for the mission he was to undertake. Having travelled via Constantinople, where he was well received by the emperor, and was particularly impressed by the great dome of Santa Sophia, he landed at Naples in June 1287 after witnessing an eruption of Mount Etna and a sea battle in the Bay of Sorrento between the navies of Charles of Anjou and of Aragon.

He arrived in Rome in early July, only to find that *Mar Papa* (Honorius IV) to whom he had been sent, had died, and that the twelve *kaltônârê* had not yet elected a successor. The cardinals were puzzled by what appeared to them as Rabban Sauma's low ecclesiastical rank, and they asked him searching questions on the origins of his church, and the location of its head, as well as on its theology, with particular emphasis on the then topical *filioque* question which had been at issue in the reunion of the Greek and Latin churches at the Council of Lyons in 1274. The credal statement made by Rabban Sauma did not altogether satisfy the cardinals on this point, while Rabban Sauma found that the subtleties of the western position escaped him, and concluded that 'the subject-matter is ultimately for the confession of wise men only'. Rabban Sauma then told the cardinals:

I have come from far lands not to dispute nor to expound the themes of the Faith; but to receive a benediction from the Reverend Pope and the shrines of the saints have I come. If it be agreeable to you that we leave the discussion and you make arrangement and appoint someone who will show me the churches here and the shrines of the saints, you will confer a great favour upon your servant and disciple.

After their grand tour of the churches and relics of Rome, Rabban Sauma and his companions went to Paris to visit the next ruler on their schedule, the king of *Frangestan*, Philip the Fair, who received them kindly, and after hearing the messages from

Arghun and Mar Yaballahah replied: 'If the Mongols, although they are not Christians, are fighting with the Arabs because of the captivity of Jerusalem, it still more behooves us to fight and to go forth in force, if Our Lord will'. As in Rome, Rabban Sauma then asked to be shown the churches and relics of Paris, 'and all that is to be found with you and not anywhere else, so that when we return we can tell and declare in the lands what we have seen'. He was duly impressed by the abbey church of St Denis, and the tombs of French kings, and also by the university of Paris where he declared there were thirty thousand students studying ecclesiastical and secular subjects, and all receiving stipends from the king. When they had remained a full month in Paris, and had seen everything else, Philip summoned them to meet him at the Sainte Chapelle, and there showed them the greatest relic of all, the Crown of Thorns brought back from the east by Louis IX.

Still in France, Rabban Sauma then went to visit 'the King *Ilnagtar*' in '*Kesonia*', that is to say Edward I of England who was then at Bordeaux in his duchy of Gascony. Edward was pleased with the letters and presents they brought him, 'And when discourse arose about the business of Jerusalem, his joy was still more increased. And he said: "We Kings of these cities carry the cross as a sign on our bodies, and we have no thought apart from this business. And my mind is gratified when I hear that somewhat of what I have thought of King Arghon has planned".' When Rabban Sauma made his usual request to be shown the churches and shrines, Edward replied: ' "So shall you say to King Arghon and all the Orientals, that we have seen something, and that there is nothing more admirable than this, namely, that in the lands of the Franks there are not two creeds but only one, that which confesses Jesus Christ, and they are all Christians." '

After spending the winter in Genoa, the home city of one of his companions, Tomasso de Anfussis, who had also accompanied the embassy of 1285, Rabban Sauma returned to Rome where the Franciscan Jerome of Ascoli had just been elected as Pope Nicholas IV. This was a very significant election since Jerome already had great experience of the east when he was apostolic legate in the Holy Land during the pontificate of Gregory X.

During his four years as pope he was to be closely concerned with efforts to spread western Christianity in Iran, and he was also responsible for sending John of Monte Corvino on the mission which took him eventually to Peking and led to the foundation of the western church in China (see chapter 5). His dealings with the il-khan Arghun were also to be marked by the baptism of Arghun's son Öljeitu under the name of Nicholas.

Rabban Sauma's stay in Rome was highly successful. He was allowed by the pope to participate in the religious services at Easter time; his religious practices and beliefs were approved as being acceptable to Rome, despite the differences in language and rite; and in return he declared himself to be in communion with the Roman Church. When Rabban Sauma left Rome he took with him the papal blessing, a number of relics, and papal letters to Arghun. He also took valuable gifts for both Arghun and Mar Yaballahah III, those for the latter including a ring from the pope's own finger, and allegedly a bull recognizing him as patriarch of all the orientals.

Rabban Sauma was accompanied on his return to Iran in 1288 by ambassadors from Philip IV of France. Arghun responded by making detailed proposals for a joint campaign in Syria, in letters which he wrote in the summer of 1289, and which were taken to Nicholas IV, Philip IV, and Edward I by a Genoese envoy, Buscarel de Giuzulfis. Only the text of the letter to the king of France has survived, but it is probably representative of Arghun's plans. After recording that Rabban Sauma had brought back an undertaking from Philip IV that 'if the armies of the Ilkhan go to war against Egypt, we too shall set out from here to go to war and to attack [the rear of the enemy] in a common operation'. Arghun went on:

And we decided [accordingly], after reporting to heaven, to mount our horses in the last month of winter in the Year of the Tiger [1290] and to dismount outside Damascus on the 15th of the first month in spring [1291]. Now, we make it known to you, that in accordance with Our honest word, We shall send our armies [to arrive] at the [time and place] agreed, and, if by the authority of heaven, we conquer these people, We shall give you Jerusalem. If, [however], you should fail to meet on the appropriate day, and thus lead our armies into an abortive action, would that be fitting? Even if you should later regret it, what use would that be to you?

Philip IV's reaction to these plans is unknown, but Edward I of England did show some interest. Buscarel de Giuzulfis visited Edward in London in January 1290 and was given a letter for Arghun expressing Edward's willingness to take part in a joint campaign, provided that the pope agreed. It is not clear whether Buscarel returned in person to Iran after this meeting, but at the end of 1290 he was associated with yet another embassy from Arghun to Edward. This further appeal resulted in the departure from England in the summer or autumn of 1291 of an embassy led by Geoffrey of Langley, who had taken part in Edward's expedition to the Holy Land in 1270–1. The detailed financial records of this mission have survived, and make it possible to trace the progress of the envoys from Genoa, where they were joined by Buscarel and his brother Percival, to Tabriz, and also to know, for example, that they took a gift of falcons to the Il-khan, who reciprocated with a leopard in a cage. But of the substance of their negotiations once they reached Iran nothing at all is recorded.

Geoffrey of Langley and his companions were at Trebizond on the Black Sea in April 1292. From there a squire, Nicholas of Chartres, and Buscarel's nephew Corradin went via Sivas to the Mongol court at Kayseri in Asia Minor, but were told that it would shortly be moving to Tabriz. The envoys resumed their journey from Trebizond and travelled via Erzerum in Armenia and around the shores of Lake Van, until they finally reached Tabriz. Unfortunately neither the date of their arrival at Tabriz nor the place of any meeting with the Il-khan is known. The mission began its return from Tabriz on 22 September 1292, and arrived back in Genoa on 11 January 1293; the date of Geoffrey of Langley's return to England is uncertain, but in 1294 he was one of the knights who accompanied Edmund of Lancaster to France; the ultimate fate of the leopard does not seem to be recorded.

Even if the official accounts of Geoffrey of Langley's mission to Iran had included diplomatic as well as financial detail, it is likely that his journey would still appear inconclusive. The Il-khan Arghun, who had laid such far-reaching plans for a campaign in Syria, died in March 1291, before Geoffrey had left England. By the time Geoffrey reached Iran Arghun's brother Gaikhatu, who was less interested in a western alliance than his predecessor, had been elected as Il-khan.

In May 1291 the city of Acre, the last great European outpost in the Holy Land, had fallen to the Egyptians, and was followed in a matter of weeks by all the remaining crusader strongholds. Although Edward I had taken the cross in 1287, collected money in aid of a crusade, expelled the Jews, arranged for the succession to his throne in case he died overseas, and decided in 1290 that he would depart on crusade in June 1293, nothing was to come of his plans. By the mid-1290s the crisis of the Scottish succession and the steady decline into war between England and Scotland, together with the war between England and France over Gascony, had set the pattern for the rest of Edward I's reign, and had brought the two western European monarchies which were most likely to contribute to a campaign in the east into direct conflict.

Even so there were some further episodes in the relations between Europe and the Il-khans. Although Arghun's son Ghazan, who seized power in Iran in 1295, was a Moslem, and his accession was marked by the attacks on Christians in his dominions which were witnessed at Baghdad by the Dominican missionary Ricold of Monte Croce, Ghazan was determined that the power of the Egyptian sultan in Syria, which his predecessors had failed to destroy in 1260 and 1281, should finally be defeated. The kingdom of Cilician Armenia still existed, and remained a Mongol ally, but only military force on the scale available in Europe would be sufficient to tip the balance.

Early in 1300 it seemed that the longed-for opportunity had come. Ghazan's armies invaded Syria, captured Damascus, and cleared the province of Egyptian forces. News of the event and pleas for military assistance were rapidly transmitted to Europe via Cyprus through the agency of Venetian merchants and Franciscan friars. The two Franciscans, for example, who arrived at Canterbury in June 1300 with news of Ghazan's victory, may also have been the bearers of the letter describing the campaign of 1300 which was written at Nicosia in February by another Franciscan, James of Ferraria, and which is preserved in the unpublished chronicle of the Premonstratensian house of Hagneby in Lincolnshire.

The news lost nothing in the telling, especially since 1300 had been proclaimed a Jubilee Year by Pope Boniface VIII, and pilgrims in search of a plenary indulgence were flocking to Rome. There is widespread evidence from chroniclers all over western Europe, and from the archives of the papacy itself, that it was believed that the Mongols had retaken Jerusalem and had even invaded Egypt. All the disappointments of the previous two centuries of crusading, and the humiliation suffered from the loss of Acre in 1291, seemed to have been wiped out at a stroke.

Disillusion came swiftly. Jerusalem had not been taken or even besieged; for no adequately explained reason Ghazan evacuated Syria within a few weeks of its conquest. He attacked it again in 1301, and planned further campaigns for the next two years, but achieved nothing. His bitterness at the failure of the European powers to provide the military assistance he had asked for expressed itself in 1303 in yet another embassy to Philip IV and Edward I, to which Edward replied tactfully that he and Philip had been at war and could not send help.

Ghazan died in 1304 but in 1305 his successor Öljeitu sent envoys to the pope, the doge of Venice, and to Philip IV and Edward I. Öljeitu had been the child baptized and named in honour of Pope Nicholas IV. He was now a Moslem, but still conscious of the advantages of a European alliance. In his letter to Philip IV he referred to the previous relations between his dynasty and the rulers of Europe, and stated that the Mongol dominions which had been divided by civil strife were now united in peace: 'From the land of the Chinese where the sun rises, to the Talu Sea, we have joined our mail lines together, in order to connect the states.'

This or a similar letter reached the court of Edward II of England in 1307, shortly after the death of Edward I to whom it had been addressed. At about the same time letters also arrived from the king of Cilician Armenia, with whom Edward I's old friend Otto of Granson had been in touch a few years before. However, by 1307 the king of England was in no position to undertake any further crusading ventures, since the war with Scotland had recently taken a turn for the worse with the beginning of Robert Bruce's efforts to expel the English from Scotland, while the scale of the war effort was placing an immense strain upon England's financial resources and administrative machine. Edward II's replies to Öljeitu's letter, in October and November 1307, were accordingly couched in generalities, wishing Öljeitu well, and hoping that he would succeed in exterminating the 'abominable sect of Mahomet'. It has sometimes been suggested that this last remark indicates that Edward II was supplied with misleading information about Öljeitu and his religious beliefs, but it was none the less in harmony with the Il-khans' aim of destroying the power of Egypt. It was said of Ghazan that one of the reasons for his invasion of Syria was religious outrage at discovering Egyptian soldiers drinking wine in the mosques of Mardin during Ramadan.

Although there was no serious prospect of an English crusading expedition either then or later in the reign of Edward II, there are some strange episodes during his lifetime which do at least show how persistent the idea of the crusade had become. In his youth Edward had been brought up against the background of the loss of Acre and his father's plans for a new crusade. In May 1293 the 9-year-old Edward had even been visited at Mortlake by the bishop of Jebail in Syria, whose diocese lay in the lordship of Peter Embriaco who maintained a precarious independence of Egyptian control until 1298, and who no doubt supplied him with tales of recent disasters in the Holy Land. At about the time of Edward II's coronation in 1308, an English poet Adam Davy wrote a Latin poem, the *Five Dreams of Edward II*, in which he depicted Edward as an invincible crusader who would recover Jerusalem. In the middle years of his reign an English Dominican, Nicholas of Wisbech, cast him in a similar role when he propagated a legend connecting Edward with a phial of holy oil allegedly given by the Virgin Mary to Thomas Becket in the twelfth century.

Anyone less fitted to be the all-conquering hero than the disastrous Edward II would be hard to imagine, but there were a few contacts between him and the real world of crusading. Early in June 1313, while on an official visit to Paris, Edward II solemnly took the cross in Notre Dame, together with Philip IV of France and many French nobles. A month later, at Poissy, the Franciscan bishop of an unnamed see in Iran left Edward's company after a visit which had lasted since the previous May. The bishop can be identified as Guillaume de Villeneuve, one of the six suffragans consecrated by Clement V in 1307–8 to serve in the newly created archdiocese of Peking/Khanbalik. Since Guillaume was described in the English household records as a messenger of the emperor of the Tartars, it is likely that his see was somewhere within the dominions of the Il-khan, and possible that he was the bearer of yet another message seeking co-operation from the king of England.

Edward II was not destined ever to embark on a crusade, and it is not known whether he had any further diplomatic dealings with the Mongols of Iran. However, Clement V had for much of his time as pope been concerned in the attempt to organize a crusade in conjunction with the Il-khan. In 1307, at about the same time that messengers from Öljeitu visited Philip IV and Edward II, an embassy also went to the papal curia. In his reply from Poitiers in March 1308 Clement V did not commit himself to any precise time for a new military expedition, but his letter reveals that Öljeitu had undertaken to supply a future crusading army with 200,000 horses and with 200,000 loads of corn on its arrival in Armenia, and to send a Mongol army of 100,000 to join the western forces in the Holy Land. In 1307 the pope's mind was also being focused upon the east by the exiled Armenian prince Hayton, who wrote at the pope's request a work entitled *La Flor des estoires de la terre d'orient*, which included detailed proposals on just how a joint enterprise with the Mongols should be undertaken. Hayton recommended that the western Christians should recapture Tripoli and make this their base, so that when the Mongols invaded Syria and took Damascus the European army should advance along a parallel route to Jerusalem: 'And in this way, because of the distance between them, peace and friendship would be preserved between the Christians and the Tartars.'

By this time the chances of an actual alliance between Europe and the Mongols were fast diminishing. The growing power of Islam within the dynasty of the Il-khans was in itself bound eventually to estrange Iran from its potential western allies. The military capacity of the Il-khans was also weakening: in January 1313 the Mongols withdrew from Syria after another campaign, which proved to be their last; in 1323 they made peace with Egypt, and by the mid-1330s the Il-khans' power in Iran itself had also disappeared.

In retrospect it is easy to see why the Mongol alliance produced no concrete results. On the whole the Mongols who lived next door to the power of Islam in Syria and in Egypt were more consistently interested in an alliance than their western counterparts, and seem usually to have taken the initiative in diplomatic relations. The problems involved in co-ordinating military action between the Mongols and armies from western Europe were formidable and almost insoluble, given the time it took to raise an army, and to transport it to the East. At critical moments both sides were often distracted by more urgent problems which made it impossible to send forces at all or in sufficient strength. There was also a degree of mistrust by each of the other's motives for wanting an alliance, especially on the western side, although it is fair to say that by the end of the thirteenth century this suspicion, born out of the fear aroused by the great Mongol invasion in the early 1240s, had largely disappeared.

There were in Europe many people whose commercial prosperity depended on trade with Moslem Egypt, and who were not anxious to see it interrupted either by the papal embargoes on trade imposed after the loss of Acre in 1291, or by an overzealous prosecution of the crusade. At one moment a European power might be on good terms with the Moslem world, at another in alliance with its enemies, all according to where the greater advantage was to be gained. When messages were reaching Europe in 1300 about the supposed Mongol reconquest of the Holy Land, King James of Aragon was negotiating with success for renewed trade privileges for his kingdom in Egypt; only a few years later, in 1307, Aragonese envoys were sent to Iran to try to negotiate an alliance with the Il-khan; by 1330 a series of seven further Aragonese embassies to Egypt had taken place.

The failure of the attempts to bring together the Mongols and the European powers should not, however, be viewed too cynically, or too lightly dismissed as inevitable. From time to time there were real chances of success. The mere fact that diplomatic contacts took place with such frequency and over such long distances is remarkable, and is testimony to the extent to which Europe's relations with the much vaster world of Asia had been transformed in the course of the thirteenth century. To the crusading propagandists, like Marino Sanudo of Venice and William Adam, who abounded in early fourteenth-century Europe, the Mongols continued to have a role in schemes for a future crusade, in one case even as late as 1332 when the Il-khans' dynasty was on the verge of dissolution. The embassy from the Great Khan which arrived in Avignon in 1338, under the leadership of the Genoese merchant Andalo da Savignone, was another reminder to Europe of the former power of the Mongols. It is no exaggeration to say that relations with the Mongols of Iran and with the more distant Great Khans in China left a mark which, in the fifteenth century, was to be an important factor in European recollections of the great age which lay in the recent past, and helped to fuel European determination to resume direct contacts with Asia.

III
Two continents and an ocean

8

Medieval Europe and Africa

Compared with the richness and complexity of Europe's relations with Asia, knowledge of Africa in the medieval period was limited to a few relatively small areas along the fringes of the continent. There is ample evidence that Europeans, especially from Italy and the Iberian peninsula, were familiar with the coast of North Africa from the eleventh century, and with Egypt in particular well before that. But beyond this coastal zone the interior of Africa was unknown, and almost totally unheard of by Europeans, while there was no conception of the vast southwards extension of the continent until this was revealed by the Portuguese voyages in the closing decades of the fifteenth century. Knowledge of East Africa was probably very slight before the late fourteenth century, although it is difficult to draw firm conclusions on this because of the ambiguity of many of the apparent references to Ethiopia and adjoining regions. Some information about the Indian Ocean was acquired by the European merchants and missionaries who sailed upon it in the thirteenth and fourteenth centuries, but there is no evidence of any systematic understanding of its patterns of trade or of the methods of navigation employed there before the end of the fifteenth century, when the Portuguese gained information from such sources as their agent Pero da Covilhã, who was sent out in 1487, and from Vasco da Gama's Arab pilot Ibn Majid. By the late fourteenth century European navigators had gained some first-hand experience of the Atlantic coastline of Morocco, and for an indeterminate distance to the south, but it was in the waters adjoining this part of Africa that discoveries of real and lasting importance had been made: the Canary Islands, and probably also the Madeira group and the Azores.

For the classical geographers Africa was one of the three continents into which they conventionally divided the world, but the only parts of the continent known in any detail were the coastal strip and immediate hinterland of North Africa, together with the delta and the valley of the Nile as far as the first cataract at Aswan. These were firmly a part of the political, religious and economic life which flourished around the shores of the Mediterranean. As the homeland of St Augustine of Hippo, North Africa made a permanent contribution to the growth of Christianity, while it made an economic contribution as a major supplier of olive oil to the lands on the opposite shore of the Mediterranean.

The Moslem conquests of the seventh century drew the economy of North Africa towards the centres of Arab power in the east, while its cultivated areas gradually declined as a result of the invasions of desert nomads and the neglect of the irrigation systems which had sustained agriculture in the past. Christianity also went into a slow but irreversible decline. There were still many Christians in Numidia in the late ninth century but these were only survivals and by the end of the eleventh century, despite the hopes of Pope Gregory VII, the last traces of North African Christianity were on the point of vanishing. Only in Egypt, in Nubia, and further south in Ethiopia did Christianity remain, but following a different allegiance from that of Rome or Constantinople. In the meantime the area of Moslem allegiance had been extended into Europe itself by the Arab conquests of nearly all of Spain in the eighth century, and of Sicily in the ninth, together with many of the islands of the western Mediterranean.

The uneasy relationship of Moslem and Christian was to last throughout the medieval period, and was enacted on both the European and African sides of the Straits of Gibraltar. At first the balance of power was in favour of Islam, sometimes reinforced by new Moslem invasions, as in the late eleventh century when the newly converted Berber tribes of North Africa (known to Europeans as the Almoravids, from the Arabic word *Murabit*—'outpost') conquered Morocco and swept through Spain, threatening to reverse the patient reconquests of centuries by the Christian communities of the peninsula. By the early thirteenth century the balance had swung in the opposite direction. Sardinia, Corsica, and Sicily had long since been reconquered. In the Iberian peninsula the historic kingdoms of Navarre, Castile, and Aragon had all come into existence before the end of the eleventh century, and the kingdom of Portugal made its permanent appearance with the capture of Lisbon on the river Tagus in 1147. Yet another wave of North African invaders, the Almohads (*Muwahhida*—'Unitarians)', entered the peninsula in 1160 and won a great victory at Alarcos in 1195, before being decisively defeated in 1212 at Las Navas de Tolosa by an army drawn from all the Christian kingdoms of the peninsula, together with some crusading knights from France.

Apart from the sheer extent of Moslem-held territory which was reconquered after 1212, many of the places acquired were of great significance for the future development of European overseas expansion. The capture of the port of Valencia in 1238, as well as the Balearic Isles between 1229 and 1235, gave Aragon the bases from which her trade with North Africa and the central and eastern Mediterranean was to grow rapidly during the rest of the thirteenth century. Meanwhile on the Atlantic side of the peninsula the kingdom of Castile took the great river port of Seville in 1248, and Cadiz in 1262. Early in the reign of Alfonso X (1252–84) Seville became the base of the new Castilian navy, a force which was to be of great international importance. In 1317 Portugal recognized the importance of its own position on the Atlantic by the creation of a royal fleet, whose admiral was one of the leading figures in the kingdom.

The rapid progress of the *Reconquista* in the Iberian peninsula allowed European pressure to be brought to bear directly on the North African bases from which Moslem invaders and reinforcements had come in the past. As early as the 1220s Castile may have had plans to invade Morocco, but it was not until 1260 that these materialized in an attack on the port of Salé on the Atlantic coast of Morocco. The enterprise was intended to be more ambitious, and at one stage Alfonso X apparently tried to persuade Henry III of England to participate, but only this one limited and temporary success was achieved. In 1291 Castile and Aragon recognized their rival ambitions against North Africa by agreeing to partition it, the western part going to Castile and the eastern to Aragon. The temporary conquest of Tarifa by Castile in 1292 was all that came of this grandiose scheme. In 1309, however, Castile took Gibraltar, the key to any future invasion of North Africa, lost it in 1333, and did not regain it until 1462. The occupation of nearby Algeciras soon after 1340 was some compensation.

It was to be expected that the kingdoms of the Iberian peninsula should be prominent in the offensive efforts against the Moslem territories in North Africa, but these were by no means all the European ventures there. The first occasion on which a military force from Christian Europe was sent to North Africa occurred as early as 1034, when the Pisans attacked the port of Bône. The city of Mahdiya in Tunisia was captured and plundered by the Genoese and Pisans in 1088; it was attacked again on several occasions in the early twelfth century before being taken and held by Roger II, king of Sicily, between 1148 and 1160. In the meantime Bougie had been assaulted by the Genoese in 1134, and Bône captured by the Genoese and Pisans in 1136. In 1270 the final crusading expedition of Louis IX of France was directed against Tunis, while on several occasions between 1282 and 1387 the kingdom of Aragon had plans to turn Tunis into a vassal state. In 1355 Tripoli was sacked by the Genoese, and in 1390 a large force of knights from France and the Low Countries, led by Duke Louis of Bourbon in the so-called 'Barbary crusade', made yet another attack upon Mahdiya.

Egypt was also a regular object of attack, beginning with the campaigns in the twelfth century by the Latin kingdom of Jerusalem. The armies of the fifth crusade in 1217 and of Louis IX in 1248 both chose the Nile Delta as their destination. Most of the crusading schemes which were put forward between the loss of Acre in 1291 and the early 1330s by such writers as Fidenzio of Padua, Pierre Dubois, Raymond Lull, Marino Sanudo, and others involved a direct attack upon Egypt, or an embargo upon trade, or naval operations against Egyptian shipping. Some of these propagandists, such as William Adam in his *De modo extirpandi Sarracenos*, written shortly before 1318, made the even more ambitious proposal of destroying Egypt's trade in the Red Sea and Indian Ocean. With the exception of the short-lived occupation of Alexandria, the focal point of Egypt's commerce with the Mediterranean, by Peter I of Cyprus in 1365, none of these schemes came to fruition.

European military activities in North Africa were not, however, exclusively hostile, since Christian mercenaries were a common feature of the armies of local Moslem rulers. There was a substantial force of Christian troops in Morocco before 1147, and in 1227, under the terms of a treaty between a Moslem pretender and Castile, twelve thousand men were authorized to serve there. In 1270 Louis IX of France, the paragon of all thirteenth-century crusaders, was none the less opposed at Tunis by a number of Christian mercenaries who included Frederick of Castile and Frederick Lanza, both presumably of Spanish origin.

Given the disappearance of a native Christian community in North Africa other than in Egypt, and the hostility between Moslem and Christian which made open proselytizing almost impossible, there was no European missionary activity of the kind which took place in Asia in the thirteenth and fourteenth centuries. There were, however, some special circumstances under which Christian clergy were able to function. The treaty of 1227, for example, gave Castile the right to build churches in Morocco, which could serve European soldiers and merchants, and even guaranteed that any converts from Islam would not be persecuted. It is not clear whether these promises were ever fulfilled, but shortly before this a number of Franciscans had gone to Morocco to make converts, in aid of which they were permitted by their order to adopt native dress. In 1233 Pope Gregory X appointed one of the Franciscans as *episcopus Marrochitanus* based at Fez. Later in the thirteenth century a number of further attempts were made to preach Christianity in North Africa, especially in Tunis whose close commercial and diplomatic links with Europe seemed to offer chances of success. At some point before 1270, for example, Louis IX sent the Dominican Andrew of Longjumeau, who had earlier been his envoy in Asia, to preach in Tunis. The Spanish Franciscan Raymond Lull preached at Tunis and Bougie in 1292 and 1307, before being stoned to death by an angry mob at Bougie in 1315 or 1316. At one stage the papacy hoped that Tunis might be brought within the area of responsibility of the bishop of Fez but this did not happen, and in the end little was achieved despite occasional successes such as the baptism of a convert from Islam in the chapel of the Genoese *funduq* at Bougie in the mid-thirteenth century.

Any propects of reintroducing Christianity to North Africa, even on a small scale, were doomed from the start, but the *funduq* or trading base at Bougie may be taken as symbolizing the most extensive and consistent form of European relations with North Africa, the practice of commerce, which overcame all political and religious barriers. In the case of Egypt, commercial relations went back at least to the Venetian activities at Alexandria in the early ninth century; in 1123 the Venetians destroyed the Egyptian fleet, and from then on seaborne trade in the eastern Mediterranean fell increasingly into Christian hands.

By the middle years of the twelfth century Genoese trade with the ports of North Africa from Tunis to Ceuta was beginning, and by the end of the century had become a routine operation. A journey to Ceuta, for example, might even be a stage in a circuit of the entire Mediterranean from Genoa to Alexandria, then to Provence, and finally back to Genoa, as in the case of Thomas de Veredeto in 1198–9. Until about 1230 European trade with North Africa was dominated by the Italian cities of Genoa and Pisa, but they were then challenged and soon overtaken by the merchants of the kingdom of Aragon, who made North Africa in general, and Morocco in particular, into a region of intensive commercial activity. The attraction of North Africa for European merchants arose from such bulky items as high grade merino wool and grain, but above all from gold bullion.

Within the interior of North Africa there was a network of caravan routes crossing the Sahara from places such as Marrakesh and Sijilmasa in Morocco to various points in the basin of the river Niger in West Africa. The Moslem world described this area to the south indiscriminately as the Sudan (*Beled es-Sudan*—'the land of the blacks'). The Moslems were in fact dealing with well-organized West African states: Ghana which flourished until its destruction by the Almoravids in 1076; and its larger successor, the empire of Mali, which was built up by the Mandingoes on the river Niger during the thirteenth century. Unlike Ghana, Mali adopted Islam, a fact which was to have an unexpected effect on European appreciation of Africa.

It was probably known even in classical antiquity that West Africa was a source of gold, and it was certainly a major preoccupation of Moslem trade with Ghana and Mali. However, even the latter were only intermediaries, since they obtained the gold from other Negro people much deeper in West Africa by the procedure known as silent barter. There was never any direct communication with the producers of the gold, so that neither the Arabs nor their contacts in Ghana and Mali knew exactly where it came from. The Arabs referred to its source as Wangara, which was probably a generic term for anywhere from which gold came. There are many places in West Africa in which gold has been mined, but it is thought that the Wangara spoken of by the Moslems of North Africa may have been a region within the savannah belt to the south of the Sahara, rather than in the coastal rain forests.

The gold of the Sudan or Wangara was of great importance to the development of the medieval European economy. It seems to have been especially significant in the Iberian peninsula where there was a serious shortage of gold. Much of it was imported by Catalan merchants from the ports of North Africa. But some also came into Europe in the guise of tribute: in 1231 the ruler of Tunis promised the emperor Frederick II a regular payment in gold in return for corn from Sicily. It may be no coincidence that in the same year Frederick minted the *augustalis*, the first gold coin to be issued in western Europe since the days of Rome, and a few years before both Genoa and Florence followed suit. Some gold also reached Europe in ready-minted form from Constantinople or Egypt, but much of the gold used in the Egyptian currency would have been of African origin, so that once again far-away Wangara came into contact with Europe.

The wealth that came out of the African interior was well known to Europeans, but any possibility of getting closer to the source of the gold was prevented by Moslem control of the North Africa coastline and the caravan routes across the desert. European merchants were sometimes allowed to go as far as Marrakesh or Tlemcen, but no farther. The few recorded cases of Europeans travelling deeper into Africa seem by their very rarity to be exceptional. Raymond Lull, for example, recorded in his

Blanquerna in 1283 that sometime before the messenger of a cardinal had joined a caravan of six thousand camels, and crossed the Sahara; in the middle of the fifteenth century a Genoese merchant, Antonio Malfante, made an attempt to do the same, in a search for the source of the gold; and in 1470 another merchant, Benedetto Dei, who was apparently connected with the Portinari company of Florence, was trading at Timbuktu on the river Niger.

There is only one known, and very dramatic, occasion on which trans-Saharan Africa came directly to the notice of European observers. This was during the pilgrimage to Mecca in 1324 of the Moslem ruler of the empire of Mali, Mansa Musa, whose exotic splendour and the large amounts of gold he lavished as he went created a sensation in Egypt. It is not known exactly how his journey was reported to Christian Europe, but there were enough resident European merchants in the North African cities he passed through for some account to be passed on, with the result that as early as 1339 Mansa Musa was shown in the world map drawn by Angelino Dulcert on the island of Majorca. In about 1375 he was recorded in a particularly elaborate world map, the Catalan atlas, also made in Majorca, which is still preserved in the Bibliothèque Nationale in Paris. In the atlas Mansa Musa is depicted seated in majesty in the midst of Africa, wearing a crown, with a sceptre in one hand, and a gold nugget in the other.

If the assessment of the extent of European contacts with the North African interior is difficult, the problem pales into insignificance when the eastern part of the continent is examined. Egypt was of course a familiar destination, at least so far as the cities of Alexandria and Cairo were concerned. Even though Egypt was less visited by western merchants in the late thirteenth and early fourteenth centuries, partly because of the papal embargo on trade after 1291 but more particularly because the trade routes across Asia were still under Mongol control, and so open to westerners, it still had many European associations. There was, for example, a commercial treaty between Genoa and Egypt in 1290, and numerous Aragonese commercial and diplomatic contacts between 1300 and 1330. In 1322 there were warehouses in Alexandria belonging to merchants from Genoa,

Venice, Marseilles, and Catalonia, while two years later the Irish Franciscan pilgrim Symeon Semeonis stayed in Cairo in a house belonging to a merchant from Marseilles, and noted the tolerated existence of a number of Christian churches in the city. From the mid-1340s European merchants turned to Egypt once again in large numbers, and from then onwards, despite the usual ups and downs of international relations, Egypt retained its place in the commerce of western Europe.

The real difficulty arises in trying to decide whether there is any firm evidence of European knowledge of, or direct contacts with, parts of east Africa beyond Egypt. The narrative of Marco Polo's travels, for example, contains references to islands which can be identified as Zanzibar and possibly Madagascar, although Mogadishu in Somaliland on the African mainland seems more likely. There is no suggestion that Marco Polo had actually been to either of these places, about which he could easily have heard while he was in Iran. He also described a Christian kingdom in East Africa which again he had not visited, but which is clearly identifiable from the context as Ethiopia.

It has often been suggested that the Christian king described in the letter of Prester John which first appeared in Europe in the mid-twelfth century is to be identified with the ruler of Ethiopia, and that a European awareness of this part of the African continent can therefore be traced back at least this far. It has also recently been argued that the letter to Prester John which was entrusted by Pope Alexander III to his physician Philip in 1177 was not in fact a direct reply to the Prester John letter, but was the result of a meeting at some previous time between Philip and men from Ethiopia somewhere in the east, or perhaps even a visit by him to Ethiopia itself. Whatever the truth of this theory, it was certainly possible in the twelfth and thirteenth centuries for Latin Christians to meet their Ethiopian counterparts in Jerusalem, where the Ethiopian Church had long maintained a community. Jacques de Vitry, the bishop of Acre from 1216 to 1228, knew of the existence of Christians in both Ethiopia and Nubia, and in 1237 the prior of the Dominican house in Jerusalem was sufficiently aware of the history of the Ethiopian Church to protest against the consecration by the Jacobite patriarch of Antioch of a new metropolitan for Ethiopia on the grounds that this function belonged to the patriarch of Alexandria in Egypt.

Ethiopia was mentioned among other possible destinations for western missionaries in papal bulls of 1245 and 1253, and in 1267 Clement IV ordered that the Dominicans should send friars to Ethiopia, Nubia, and India, and that these should be accompanied by a member of their order, a certain Vazinpace, who had already been to these regions. When John of Monte Corvino set out in 1289 on the journey which took him to China he carried letters of recommendation to the emperor and to the metropolitan of Ethiopia, and in the letter he wrote from Peking in 1306 he said that he had received an invitation to go to Ethiopia. In about 1315–16 two Dominicans, Raymond Etienne and William Adam (the future archbishop of Sultaniyeh in Iran), travelled in parts of the Indian Ocean, visited the island of Socotra, and had the opportunity to visit Ethiopia as well; and in 1323 the French Dominican Jordan of Séverac wrote from India of his own wish to visit Ethiopia.

This is an apparently impressive list of references to Ethiopia, however, on closer examination many such references either cannot be confirmed or turn out to be highly dubious or altogether mistaken. If William Adam, for example, had actually been to Ethiopia, there is no resulting papal correspondence to demonstrate the fact. Another story commonly met with, and relating to the same period as Adam's travels, is to the effect that eight Dominicans preached in Nubia and Ethiopia at some point during the pontificate of John XXII (1316–34); but this appears to rest on a confusion of evidence, and is not recorded before the early sixteenth century. Similarly, the alleged appointment of another Dominican, Bartholomew of Tivoli, as bishop of Dongola in Nubia in about 1330, and his subsequent journey to Ethiopia are both spurious, and may in some way be based on the career of Bartholomew of Podio, bishop of Maragha in Iran.

It is just possible that European merchants may have penetrated to Nubia or Ethiopia in the fourteenth century. The best-known evidence for this appears in the *Book of Knowledge of All the World*, written by an anonymous Spanish Franciscan in the late 1340s, and in the *Songe du Vieil Pèlerin*, by the French crusading propagandist and chancellor of Cyprus Philippe de Mézières, which was composed in 1388–9. The Franciscan claims to have visited Dongola, and to have met Genoese merchants there, while de Mézières refers to information on the same region allegedly gained from a traveller named Bragadin. For reasons connected with the literary form of their works, however, neither writer can be taken seriously as an authority on travel, and their statements are best treated with great caution.

One significant pointer to the nature of European awareness of Ethiopia lies in the fact that until the fourteenth century European travellers invariably sought the Christian king of the Prester John legend in some part of the Asian continent rather than in Africa. Prester John was still given an Asian context in the middle of that century by the author of the travels ascribed to Sir John Mandeville, but this was a literary work based on the experiences of earlier genuine travellers, and on a variety of fictions and fabulous tales of great antiquity. The last actual European traveller to locate Prester John in Asia was Odoric of Pordenone in the 1320s, whose travel narrative was to be one of the sources used by the compiler of Mandeville.

The identification of Ethiopia as the centre of Prester John's power seems to have resulted in part from the repeated failures to find either him or his descendants in Asia, but more positively from the stay in Genoa in about 1309 of an Ethiopian embassy which had just visited Rome and Avignon. The envoys were questioned closely by the Genoese scholar Giovanni da Carignano, who then incorporated their information either into a treatise on Ethiopia or into a map with captions, now lost. The earliest surviving map to depict Prester John as an African ruler was made on Majorca in 1339 by Angelino Dulcert, more properly called Angellino Dalorto, who probably came from Genoa, and might have had access to the work of Carignano.

A number of other fourteenth-century maps also show some knowledge of both Nubia and Ethiopia, but firsthand information on this part of Africa is still hard to find. A Florentine named Antonio Bartoli may have visited Ethiopia late in the century, and an embassy connected in some way with the duke of Berry in France may have been there before 1432, but there is no reliable confirmation of either of these episodes. Ethiopia did not become of any real interest to Europe until the middle of the fifteenth century. Delegates from the Ethiopian Church had attended the Council of Florence in 1441, and are thought to have been one of the sources of information for the map known as *Egyptus Novelo* which was produced in Florence for King Alfonso of Aragon in the early 1450s. The king of Aragon had already in 1428 received an embassy from the ruler of Ethiopia proposing an alliance against Islam; in 1450 Alfonso revived the idea, and also interviewed the Italian traveller Pietro Rombulo, who had lived in Ethiopia between 1407 and 1444, and who later gave a lengthy report of his experiences to the Dominican Pietro Ranzano, who embodied it in a vast and rambling compilation, the *Annales*. The world map by Fra Mauro of Venice which was completed in 1460 has further information about Ethiopia, but its sources are not known. Despite possible attempts by European merchants and missionaries to visit Ethiopia in the closing decades of the fifteenth century, it was still a country shrouded in mystery when the Portuguese sent their envoy Pero da Covilhã in 1487 to gather information about the Indian Ocean and its environs, before embarking on the final stages of their exploration of the sea route to India.

There were few opportunities before the thirteenth century for Europeans to acquire firsthand knowledge of the west coast of Africa, and of the adjacent waters of the Atlantic. From time to time ships from northern Europe, such as those of the Vikings, and a number of naval expeditions associated with the first and second crusades, did sail south, but so far as is known all of these went no further than the straits of Gibraltar, through which they passed eastwards into the Mediterranean. Because of the continued control of the straits by Moslem powers, and also because of the great difficulty in sailing westwards against a strong adverse current and the prevailing winds from the Atlantic, very few Mediterranean-based vessels went in the opposite direction. The political barrier to passage through the straits of Gibraltar was briefly lifted after the capture of the port of Almeria by Castile in 1147; it closed again with the growth of the Almohad empire later in the century, and did not finally disappear until territory on the Spanish side of the straits and the major Atlantic ports of the peninsula returned to Christian control in the years after the great victory at Las Navas de Tolosa in 1212.

Although the reconquest was chiefly the work of the kingdoms of Castile and Aragon, a contribution of considerable and lasting importance was made by Italians. Genoese and Pisan ships had taken part in the capture of Almeria; Genoese merchants were established in Castile from the middle of the twelfth century; Genoese shipwrights helped to build the Castilian fleet at Seville in the 1250s; and in 1264 Ugo Venta was appointed as the first of several Genoese admirals of Castile. There was a similar pattern of Italian influence in Portugal where the first admiral of the Portuguese royal fleet, appointed in 1317, was another Genoese, Manuel Pessagno, who was to be succeeded in the office by five generations of his family.

Manuel Pessagno's career in Portuguese service was of particular importance in the exploration of the Atlantic in the following decades, but it has a wider significance too, since he was the brother of Antonio Pessagno who spent a long period in England as a merchant and banker to the crown during the reign of Edward II, and on occasions supplied shipping as well. Manuel and Antonio, together with a third brother, Leonardo, represent very neatly the whole range of commercial, financial, and nautical skills which were possessed by Italians in the early fourteenth century, and which could be made available to others. In the fifteenth century other Italians such as Cadamosto, Cabot, and of course Columbus, were to play very similar roles.

The beginnings of ocean navigation by Mediterranean-based ships can be traced back to the mid-twelfth century, when a number of Genoese vessels probably ventured through the straits of Gibraltar to ports on the Atlantic coast of Morocco. In 1235 the Genoese, in a significant anticipation of the Portuguese conquest in 1415, captured and ransomed for a huge sum one of the keys to control of the straits, the Moroccan city of Ceuta; in 1260 some of their ships took part in the Castilian attack on the Moroccan Atlantic port of Salé; in the 1270s Genoese trading galleys began what soon became regular sailings from the Mediterranean to the ports of the Low Countries and southern

England; and in 1291 the Genoese brothers Ugolino and Vadino Vivaldi sailed through the straits of Gibraltar in two galleys, with the declared intention of opening a sea route to India.

Although the Vivaldi never returned to tell of their experiences, the reality of their voyage is well attested by notarial instruments drawn up before they departed, and by a passage in a treatise written in 1311 by the Paduan scholar Petrus de Abano. It has been suggested that Dante was thinking of the Vivaldi, then a recent memory, when he mentioned the voyages of Ulysses (*Inferno*, xxvi) and there is also an apparent reference to the brothers in the *Book of Knowledge of All the World*. That the Vivaldi sailed off somewhere in 1291 therefore seems certain: on the other hand, just what their intentions really were and how far they went towards achieving them raise other problems, to which many different answers have been given.

It has even been suggested that in voyaging *ad partes Indiae per mare oceanum* the Vivaldi were attempting to sail westwards across the Atlantic with the same object as Columbus two centuries later. This particular conclusion has not been widely accepted, but an intended sea journey to India, involving a circumnavigation of Africa and a crossing of the Indian Ocean, again a full two centuries before it was actually achieved, seems at first sight only slightly less implausible. There are many possible objections to this interpretation: the enormous distance to be covered through unknown waters; the unsuitability of thirteenth-century ships for such a voyage, which was undertaken even in the fifteenth century with only a very bare margin of safety; and the vagueness in contemporary geographical usage of the word 'India', robbing it of any precision as the declared destination of the Vivaldi.

However, it is too easy to consider the problem simply in the light of later geographical knowledge. In the thirteenth and fourteenth centuries no one in Europe was aware of the great length of the African coastline; equally there was no theoretical opinion, before the rediscovery of Ptolemy's *Geography* in the early fifteenth century, to suggest that Africa could not be circumnavigated. There were indeed a number of writers at about the time of the Vivaldi voyage who may have thought that such a voyage was possible: Raymond Lull, for example, seems to have taken it into account in drawing up his scheme for a great new crusade against the Moslem world; Petrus de Abano and William Adam may have been of the same opinion. If the Vivaldi really did plan to circumnavigate Africa as part of a journey to India, their underestimate of the distance was no more grievous a mistake than the set of erroneous geographical conceptions which set Columbus off on his first voyage in 1492, with the difference that Columbus was lucky enough to discover something, and returned home to tell the tale.

There are, however, a number of other considerations which give at least circumstantial support to the argument that the Vivaldi really were attempting to open a sea route to India in 1291. There is little doubt that they began their journey by attempting to sail southwards along the western coast of Africa, since they are known to have passed Cape Nun, after which they disappeared from sight and from record. It is probably also significant that Genoese international trade was very active in the late thirteenth century, and that a number of Genoese commercial families, including the Vivaldi, were involved in direct trading relations with India via the land routes through Iran, and sometimes via the Indian Ocean itself. In 1315, for example, Benedetto Vivaldi left Genoa on a trading venture to India, where he died before 1322. This journey may also have some connection with the garbled accounts of a certain Sorleone Vivaldi, allegedly the son of Ugolino, who went on a quest for his father along the eastern coast of Africa, evidently in the hope that he might have succeeded in circumnavigating the continent.

It was probably no accident that the Vivaldi chose to attempt their voyage in 1291, since this was the year when the papacy first placed an embargo on Christian trade with Egypt in retaliation for the Moslem capture of Acre. European merchants could readily obtain their supplies of eastern spices from the Mongol dominions in Iran, and were already trading less with Egypt than in the past, but there may none the less have been an incentive for merchants such as the Vivaldi to try to open a direct sea route to India which would effectively bypass Egypt altogether. If this was their motive, the behaviour of the Vivaldi was comparable to that of the Genoese sailors who in the same year were recruited by the Il-khan of Iran to interrupt Egyptian trade in the Indian Ocean by means of a naval blockade; and in the early fourteenth century, as noted earlier, a number of European crusading propagandists chose the same weapon. While there is no means of proving exactly what the Vivaldi hoped to achieve, there are good circumstantial and general grounds for arguing that a sea journey to India really was their intention, so that there is a remarkably close parallel between their voyage and those of Diaz and da Gama in 1487 and 1498.

The voyage of 1291 was not an isolated event, but the beginning of a series of Atlantic expeditions during the fourteenth century. The best-documented of these is the rediscovery of the Canary Islands, which had been known in classical antiquity as the Fortunate Islands, and which had been visited by Moslem sailors as recently as the twelfth century, if the story of the eight adventurers of Lisbon is to be believed. It has been suggested that the Vivaldi themselves may have visited one of the islands of the Canary group, but there is no firm evidence to support this, and the credit for their rediscovery is generally given to Lancelotto Malocello of Genoa. Dates as early as 1270 and 1312 have been suggested for this event, but the researches of Professor Verlinden have shown that it took place in or shortly before 1336 when Malocello was in Portuguese service, and that his voyage was probably one of a number organized by Portugal's Genoese admiral Manuel Pessagno. The island of Lanzarote in the Canaries, which was named after Malocello, was first recorded on a map by Angelino Dulcert in 1339.

It has been argued that other expeditions from Portugal, also under the influence and command of Genoese, discovered two more groups of Atlantic islands, Madeira and the Azores, possibly during a voyage in 1341 or later in the same decade. The evidence for these discoveries is mainly derived from material in the *Book of Knowledge of all the World*, which Verlinden has dated to the late 1340s, and from the Laurentian portolan, a world map which is generally believed to date from 1351. Both discoveries were certainly possible. Madeira in particular was not far to the north of Canaries, although slightly farther out to sea, and was a very likely discovery once the Canaries became known. The Azores were not so accessible, since they were due west of Lisbon and about 1,000 miles out in the Atlantic. However, it is likely that by the 1340s the galleys which had been used by the Vivaldi, and probably also in early fourteenth-century Portuguese voyages, had given way to sailing vessels. These would have been more suitable for Atlantic sailing, and it is conceivable that in the course of a return journey from the Canaries one of these, under the impetus of the prevailing winds and currents, made an unintended sweep far out into the ocean which led to the accidental discovery of the Azores. Such a voyage would have been an anticipation of the sea route known as the *volta da Guiné*, which was regularly followed from the end of the fifteenth century by ships returning to Europe from India. These are plausible but unproven arguments. The *Book of Knowledge* and the Laurentian portolan are both controversial in themselves, while the problem is further complicated by arguments over the authenticity of documents which were preserved in Portugal by nineteenth-century descendants of the Pessagno family.

Whatever the real nature of the Portuguese achievements in the fourteenth century, interest in the Atlantic waters adjoining the west coast of Africa was certainly not confined to Portugal and its Genoese agents. A Catalan voyage to the Canaries took place in 1342, and in 1344 a Castilian attempt to obtain a grant of possession of the islands from the papacy provoked a strong Portuguese protest. However, about sixty years later in 1402 the settlement of the islands on behalf of Castile was begun by two French adventurers, Gadifer de la Salle and Jean de Bethencourt.

It is far more difficult to assess the extent of European voyaging along the west coast of Africa itself. It is known, for example, that in 1346 a Catalan sailor, Jaime Ferrer, set out from Majorca in search of the *Riu del or* ('River of Gold'). He did not return, but his voyage was remembered on Majorca, and was recorded there in about 1375 on the Catalan atlas.

The *Riu del or* evidently had something to do with the source of the West African gold whose existence was already widely known in the Iberian peninsula, but whether it was a real destination or one which was only rumoured to exist is quite another question.

The answer to it is in turn bound up with the problem of whether or not Europeans had any direct knowledge of that part of West Africa which is referred to as *Gunaia* or *Ganuya* in various four-teenth-century maps and treatises, and which was known as Guinea to the Portuguese who visited it in the fifteenth century.

The alleged discovery of the Gulf of Guinea by sailors from the French port of Dieppe in 1364 is unknown before the seventeenth century, and seems to be one of the many claims and counter-claims which were then being made by various European nations in attempts to establish priority of discovery. A more plausible-seeming case can be based on the *Book of Knowledge of the World*, whose author claims to have sailed down the coast in an Arab vessel, and to have visited both the River of Gold and the kingdom of Guinea, on both of which he supplies circumstantial but rather vague details which makes it seem as if he had actually been there. However, as will be argued in Chapter 10, there are good reasons for believing that the *Book of Knowledge* was essentially a literary compilation, and not the record of genuine travel by its author, either in Africa or elsewhere in the world. Much of his information on Africa could have been derived from Moslem sources, although none has been specifically identified: it is worth remembering that the Moslems of North Africa had extensive trading connections with West Africa via the routes across the Sahara (but not necessarily by any coastal routes, as claimed by the Spanish Franciscan), and that in the 1350s, within a few years of the composition of the *Book of Knowledge*, one of the greatest of all Arab travellers, Ibn Battuta of Tangier, was to cross the Sahara to Mali, and later wrote a detailed account of his experiences there. It is also important to emphasise that geo-graphical expressions such as 'Guinea', 'Sudan', 'Ethiopia', and also 'India' which have a precise meaning in the present century were very imprecise in medieval usage, so that evidence in which they are employed has to be used with care.

Equal care has to be applied to another source of evidence on medieval European knowledge of the coastlines of Africa, the famous world map which is usually dated to about 1351, and which is known as the Laurentian Portolan because of its preser-vation in the Medici library in Florence. Apart from including a very accurate outline of the coasts of the Mediterranean and Black Seas, and a recognizable picture of the Atlantic shores of France, Spain, and Morocco, the map also depicts various groups of Atlantic islands and, more important, it appears to show a rough approximation of the true shape of the African continent. The eastward inclination of the coastline after passing the bulge of West Africa is carried much too far to the east, and the southwards extension of the continent is therefore badly out of proportion, but otherwise the shape is recognizable as that of Africa. No adequate explanation of this phenomenon has been provided, and none is offered here. There is no reason to believe that anyone had ever circumnavigated Africa, and hence knew its true shape, and the best answer is either that the map was modified in the fifteenth century as more became known about Africa, or that the outline is the result of a fortunate accident of draughtsmanship, perhaps assisted by the assumption that Africa could, in theory at least, be circumnavigated.

European knowledge of Africa in the medieval period was very incomplete, and therefore presents many problems of interpretation for the modern scholar. There was a great deal of commercial contact with the coastal regions of North Africa, an important part of which was the trade in gold which stimulated the European economy, and, helped to stimulate fourteenth- and fifteenth-century Europeans to make an active search for the West African sources of the bullion. European trade with Egypt suffered fluctuations, particularly in the late thirteenth and early fourteenth centuries, but then recovered. In the fifteenth century the port of Alexandria was one of the major sources of eastern spices for the European market, the Venetian trade with Egypt reaching a peak in the 1490s on the very eve of Vasco da Gama's first voyage to India. Whatever the motivation of that voyage may have been, it was certainly not brought about by any overall shortage of spices for sale in Europe, or by the supposed pressures caused by the Turkish conquest of Constantinople in 1453. By the early fifteenth century sporadic contacts with, and sparse knowledge of, the Christian communities in East Africa were turning into a definite awareness that here was the location of a ruler who could be associated with Prester John, who might be an ally in future military operations against the world of Islam. The vagueness of definition of 'Ethiopia' also led to the belief that a Christian realm might extend right across Africa from east to west, and in the rear of the Moslem lands of North Africa and the Sahara.

The search for Christians and gold helps to explain the persistent European interest in the west coast of Africa. Many ostensible destinations, such as the River of Gold or Guinea were places probably known only through hearsay, and did not necessarily correspond with the places which bear these names today. Their appearance on maps and in geographical treatises should be considered in association with other locations like the wholly fictitious Atlantic islands of St Brendan, or of Brasil, the Island of the Blest, which also played their part in stimulating exploration. On the other hand, there were some perfectly genuine voyages down the coast of West Africa, notably those of the Vivaldi and Jaime Ferrer. It is possible that one or other of these sailed past the famous Cape Bojador, whose passage in 1434 by the ships of Henry the Navigator is taken as both a literal and a figurative turning-point in the history of fifteenth-century discovery. But here again there is a problem of definition, since it is not always clear whether medieval references to Cape Bojador are to the cape now known by that name, or instead to Cape Juby, about 150 kilometres to the north-east. However, if anyone did pass Cape Bojador in the fourteenth century, he did not return to tell of it: in this sense it remained a real point of no return until the fifteenth century.

The most enduring discoveries in the vicinity of the west coast of Africa were the Atlantic islands. The Canaries were certainly discovered, and their exploration begun, by the middle of the fourteenth century; the discovery of Madeira and of the Azores is less certain but probable. These were discoveries of a very practical kind, since they created opportunities for colonization and commercial exploitation by the kingdoms of the Iberian peninsula, especially Portugal, which needed land for the production of grain for their own use, and of sugar for sale on the European market. But the islands were also an essential link in the chain of communications which led at the end of the fifteenth century to the opening of a feasible sea route to India, and of another to the continent of America, as yet unsuspected. In this sense the major outcome of medieval European contacts with Africa and its ocean margins was a growing interest in the waters of the Atlantic, which was to have totally unforeseen consequences both for Europe and for the world at large.

9

Medieval Europe and North America

One of the consequences of medieval European attempts to learn more about Africa was the discovery, in the waters of the Atlantic adjoining the continent, of one or more groups of islands which were to be of great importance to future exploration. In the North Atlantic a superficially similar pattern of events unfolded. Here, too, islands were discovered, and beyond them, far to the west of Europe, a new land of great promise which was given the name of Vinland, and almost certainly formed part of the North American continent, was found and briefly settled. However, there were major differences. Whereas Africa, despite its many remaining mysteries, had been regarded since classical antiquity as one of the three continents of the inhabited world, Vinland was found as a wholly unexpected by-product of a process of North Atlantic exploration which had already been in progress for several centuries, and for all its discoverers knew it was just another island to add to a long catalogue. There is no evidence that the existence of Vinland was ever widely known outside Scandinavia and its Atlantic outposts in Iceland and Greenland, and the knowledge consequently had little or no influence on the new phase of Atlantic exploration which began during the fifteenth century. Even then it was only slowly realized that the lands across the Atlantic belonged to a large and hitherto unknown continent. North America did not, therefore, form a central part of the medieval expansion of Europe, and must instead be treated as one aspect of European exploration of the North Atlantic.

While the details of Irish voyaging in the waters around Ireland and Britain in the sixth and seventh centuries are hard to disentangle from the literary form of the *imrama* and the saints' lives in which they are recorded, there is no doubt about the general nature of their achievement. Whether or not, for example, the sixth-century Irish monk Cormac, from St Columba's community on Iona, should be credited with visiting the Orkneys and Shetlands, and more particularly with the discovery of the Faeroes, it is clear that Irish hermits had settled on the latter islands by AD 700 at the latest. The evidence provided by the Irish scholar Dicuil shows that Irish monks had also reached the island of Thule, or Iceland as it was later to be known, by the closing years of the eighth century.

The date at which Irish monks first reached Iceland is unknown, but has been suggested that the arrival of the Vikings in the Faeroes in the early years of the ninth century persuaded the Irish who were already there to go in search of new islands in the Atlantic, or to settle in a place such as Iceland of which they had some previous knowledge. Even without such an advantage the distances between one island group and another were short, so that there was always a possibility that the discovery of one would at some stage be followed by that of others. From the Shetlands to Greenland there was no sea passage much longer than 250 miles, and to reach the outlying islands of the American continent involved only another short journey across the Davis Strait, although to arrive at any destination of value would take much longer. These possibilities applied equally to the Irish monks and the Viking raiders, but there was never any certainty that any particular group of seafarers would make all the possible connections.

The islands around the coasts of Britain and Ireland were the key to the discoveries in the North Atlantic of both the Irish and the Vikings. Although many of the settlers of the Faeroes and Iceland came from Norway, and the Norwegian Ohthere was to sail as far north as the White Sea at the end of the ninth century, Norway itself was not the most likely starting-point for the initial discovery of islands far out in the Atlantic. Iceland lay 600 miles to the west of Norway, and to reach Greenland by the most direct route, passing to the south of Iceland, required a journey of about 1,000 miles from the Faeroes through some of the most dangerous seas in the world. Such voyages were possible once the initial discoveries had been made and sailing directions were known, but they were not feasible earlier.

Viking settlement of the Faeroes seems to have begun early in the ninth century, and less than two generations later was followed by that of Iceland. Later Icelandic sources identified three separate voyages as contributing to the Viking discovery of Iceland: those of Naddod who, significantly, seems earlier to have been in the Faeroes; of a Swede named Gardar Svavarsson; and of a Norwegian named Floki who sailed via the Shetlands and the Faeroes. The exact order of these voyages is not important, but they evidently took place between about 860 and 870, and were followed by extensive settlement which was to fill up all the usable land in Iceland by about AD 930, and which represents the first large-scale movement of population from any part of western Europe into entirely new territory.

The evidence of the twelfth-century *Landnámabók* shows that most of the settlers of Iceland came direct from Norway, but some also came from the islands around the coast of Scotland and from Ireland, so that there was a small Celtic element in the colony resulting from previous intermarriage, and from the importation of Irish slaves. What happened to the handful of Irish monks who were already in Iceland when the Vikings came, and whose own discovery of Iceland had probably been known to the Vikings even before the 860s, is unknown. The suggestion that they might have emulated the alleged exploits of St Brendan, and sailed off to America as the creators of a mysterious *Hvítramannaland* or 'White Man's Land', where they were ready to greet later comers, is based only on some very ambiguous references in one of the versions of Eric the Red's saga. At any rate the Irish monks appear to have left few traces behind them in Iceland.

When the first recorded sighting of Greenland was made around AD 900 by a certain Gunnbjorn, who had apparently been blown off course while on his way from Norway to Iceland, the settlement of Iceland was still incomplete. Gunnbjorn's Skerries, as Greenland was at first known, were of little interest to anyone in Iceland until all the good land there was used up, and it was time to look further afield. The first attempt to settle Greenland appears to have been made in 978, and to have failed totally.

However, there was another reason for the search for new land, and this, in the early 980s, brought a certain Eric

Thorvaldsson, better known as Eric the Red, to Greenland. Whatever the truth of the argument that some of the early settlers of Iceland were refugees from the newly won authority of Harald Fairhair, king of Norway, after the latter's victory at Hafrsfjord in about 892, there were certainly others who fled the consequences of crimes. Eric and his father had originally left Norway 'because of some killings'; once in Iceland the pattern was repeated until in 982 Eric was exiled from Iceland for three years, and decided to spend the time in exploring the mysterious land found by Gunnbjorn. It soon became apparent that it was not a group of islands but a vast land mass with high mountains, and a great ice sheet in the interior.

Paradoxically Eric gave this forbidding land the name of Greenland. Yet, when compared with the barren landscape of Iceland, there were definite attractions for would-be settlers. Along the west coast there were many fjords at whose heads were good pasture land, and even small birch trees and willows. The summer climate was favourable for anyone living in these districts, while those who had lived in Iceland could learn to cope with the severity of the winter. Returning to Iceland at the end of his exile, Eric organized a party of colonists who set out for Greenland in twenty-five ships in the year 986. Only fourteen ships reached Greenland, the rest either being sunk by storms or turning back to Iceland, but the foundations were now laid for what became known as the Eastern Settlement on the southwestern coast of Greenland, with its focal point at Eric's own homestead of Brattahlid at the head of the fjord he had named after himself. By the turn of the century other groups of settlers had set up the Western Settlement about two hundred miles to the north-west, and most of the suitable land had been occupied.

The colonists of both Iceland and Greenland settled down to the routine of existence within a remarkably short time. Life was never easy, especially in Greenland where the climate was far more extreme, and depended heavily on the raising of cattle and sheep. In Greenland the hunting of seals and walrus was also very important, but it seems to have been possible to grow a certain amount of grain there (probably barley) in the more favourable climatic conditions which prevailed until the end of the thirteenth century. To the outer world Greenland became known chiefly as the source of walrus and narwhal ivory, as well as of falcons and the occasional polar bear skin.

Not all the inhabitants of Greenland were as reluctant to become Christians as Eric the Red. The gift of a polar bear to Sigurd the Jerusalemfarer, king of Norway, in 1125 was made as an inducement for the king to sanction the appointment of a bishop for Greenland. This duly took place in 1126, with the new bishop, Arnold, establishing his see at Gardar in the Eastern Settlement. Christianity had probably reached Greenland at a very early stage in the history of the colony, but there was none of the drama associated with the formal decision taken in 999 or 1000 that the Icelanders should embrace the new faith. Iceland was to have two dioceses, one at Skalholt from 1056 and the other at Holar from 1106. Both dioceses, and later that of Gardar, formed part of the ecclesiastical province of Hamburg, whose archbishop had been given authority over Iceland, Greenland, and all of Scandinavia by the papacy in 1047, a decision which indicates that the pope was well informed about the Viking settlements in the North Atlantic. In 1153 the three sees came under the newly founded archbishopric of Nidaros in Norway, which may have contributed in later years to their growing isolation, and to that of the colonies in which they lay.

In the mid-thirteenth century the Norwegian author of the *Speculum Regale* remarked that men went to Greenland for three reasons: 'competitive spirit (and thirst for fame), curiosity, and the lust for worldly goods.' If we add land hunger, as well as the pressures of politics, personal quarrels, and crimes, this is probably a reasonably fair explanation of the Viking settlements not only in Greenland but elsewhere as well. Yet none of this would have been feasible without the existence of ships of a kind peculiarly well suited to the demands of ocean voyaging, and at a time when, with the possible exception of the Irish *currach*, there was no other type of vessel in Europe capable of performing and, even more important, of repeating such voyages.

Modern ideas of Viking ships are inevitably coloured by the notion of the longship, of which the ninth-century Gokstad and Oseberg ships are splendid surviving examples. The Atlantic crossing made in 28 days in 1893 from Bergen to Newfoundland by a replica of the Gokstad ship showed how effective a design this was. But the Gokstad ship was a coastal vessel of shallow draught, whereas the type of vessel used for the crossings to Iceland and Greenland, and later to Vinland, was the *hafskip* or *knörr*, shorter, broader, and deeper than the *langskip*, and capable of faster speeds in high winds. The *hafskip* was intended for carrying cargo or people with their animals and other possessions over the open sea for long distances, and without it the creation and survival of the Iceland and Greenland colonies would never have been possible. The development of Viking ships is now thought to have occurred over a long period of time, with the final stages being reached in the late eighth and early ninth centuries, at about the same time that the Vikings were starting to raid Britain and Ireland, and beginning to settle in the western isles of Scotland and the Faeroes. These early voyages probably in themselves contributed to the refinement of existing ship designs.

Techniques of navigation were devised by the steady accumulation of experience rather than by the use of instruments, the compass, for example, being unknown in northern waters until the thirteenth century, and of limited value there because of the magnetic variation from true north. Little is known for certain about Viking methods of navigation, but they seem to have included observations of the sun and the Pole Star, as well as of the flights of birds and other indications of nearby land. These added up to a system of dead reckoning, apparently based on the principle of latitude sailing by which a sailor tried to steer his ship on approximately the correct line of latitude until he reached his destination; if he missed his target or guessed that he was in its vicinity, he could then make an appropriate adjustment either to the north or south. Thick cloud or bad weather could make observations difficult or drive a ship off course, as often happened, the Viking ship being liable to drift to windward. This tendency was a factor in many of the accidental sightings of unknown land that occurred in the Viking exploration of the North Atlantic. On the whole the Vikings were well served by these rough and ready methods of navigation: in many respects

the methods used by European sailors in the fourteenth and fifteenth centuries were not greatly different, despite their use of
the compass, and the growing availability of charts and other
instruments.

One of the most dramatic and contentious issues in the entire
history of medieval European expansion is the apparent Viking
discovery of a portion of the North American continent. Of the
two sagas which record this event and its aftermath, the *Greenlanders' Saga* is now thought to date from the latter part of the
twelfth century, and *Eirik's Saga* from the middle of the thirteenth. It is now generally accepted that the *Greenlander's Saga* is
the more reliable, and that *Eirik's Saga* was a version carefully
edited to give added importance to the role of Eric the Red and his
family.

According to the *Greenlander's Saga*, Bjarni Herjolfsson, an
Icelander who was following his father to Greenland shortly after
the first colonizing voyage of 986, lost his way in gales and fog,
and found himself off a hilly and forested coastline far to the
south-east of his intended course. Realizing that this could not be
Greenland he set sail to the north, and found another land, this
time low-lying and wooded, which he again rejected; after a few
more days' sailing Bjarni sighted a land of high mountains and
glaciers which he decided did not meet the description of Greenland which Eric the Red had given in Iceland. Bjarni then sailed
for four days before a south-westerly gale, and finally reached
Greenland, landing by luck at Herjolfsnes where his father had
just settled. Bjarni settled down there in his turn, and ended his
days as a peaceful farmer, totally unaware of the importance of
his discoveries.

At some point in the 990s Eric the Red's son Leif bought
Bjarni's ship in order to retrace the latter's voyage, and explore
the new lands to the west and south. There were no sailing directions, and it was a matter of chance whether Leif would make his
way to the same locations. According to the *Greenlanders' Saga*
his first landfall was the land of ice and rock which Bjarni had
seen last, which Leif now named as *Helluland* or 'Slab-land'; he
then came to the land of low ground and forest which was called
Markland or 'Forest-land'; finally he reached another land,

attractive and with a mild climate, where he decided to spend the winter. Here the Vikings found salmon in the rivers, grass for their cattle, and grapes and timber with which they loaded their ship. Leif named this land *Vinland* or 'Wineland' after its produce. The following spring they set sail for Greenland, and arrived there after an easy voyage.

Leif apparently never returned to his discoveries, but in the following years there were several more voyages from Greenland to Vinland. Leif's brother Thorvald led the first, spent the winter in the houses built by Leif, explored some of the surrounding country, and encountered the native people, whom the Vikings called *skraelings* or 'wretches', one of whom killed Thorvald with an arrow. Thorvald's brother Thorstein then attempted to sail to Vinland to recover his brother's body, but failed because of bad weather, and died of disease in Greenland after his return. Thorstein's widow Gudrid married an Icelander, Thorfinn Karlsefni, and together they set out to found a permanent colony in Vinland, again using Leif's houses. Like Thorvald before them they spent two winters in Vinland, where Gudrid gave birth to a son named Snorri. The hostility of the *skraelings* was, however, too much for them, and they returned to Greenland. Snorri and his parents later moved to Iceland where Snorri's descendants included a twelfth-century bishop of Holar, Brand Saemundarson (1163–1201), during whose time the *Greenlanders' Saga* is thought to have been written, possibly even by Brand himself. The saga also records one more voyage, by Eric the Red's daughter Freydis, who reached Vinland but later returned to Greenland after instigating the murder of her partners in the venture, and killing several of their womenfolk herself. With this voyage the attempts to settle in Vinland, so far as these are recorded in the sagas, came to an end. While the account given in *Eirik's Saga* differs in detail, and glorifies the role of Leif Ericsson and his family, making Leif for example the first discoverer of Vinland rather than Bjarni, the basic story is the same.

Written evidence for the Viking discovery of Vinland also occurs in the history of the archbishops of Hamburg written in about 1075 by Adam of Bremen, in which the author claimed to have obtained his information from the king of Denmark, and spoke in glowing terms of the wild grapes growing there, and also of self-sown wheat. Much argument has been devoted by modern scholars to the details of the accounts of Vinland, especially to the tales of grapes and wheat. There may be some element of truth in such stories, but it is not necessary to take them too literally. It was natural that men who were hoping to encourage others to settle in a new country, and were also trying to show the value of their achievement should praise its virtues to the skies, just as the attractions of Greenland had been stressed earlier. Vinland, as it appears in the sagas, is rather like the wondrous islands visited by St Brendan; none the less it was also a very real land, as the descriptions of the native inhabitants and of their hostility make clear. It was certainly no Garden of Eden.

However sceptical one may be about some of the details in the sagas, there is no serious doubt that they do represent accounts of genuine voyages to parts of the North American continent, and of a series of short-lived attempts at settlement there. The real problems lie in determining when these events took place, and where the different places named in the sagas were located. There are no dates in the sagas, but the starting-point for the events described, the settlement of Greenland, is generally agreed to be in the years 985–6; Leif Ericsson's voyage to Vinland can probably be dated to around the year 1000, and the remaining voyages to a short period of years thereafter. The precise dates do not matter greatly. What is clear is that the attempt to establish a colony in Vinland had ended within the early decades of the eleventh century, and so far as can now be judged it was never resumed. Vinland really was a case of 'a colony too far', without the resources to maintain itself against the known hostility of the native population (who are probably to be identified with the North American Indians known to much later generations of settlers rather than with any of the Eskimo peoples), and with a long and precarious line of communication with its mother country, Greenland, which was itself on the far limit of viability.

No exact locations can now be ascribed to the various lands named in the sagas, and they were probably never very precisely known at the outset. The most likely site for Helluland is the coast of Baffin Island across the Davis Strait from Greenland, although the northern shore of Labrador has also been suggested; Markland seems to fit with southern Labrador; but where to locate Vinland is another problem altogether. It was evidently to the south of Markland, but how far south it is impossible to say. Attempts have even been made to place it in Florida, but on the whole the vicinity of Newfoundland and New England seems more probable. Much depends on whether the name Vinland is to be identified with grapes and wine, as the sagas and Adam of Bremen appear to suggest, or whether, as some modern scholars have argued, the word *vin* refers instead to grassland.

It is unlikely that the argument over Vinland's location will ever be settled definitively, and perhaps, like the actual date of its discovery, an exact answer is not vital. There have, however, been many attempts to provide archaeological proof of the Viking presence. Some of these have turned out to be practical jokes; others such as the Kensington rune-stone to be fraudulent; and some to be the result of the misinterpretation of genuine evidence. A good example of the latter is the famous Newport Tower in Rhode Island, which was once acclaimed as Viking in origin but has now been identified as a windmill from the seventeenth-century colonial period.

The site at L'Anse aux Meadows (originally L'Anse au Méduse or 'Jellyfish Creek') in northern Newfoundland, which was discovered in 1960 by the Norwegian Helge Ingstad, and excavated between then and 1968, has provided archaeological evidence which must be taken much more seriously. The foundations of buildings resembling those in Greenland and a few artefacts of Norse type have been found, while Carbon 14 tests on samples of organic material have yielded dates consistent with an eleventh-century origin. It is now increasingly accepted that the L'Anse aux Meadows site was occupied by Vikings, and that the occupation was short, but there is nothing to prove that it was the actual place inhabited by Leif Ericsson and his successors, convenient as such a conjunction would be.

Apart from the existence of Viking relations with North America which is revealed in the Vinland sagas, and partially confirmed by the archaeological discoveries in Newfoundland, there is little further firm evidence. A reference in the Icelandic annals under the year 1121, about a century after the events just described, records that a Bishop Eric set out from Greenland in search of Vinland. However, there was no bishop in Greenland until 1126, and Bishop Eric is not otherwise known with certainty, so that this evidence is inconclusive. Later in the twelfth century the Icelandic monk Nikolus Saemundarson, who died in 1158, wrote a geographical treatise in which he referred to Helluland, Markland, and Vinland, but with so little supporting detail that he clearly had no real knowledge of these places. The thirteenth-century literary sources are not much more helpful. The work known as the *Speculum Regale*, for example, which has important information about Greenland, makes no mention at all of Vinland. Snorri Sturluson's *Heimskringla*, a history of the kings of Norway which was completed in about 1225, contains a considerable amount about the discovery and settlement of Vinland, inserted in its correct chronological place in the narrative. Much of this material seems to be related to the Vinland sagas which were then being committed to writing, and is not of independent value as evidence, but it is possible that there may also be traces of more recent knowledge of Vinland. The only reference to any part of North America which is clearly of contemporary origin occurs as late as 1347, when the Icelandic annals recorded the arrival in Iceland of a Greenland vessel which had been blown off course while returning from Markland. This suggests that Markland at least was the object of occasional visits from the Greenland colony, probably in search of timber of which Greenland was desperately short.

Although Vinland has only a very shadowy existence in the historical records which have come down to us from Iceland and Greenland, there is some evidence which suggests that the Vikings continued to explore the North Atlantic lands after the apparent failure of the Vinland venture. A rune-stone found in Greenland in 1824, for example, revealed that a party of Norsemen had reached approximately 73 degrees North at a date which is variously interpreted as 1135 or 1333; there is also evidence that in 1266 another group went as far north as 76 degrees. On the other hand, there is nothing to show that the Vikings ever managed to traverse the whole of the northernmost coast of Greenland, a point of some significance since the now-discredited Vinland Map purports to show the entire coastline of Greenland. Occasional finds of artefacts in the Canadian Arctic have suggested that Viking explorers may have visited the lands to the west of Greenland. Two sites on Ungava Bay in northern Quebec which appeared to be promising examples of Viking activity have now been eliminated, but recent discoveries at a site on Ellesmere Island at 79 degrees North, and only 800 miles from the North Pole, are still being assessed by archaeologists. In 1194 the Icelandic annals record that a crew from Iceland discovered land five days' sail to the north, to which they gave the name of *Svalbard* ('Cold Coast'). This has variously been identified with the island of Spitzbergen (to which the name Svalbard is applied today), with Jan Mayen Island, and with a portion of the uninhabited and uninviting north-east coast of Greenland (possibly in the vicinity of Scoresby Sound). Nearly a century later, in 1285, the brothers Adalbrand and Thorvald Helgeson made a discovery to the west of Iceland which was probably a part of the east coast of Greenland, which had never been much visited by the Viking colonists from the western side of the island.

It is impossible to draw any firm conclusions on the full extent of Viking exploration of the islands and mainland of the northern and western parts of the Atlantic from such scattered and often ambiguous evidence. However, any new ventures depended on the maintenance of their existing Atlantic colonies in Iceland and Greenland. Iceland survived the medieval period as a viable community, but the Greenland settlements disappeared altogether at some point during the fifteenth century. The failure of the Greenland colony is a much debated subject, but one reason was certainly its remoteness from Europe, and the difficulties in getting there. The fact that the available land in both the East and West Settlements was fully occupied by about 1030 removed any incentive for further settlers to come from Iceland or Norway. But the hazards of the journey were also great. From the very beginning shipwrecks were frequent, while the ships used by the Greenlanders were often small and ill-found because of the shortage of timber. A character in *St Olaf's Saga*, who was about to set out for Greenland, is reported to have remarked: 'Now it may

happen, and it is not unlikely, that we shall never reach Greenland, but be driven to Iceland or other countries'; in 1276 Pope
John XXI wrote to the archbishop of Nidaros in Norway that 'it
is hardly possible within a span of five years to make the journey [between Nidaros and Gardar in Greenland]'; and in 1279
Nicholas III told the same archbishop that 'the island on which
Gardar is situated is visited only infrequently on account of the
cruel ocean'.

While there was certainly some exaggeration in these remarks,
the history of the diocese of Gardar reveals very clearly the
tenuous communications between Greenland and the mainland
of Europe. When Bishop Helgi, for example, died in 1230, a new
bishop was not consecrated until 1234, and did not reach his
diocese until 1239. In 1343 a new bishop was even appointed in
Norway on the reasonable assumption that his predecessor, who
had gone to Greenland as long ago as 1315, must have died, only
to discover that the latter was very much alive. After the last
resident bishop of Gardar died in 1378 the diocese had a shadowy
existence until 1492 when Pope Alexander VI decided that perhaps the bishop-elect should actually go there, but did nothing
about it.

It is often argued that the assertion of the authority of the king
of Norway over Greenland in 1261 and over Iceland in 1262
caused the decline of both colonies by depriving them of control
over their political and economic affairs. However, such a simple
explanation of Greenland's decline as neglect by a distant royal
overlord will not really suffice. Sailings of ships between Greenland and Norway may have been few after 1261, but so had they
been before. Trade seems to have been relatively unimportant to
the Greenland economy which was largely self-sufficient, while
there was no Greenland product that the outside world could not
live without. The surrender of independence by Iceland and
Greenland appears less significant if it is remembered that the
power of the Norwegian monarchy to intervene in other areas of
Viking settlement, such as the Isle of Man and the Hebrides, was
coming to an end at almost exactly the same time.

There is, however, some fourteenth-century evidence of at
least a temporary interest in Greenland on the part of both

secular and ecclesiastical authorities in Norway. In 1325, for example, traders from Bergen and Trondheim formed a joint association to trade with Greenland, possibly at the instigation of the king; in 1327 the papal tax collectors for Norway reported that they had received the tithe of the diocese of Gardar which was paid in the form of walrus ivory, and later sold in Flanders; in 1341 the bishop of Bergen authorized Ivar Bardarson to visit and report on conditions in Greenland, which he did, recording among other things the activities of the king's official representative there; and in 1355 a certain Poul Knudsson was appointed by the king of Norway to go there with a crew to stave off some calamity.

The crisis which inspired this latter decision is not mentioned specifically, but was probably connected with the impending or actual destruction of the Western Settlement, the more northerly of the two. One reason for this event was the deterioration in climate which is now generally recognized to have taken place in the Arctic during the thirteenth century, and which probably had effects in Europe in such forms as the great famine of 1315–17, and the advance of the alpine glaciers. The cooling was no more than a few degrees, but it was enough to make a dramatic difference to life in Greenland. In the mid-thirteenth century the author of the *Speculum Regale* wrote of the great icebergs that were to be found at sea, and of the ice-floes lying to the north-east of Greenland which made it necessary for a ship sailing there to pass around the ice to the south-west and west. Ivar Bardarson's account of his sojourn in Greenland stressed that the direct course to Greenland due west from Iceland, which had been followed by the original settlers, was no longer possible because of the encroachment of the ice sheet. One other consequence of the change in climate was the movement south of the Eskimo population of Greenland, bringing them into more frequent contact and possibly into conflict with the Viking settlers. Whatever the precise reason, the Western Settlement probably succumbed at some stage between 1341 and 1364, the terminal dates of Bardarson's account.

Life continued in the Eastern Settlement, even though it was now cut off from the northern hunting grounds, and was also attacked by the Eskimos in 1379. In 1385 an Icelander named Bjorn visited Greenland, and found life there normal, and in 1409 two priests testified that they had been present at a properly conducted marriage ceremony in Greenland in September 1408. Again there is the appearance of normality, but it is significant that in both cases the outsiders were in Greenland only because they had been blown off course while sailing to Iceland. Clearly few people any longer went to Greenland from choice. With the possible exception of an expedition sent out by the king of Denmark in the early 1470s, which may have reached the east coast of Greenland, the side never occupied by the Vikings, the legal record of 1409 is the last positive evidence of any contact between Greenland and Scandinavia.

It is uncertain just when the Greenland colony finally came to an end. Finn Gad, the most recent historian of Greenland, has argued from the style of clothing excavated from graves at Herjolfsnes that a population of European descent survived in Greenland until well into the fifteenth century, perhaps as late as 1480. Other scholars would prefer an earlier date. Many suggestions have been made as to the fate of the settlers: death from disease and physical degeneration, or in conflict with the Eskimos; intermarriage with and absorption by the Eskimos; or even a mass migration to the Vinland discovered by their ancestors centuries before. The only certainty is that no one knows the answer.

Knowledge of the existence of Greenland had been general in medieval Europe, even if very few people actually bothered to go there. What is far more interesting however, and of greater significance for a study of the medieval expansion of Europe, is to find out whether the Viking discoveries in Vinland ever became known outside Scandinavia, and whether in turn such a knowledge had any bearing on the fifteenth-century voyages of discovery in the Atlantic.

For a year or two after the publication in 1965 of the Vinland Map, dated by its editors to the 1440s, the answer appeared to be positive. Then doubts set in and the Vinland map is now commonly considered to be a twentieth-century forgery, which it is accordingly unnecessary to discuss in any further detail. (But, see the Preface to this book.) It is significant, however, in the sense that it is merely the latest in a seemingly never-ending series of attempts to prove not only that Vinland was known in Europe before Columbus, but that Columbus was anticipated by so many others that it is a wonder he did not have to join a queue in mid-Atlantic. The various items of evidence may be classified as certain, just possible, highly improbable, and preposterous: since the enthusiastic supporters of particular theories will naturally argue that their arguments are sound while everyone else's are absurd, the following brief catalogue will certainly not satisfy everyone who may read it.

The one reliable piece of evidence is Adam of Bremen's account of Vinland written in the 1070s, which is generally accepted as authentic because of his close connection with the Danish court, and the authority then exercised over Scandinavia by the archbishops of Hamburg-Bremen, even if some of the details may be disputed. Adam's description is, however, too early to have had any likely influence on the events of the fifteenth century. Just possible, but not convincingly so, is the suggestion by some scholars that the appearance of 'Finland' among the dominions of the king of Norway listed by the Anglo-Norman historian Orderic Vitalis in his *Historia Ecclesiastica*, written before 1143, is a mistake for 'Vinland'.

The highly improbable category contains just one item, the anonymous mid-thirteenth-century geographical treatise contained in Trinity College Dublin MS 347, which was recently discovered and edited by Professor Marvin Colker, with the very cautious suggestion that it might contain a reference to Vinland. After his description of Norway the author wrote that: 'Norway has two very distant islands to the northwest. Because of the cold of these islands, the bones of fish and animals are greased with fish fat and then used for fuel. The inhabitants have cattle and many sheep.' These two islands are almost certainly Iceland and Greenland. But the author then added the following intriguing information:

Furthermore there is an island discovered in our time at the northern part of Norway. To this island persons go in a doublesided ship and return from there within a five-year period. The island is spacious, very abundant in people, but they are pagans. Excellent gold is found in great abundance on the shores of rivers and of the sea. In the summer the people of the island do not know the darkness of night, and in the winter they are completely deprived of light. But about Christmas time, as I have learned from a man who stayed two years on the island and is now still living in Denmark, the people receive light from Aurora Borealis.

The description of the climate and the island's northern location do not accord with anything known about Vinland, which could not in any case, as Professor Colker points out, be referred to as 'discovered in our own time'. The island might perhaps be connected with the mysterious *Svalbard*, or be somewhere in the vicinity of the White Sea in northern Russia which the Norwegian sailor Ohthere had begun to explore as long ago as the ninth century. Although Vinland has no part in the treatise, it is none the less worth further examination since its author seems to have been writing in the immediate aftermath of the Mongol attacks on eastern Europe, and was also interested in the activities of Christian missionaries in Russia and the Baltic lands.

The preposterous tales of pre-Columbian contacts with North America are infinitely varied, and are treated almost as articles of faith by their upholders. At either end of the chronological spectrum they include the argument that the Irish monk St Brendan sailed across the Atlantic 500 years before the Vikings, and the belief that in the fifteenth century there was extensive Portuguese voyaging and discovery in the Atlantic, the results of which were kept secret for reasons of state policy. In fairness to the eloquent supporters of St Brendan, the remote possibility of an Irish crossing of the Atlantic should be admitted, but in the absence of unambiguous archaeological evidence from the North American continent it is impossible to go any further than this. On the other hand, while the claims about fifteenth-century Portuguese voyages contain much that is unprovable, there is none the less a real problem which will be discussed in a later chapter.

The remaining stories include the claim that a Welsh prince named Madoc discovered and colonized America soon after 1170; that the Poul Knudsson expedition which was ordered to go to Greenland in 1355 went on from there to Vinland, and explored as far westwards as the modern Minnesota; that in the

1360s an English Franciscan, Nicholas of Lynn, visited Greenland and the Canadian Arctic and later recorded his experiences in a geographical treatise, the *Inventio Fortunata*, which also contained details of Vinland; and finally that in the 1390s two Venetians, Antonio and Nicolo Zeno, made voyages to Greenland and to the North American mainland. All of these are generally regarded as fabrications dating from the period after 1492, and therefore having nothing directly to do with the geographical knowledge possessed by medieval Europe.

The Madoc legend seems to have derived from sixteenth-century attempts to demonstrate the Welsh contribution to the glories of the Tudor dynasty, and English priority over other rivals for territory in North America. The legend was further embellished in the eighteenth century by the Welsh antiquarian and literary forger Edward Williams, alias Iolo Morgannwg, before being systematically demolished by Thomas Stephens in the nineteenth century, and more recently in the witty and learned studies of Professor G. A. Williams.

The story of the alleged Poul Knudsson expedition to America (which in reality may not even have gone to Greenland) originated with the supposed discovery at Kensington in Minnesota in 1898 of a rune-stone recording the presence there in 1362 of a party of Swedes and Norwegians. Scholarly opinion is virtually unanimous that the Kensington rune-stone, which continues to have its ardent supporters, is a forgery made only shortly before its 'discovery'. It is significant that in 1892 there had been celebrations of the fourth centenary of the discovery of America by Christopher Columbus; that in 1893 the pride of Scandinavian Americans had been salved by the sailing of a replica of the Gokstad Viking ship across the Atlantic, and through the Great Lakes to Chicago, where it was put on display at the World's Fair; and that the state of Minnesota contained many recent immigrants from Scandinavia.

The *Inventio Fortunata* of Nicholas of Lynn, whose alleged travels have even been worked into the Kensington rune-stone saga, is not extant, and is known only from references to it in the late fifteenth and sixteenth centuries. The historical Nicholas of Lynn was a Carmelite, not a Franciscan, who worked in fourteenth-century Oxford, and did not so far as is known travel anywhere out of the ordinary. He did, however, compose his *Kalendarium* in 1386, a calendar for dates between 1387 and 1462 which was known to, and used by, Chaucer. From this slender foundation a wholly fanciful career seems to have been built up for Nicholas by later writers.

Many attempts have been made to show that the final example, the Zeno narrative, is based on genuine travel. A journey to Greenland by two fourteenth-century Italians would be plausible enough in itself, were it not for the fanciful details with which Greenland is described. However, the narrative moves further into fantasy with an account of how the brothers accompanied a mysterious nobleman, Prince Zichmi, to an equally mysterious western land named Estotiland. Zichmi has been identified with Henry Sinclair, earl of Orkney, who died in 1404, and Estotiland with Nova Scotia, but the arguments do not carry conviction, and it is generally believed that the entire narrative was invented by the Nicolo Zeno who first published it, together with a map, at Venice in 1558. Probably he was trying to annex some of the glory of discovering the New World for his own family as well as for his native city.

When stories such as these and the forged Vinland Map are eliminated, it is clear that there was little or no knowledge in late medieval Europe of the lands which we now know as North America. The sagas of the Greenlanders and of Eric the Red, which had been composed in Iceland, and in which the most detailed account of Vinland would have been found, were entirely unknown, and even if they had been known would probably not have been understood. It is quite possible too that by the fourteenth and fifteenth centuries Vinland, if it was remembered at all in the Scandinavian world outside Iceland, had become a semi-mythical land. Another likely explanation of the European failure to learn of the Viking discoveries in North America is that they took place at a time when Scandinavia was not yet fully a part of western Christendom, and was therefore in a sense out of phase with the rest of Europe.

There is, however, a more fundamental problem deriving from the differing ways in which the Atlantic, the lands bordering it, and the islands within it were understood in Scandinavia and elsewhere in Europe. The common belief among Scandinavian writers, which can be traced back to the twelfth-century Icelandic geographer Nikolus Saemundarson, was that the Atlantic was an enclosed sea, like the Mediterranean. Greenland was attached by a land bridge to the mainland of Europe somewhere to the north of Norway; Helluland lay to the south of Greenland; next to it was Markland; and not far away was Vinland 'which some think to be connected to Africa'. The Atlantic equivalent of the straits of Gibraltar lay between Markland and Vinland in a passage connecting it with the great ocean running around the world. With the exception of the land bridge between Greenland and Europe, which passed into the cartography of southern Europe in the 1420s via the Danish cartographer Claudius Clavus, none of these ideas was current outside Scandinavia. The usual opinion elsewhere, beginning with Adam of Bremen's attempt in the eleventh century to make sense of the information he had obtained at the Danish court, was that the Viking discoveries in the Atlantic consisted entirely of islands. Iceland lay to the north of Norway; Greenland further east; and Vinland (which Adam was the only non-Scandinavian writer to describe) was placed further east again. Finn Gad, the modern authority on the history of Greenland, has remarked that 'it may almost be said that the further south you lived, the more northerly and easterly was your idea of Greenland'.

For some European observers, unconsciously echoing the opinion of the great twelfth-century Moslem geographer Idrisi that 'no one knows what exists beyond this sea, no one has been able to learn for certain, because of the dangers to navigation caused by the impenetrable darkness, the great waves, the frequent storms and violent winds, and the multitude of sea monsters', the Atlantic was a desolate and empty place. Men of such varied backgrounds as the Ostman, descended from the earlier Viking settlers of Ireland, who petitioned his overlord Edward I of England in 1290; the fourteenth-century English chronicler Ranulf Higden; and Gilles le Bouvier, the chief herald of Charles VII of France, who wrote his *Livre de la Description de Pays* in the 1450s, all regarded Ireland as effectively the end of the world, beyond which nothing else existed to the west.

But this was not a universal perception of the Atlantic. Gilles le Bouvier added the significant remark that some men said that if a ship were to sail to the west it would eventually reach the land of Prester John, while even Idrisi had qualified his terrifying account of the 'green sea of darkness' by saying that the Atlantic contained many islands, some inhabited and others deserted. This was really how the Atlantic was regarded by many practical navigators in the early part of the fifteenth century. The island group of the Canaries, and probably Madeira and the Azores, had been discovered by earlier generations of sailors. The Viking landfalls in North America had come and gone, leaving hardly any trace behind them, but the other Viking discoveries, in Iceland and Greenland, were still remembered, even if the Greenland colony itself was then on the point of dying out. Some of the marine charts which were drawn in the fourteenth century bore representations of other islands, such as those of St Brendan, Brasil, and Antilia, whose existence was less certain, but which none the less helped to stimulate new voyages of discovery. For new generations of European navigators, from Portugal, Castile, England, and perhaps elsewhere, the prospect of Atlantic islands, those already known and those that might be awaiting discovery, was a very real one indeed.

IV
Europe and the world: *c*.1100–1450

10
Scholarship and the imagination

Before discussing the fifteenth-century phase of the expansion of Europe, symbolized by the opening of the sea routes to India and America, it is essential to pause and examine the geographical ideas and perceptions of the world which were current in Europe as it entered upon the fifteenth century. This chapter offers more of a series of impressions than any attempt at a systematic analysis of these questions, which would require a book to themselves, but one fairly safe conclusion is that there was in medieval Europe no such thing as a generally accepted view of the world. Then, as now, an individual's ideas of the outer world could be influenced by the opportunities for firsthand observation and the testing of evidence, by the nature of the written and visual material available, by the intelligence of the observer and the reader, and, in the case of a writer, by the kind of audience being addressed, and by what that audience wanted to believe. The result was a great variety of ideas, not necessarily consistent with one another, and an erratic line of development which led, by the early fifteenth century, to the coexistence of new ideas and factual information with notions derived from a tradition reaching far back into classical antiquity. The modification or the replacement of the received ideas and perceptions of earlier generations was to remain a slow process even after the discoveries of the fifteenth and sixteenth centuries gradually made it evident that the world was a bigger and more complex place than anyone had ever imagined.

The geographical ideas with which medieval Europe had begun the first great phase of its expansion, in the eleventh and twelfth centuries, differed little from those of the late classical and early medieval periods which were discussed in the first chapter, except that, potentially at least, western Europeans were now able to visit the eastern Mediterranean and see for themselves the current reality in Constantinople, Syria, Palestine, or Egypt. Yet geography as a subject for study still had no independent status and was commonly treated either as a peripheral adjunct to the universal histories which were coming into fashion in the twelfth century, or in the following century as a part of the encyclopaedias of human knowledge which were then being written. A highly intelligent and well-informed historian such as Otto of Freising, whose universal chronicle *The Two Cities* was written in Germany between 1143 and 1147, could therefore begin his work with a description of the world taken directly, by his own admission, from the fifth-century historian Orosius, to whom he referred his readers for any further information they might require.

Honorius of Autun in his *Imago Mundi*, written and revised between 1110 and 1139, supplied an account of the world which began with the four rivers issuing from Paradise, and contained many details drawn from biblical geography. The *Liber Floridus* of Lambert of St Omer, composed in about 1130, adhered to the familiar classical notion of climatic zones; Lambert appears to have considered the earth as a sphere, since he was aware that different constellations of stars would be visible to the north and south of the equator; he believed in the existence of the antipodes but did not allow that they might have a human population, and ensured their inaccessibility by dividing the earth around the equator by a great belt of ocean, impassable because of the heat of the sun. Alongside these basic principles of world geography there existed, as commonplace ideas, the notions of a terrestrial paradise and of various monstrous and wonderful races of men; at least forty such marvels have been identified in medieval works.

One of the most common forms of representation of the earth was in the *mappae mundi*, of which over a thousand have survived. Despite their name these were not world maps in the sense that the term began to acquire in the fourteenth and fifteenth centuries, or in which it is understood today. The *mappae mundi* were instead schematic in form: it has been suggested, for example, that they bore the same sort of relation to reality as a modern map of the London underground. Many of the *mappae mundi* were of the kind known as the T-O, or Sallust, or Noachid type, in which the classical idea of the *orbis terrarum*, comprising the three continents of Asia, Africa, and Europe, was joined to the idea derived from the Bible, that the continents had been distributed between the descendants of the sons of Noah. The world was depicted as a flat disc surrounded by the world ocean, forming the O shape; this was internally divided by the T with east at the top, the stem of the T representing the Mediterranean separating Europe and Africa, while the cross of the T was formed by the river Don (the classical Tanais) and the Nile, dividing Europe from Asia and Asia from Africa respectively. Another common type of schematic map was originally associated with the *Commentary on the Dream of Scipio* by the early fifth-century writer Macrobius, and was designed to illustrate the position of the zones of climate on the face of the earth.

The T-O map was a basis to which a great deal of both real and imaginary information could easily be added. Examples of these more elaborate *mappae mundi* can often be found incorporated into literary works, while a few especially fine ones, such as the Hereford map of the late thirteenth century and the Ebstorf map of about 1240, were evidently designed to stand alone. Such maps would commonly represent Jerusalem as the centre of the world, and depicted the terrestrial paradise, as well as the monstrous races of men in their appointed places: twenty of the latter are to be found in the Hereford map, and twenty-four in the Ebstorf. Just as the geographical theories current in the twelfth century came mainly from classical writers such as Isidore of Seville and Orosius, so the fanciful details contained in the *mappae mundi* also had a classical origin. The Elder Pliny, Solinus, and the anonymous author of the *Physiologus* of about AD 200 supplied much of the information, but the origins of some of it went as far back as the fifth century BC and the wondrous tales about India recorded by the Greek writer Ctesias.

It is hard to establish with certainty before the thirteenth century whether there was a clear understanding of the spherical shape of the earth. Lambert of St Omer and Bede had known this fact, but attention has already been drawn in Chapter 1 to the ambiguity of Isidore of Seville's description of the world, which he seems to have thought of as a flat disc rather than a sphere, and it is likely that such ambiguities were preserved in this later period which derived so many of its geographical theories at second hand. There has also been considerable scholarly debate as to whether the artists who drew the *mappae mundi* were trying to convey the idea of a sphere. No definite answer is possible, but even allowing for the facts that the *mappae mundi* were very formal representations of the world, and that to someone unfamiliar with the concept of map projections it would not be immediately obvious that a twentieth-century world map was intended to depict a curved surface, it remains likely that most of those who saw a twelfth- or thirteenth-century *mappa mundi* would probably not have understood it as a sphere.

The element of what we would now call fantasy which entered into much medieval geographical writing and cartography can readily be illustrated by beliefs such as the literal existence of an earthly paradise, or by the monstrous races, of which the tribes of Gog and Magog enclosed by Alexander the Great behind a gate of brass in the Caucasus mountains were some of the most spectacular. Another outstanding example is the famous *Letter of Prester John* which first came to the attention of Europe in the second half of the twelfth century, later circulated in several versions in numerous languages, and was regarded as having come from a genuine Christian ruler who might one day recover the Holy Land (see Chapter 3). Any western visitor to Asia after the continent had been made accessible by the Mongol conquests in the thirteenth century would be expected to remain alert for signs of Prester John and his kingdom, and at the very least could not avoid expressing an opinion on the matter. Carpini mentioned Prester John as the ruler of Greater India but did not claim any positive evidence for his existence, while Rubruck dismissed all the tales he heard about Prester John as baseless rumours put about by the Nestorians whom he met. However, the discovery of Christian communities in many parts of Asia continued to raise hopes that one day Prester John, or a king connected with him, would be found. In the 1290s John of Monte Corvino seems to have believed that Körgis or George, the Nestorian Christian ruler of the Öngut, a Turkish people in northern China, was of the same family as Prester John. The story told to Rubruck about a certain Ung Khan may derive in part from a ruler of the same people, but is more likely to have been a reference to the Ung Khan who was one of the allies of Genghis Khan early in the thirteenth century. Prester John inevitably figured in the narrative of Marco Polo's travels where this identification with the earlier Ung Khan was made, and in which Prince George of the Öngut was described as sixth in line of descent from Prester John. Marco Polo's account of Prester John is scattered through his narrative, and is based on a confused version of past historical events rather than on the fabulous details contained in the *Letter of Prester John*. Prester John was also mentioned in Odoric of Pordenone's account of his travels in the East, written in 1330, but this proved to be the last reference to him in an Asian context: in future he was to be identified with Ethiopia.

Needless to say no Prester John with the characteristics of the king in the *Letter*, or ruling over a kingdom with the splendours and marvels there described was ever found in Asia or Africa. There is now no doubt that the *Letter* was a skilfully composed literary fabrication with sufficient historical reality behind it to make it plausible to its early readers, and perhaps to have inspired the letter in the first place. Despite a great deal of research during the past century, the identity of the author and the place of the letter's composition remain unknown. Attempts to show that it was connected from the very beginning with the Christian kingdom of Ethiopia have not proved convincing, since the terminology of the letter and the quests of European travellers for its author associate the document firmly with Asia. The battle won by Prester John, which was reported by Bishop Hugh in his interview with the pope in 1145, has been identified with the victory near Samarkand in 1141 of Yeh-lü Ta-shih, the founder of the Central Asian empire of Kara-Khitai, over the Seljuk Turkish sultan Sanjar. Neither of these rulers was a Christian. Similarly, the story of the King David, who was said in 1221 to be connected with Prester John and to be advancing through Asia, may derive either from vague accounts of the conquests of Genghis Khan or from the activities of Küchlüg, one of his enemies who had escaped westwards from Mongolia, and had conquered the empire of Kara-Khitai before being destroyed by a renewed Mongol attack. Küchlüg may once have been a Christian, but he came no closer to Prester John than that.

Examination of the text of the *Letter* has shown that it contains material drawn from the legends of Alexander the Great, from accounts of the marvels of the East, and from the works of Ekkehard of Aura (d.1125) and Marbod of Rennes (d.1123), all of which were familiar parts of medieval Latin literature. A number of Greek references have been accounted for as loan-words or as titles. Professor Slessarev, the author of the most detailed modern commentary on the *Letter*, has made the tentative suggestion that it was based on some of the stories of the apostle St Thomas and India, which were then skilfully combined with other available written sources, and given some plausibility by the recent dramatic events in central Asia, and by the urgent need of military assistance in the Holy Land after the fall of Edessa in 1144. The authorship of the *Letter* remains a mystery, apart from the likelihood that its author was a cleric working in western Europe and with access to Latin writings. The suggestion that the author was archbishop Christian of Mainz has been examined and found wanting, but the possibility of a German origin has been revived by Professor Hamilton's recent argument that the *Letter* may have been commissioned in the 1160s by Rainald of Dassel, archbishop of Cologne and chancellor to the emperor Frederick Barbarossa. According to this view the *Letter* was intended as imperial propaganda in the battle between Frederick and the papacy by demonstrating the supremacy of a priestly king. Whatever the origin and the immediate purpose of the *Letter*, it appeared in Europe at a time when there was a strong propensity to believe the story it told, while many of its details described the kind of marvels that Europeans expected to find in the East. Even when the experiences of European travellers in Asia made it clear that Prester John was not to be found there, the story did not lose its fascination. Like other wonders, Prester John's location was simply moved on elsewhere.

From the twelfth century there were, however, various new sources of geographical information. The earliest of these to become available to Christian Europe was through the medium of translations into Latin from Arabic of scientific works which were either of Arabic origin, or were themselves Arabic translations of classical Greek writings. After the conquest of the city of Toledo in Spain in 1085, and the formation of the Norman kingdom of Sicily, scholars from western Europe flocked to these former centres of Moslem learning, and particularly to Toledo, to search for and translate works on mathematics, medicine, and astronomy. For present purposes some of the most important translations were those of the ninth-century *Khorazmian Tables*, made in 1126 by Adelard of Bath, and of the *Toledo Tables*, made by 1140. These made available the classical Greek theories and calculations of latitude and longitude, together with the improvements which had been made by later Arab astronomical observations. In 1175 one of the leading works of classical antiquity, the *Almagest*, the Arab version of Ptolemy's *Syntaxis Mathematica*, was translated by Gerard of Cremona, and became known to Latin Europe for the first time. There was now the potential for a great advance in geographical theory.

At an empirical level the travels of European envoys, missionaries, and merchants in central and further Asia in the thirteenth and fourteenth centuries permitted the accumulation of an enormous amount of detailed, and often very accurate, information about parts of the world which previously were totally unknown in Europe. The writings of men such as Carpini, Rubruck, and John of Monte Corvino contain evidence of serious attempts by westerners to come to terms with an alien world which they often judged with a remarkable degree of sympathy. Carpini and Rubruck in particular stand out as highly intelligent and perceptive observers of the society and customs of the Mongols and their subject peoples. Marco Polo might also appear in the same light, were it not for the difficulties posed by the literary form in which his narrative was composed by Rustichello of Pisa. European accounts of regions for which little or no advance information, and hence preconceptions, existed, could often be particularly objective. This is very noticeable in the case of China, whose classical description as the land of the Seres where silk originated did little to prepare visiting Europeans for the size and sophistication of its cities and seaports. They realized that they were in the midst of a society which, even in the aftermath of a destructive conquest by the Mongols, possessed a degree of organization far ahead of any of the European states of the time. Even though China contained only a tiny minority of Christians, most of whom were Nestorian heretics, and the number of converts appears to have been small, it was not regarded as the abode of infidels in the same way as the Moslem world of the eastern Mediterranean and central Asia. Some echoing chord may have been struck, for example, by the Buddhist practice of monasticism, while Carpini's confusion of the Buddhist scriptures with those of Christianity has already been noted in Chapter 4. Even allowing for the possibility that letters sent back to Europe by merchants and missionaries resident in China were subject to imperial censorship, and therefore had to avoid offence, westerners in China were deeply impressed by what they saw. Marco Polo and John of Marignolli, for example, described the great cities and palaces they visited. Chinese technical mastery was also witnessed, from Marco Polo's account of the quality and cheapness of Chinese porcelain, to the great seagoing junks, complete with watertight bulkheads, which were mentioned by himself and Jordan of Séverac.

European travellers could also be critical of received ideas when these conflicted with their own observations or enquiries. The sceptical attitude often adopted towards the Prester John legend is one good example, but so also is Rubruck's disbelief in the existence of the monstrous races described by Pliny and Solinus, and his rejection of the traditional belief that the Caspian Sea was a branch of the encircling world ocean, while Marco Polo noted the deception practised by those who claimed to have brought pygmy men from the Indies. John of Monte Corvino's letter written while he was *en route* for Peking provides a generally accurate account of India, which includes the following significant passage: 'As regards men of a marvellous kind, to wit, men of a different make from the rest of us, and as regards animals of a like description, and as regards the Terrestrial Paradise, much have I asked and sought, but nothing have I been able to discover.' John of Marignolli who visited India in the late 1340s on the way home from China, devoted several pages of his description of the country to a reasoned denial of the existence of the monstrous races. He concluded that the truth was that 'no such people do exist as nations, though there may be an individual monster here and there'. The people he asked about these races had even asked him in turn whether such existed in his own homeland. He also noted that the tales of the *sciapods*, who were said to have one large foot with which they shaded themselves, could be explained by the Indian use of parasols to keep off the sun. He even took one back with him to Florence.

Marignolli also contradicted the standard belief of the time that the torrid zone on either side of the equator was impassable because of heat. The same conclusion was implied, though not stated directly, by other travellers such as Marco Polo and Jordan of Séverac, when they understandably remarked on the intense heat of India. Another significant point is that many of the Europeans who visited the southern part of India, or Java and Sumatra, observed that the Pole Star was scarcely visible or not visible at all above the horizon, thereby confirming if they had wished to draw this conclusion, the spherical shape of the earth: Marco Polo, John of Monte Corvino, Jordan of Séverac, and John of Marignolli all noticed this phenomenon. Monte Corvino commented that if he had been on a high enough point he 'could have seen the other Pole-Star [*sic*] which is in the opposite quarter', while the language used by Polo and Marignolli implies that they had actually travelled south of the equator. None of them directly addressed the problem of the antipodes apart from Marignolli, who expressly denied that the antipodes could be inhabited, and seems to have denied the very existence of land beyond the equator. These European experiences in India and the islands to the south-east of it, therefore, had major implications for certain important matters of geographical theory.

That new information was being acquired from various quarters is quite clear, but it is another matter entirely to assess the extent to which it was absorbed into and modified European perceptions of the world. There are some examples of valuable sources of information which were potentially available to European scholars but in practice had no influence at all. The *Geography* of Claudius Ptolemy, for example, which represented the peak of classical learning in its field, and had been translated and commented upon by writers of Arabic, was not discovered and translated by any of the scholars who went to Toledo, and did not become known to western Europe until it was translated from Greek early in the fifteenth century. Similarly, the work which contained the best of Arabic learning, the *Book of Roger* written in Palermo in about 1154 by the geographer al- Idrisi of Ceuta on behalf of Roger II, the Norman king of Sicily, remained entirely unknown elsewhere in Christian Europe, and has been translated and edited only in very recent times. Another even more detailed work which Idrisi wrote in 1161 and dedicated to William I of Sicily has disappeared altogether, apart from a short summary.

Neither is it difficult to find examples of European authors writing at a time when new information about the world was beginning to circulate in Europe who either knew nothing of it or took no notice of what they heard. Snorri Sturluson, the Icelandic author of the *Heimskringla*, a history of the kings of Norway finished about 1225, began his work (whose very title means 'the orb of the world') with a short description of the world derived directly from the pattern of a T-O map. Although he gave an account of the discovery of Vinland, he found nothing inconsistent with this basic picture. The comparative isolation of Scandinavia, and the date at which Sturluson was writing are perhaps sufficient explanation. Initially more surprising is the Florentine author Brunetto Latini, who wrote his *Livres dou Tresor* in France and in French in the 1260s. He devoted only a short part of his work to geography, under the revealing title of *Mappemonde*, a section which shows not a trace of the Asian discoveries of Carpini and Rubruck which were then becoming known in France, and is full of borrowings from Solinus, many of them inaccurate. As late as the 1320s the English chronicler Ranulf Higden began his *Polychronicon* with a lengthy geographical treatise drawn almost entirely from classical sources, apart from a section on Ireland taken from Giraldus Cambrensis. Although he knew of the work of the thirteenth-century French encyclopaedist Vincent of Beauvais, there is no sign of any of the recent information he might have found there. At one point Higden, like Latini, described his written work as a *mappa mundi*, while manuscripts of the *Polychronicon* are also well known for including a drawn *mappa mundi* of the conventional kind.

On the other hand, it is also easy to demonstrate that new information did pass into wider circulation. The classic example of this is the treatise known as *De Sphaera Mundi* which was produced in Paris in about 1220 by the English scholar John Holywood (*Sacrobosco*). This was entirely unoriginal, drawing much of its material from the ninth-century Arabic writer al-Farghani. But this was precisely its significance, since it was written as a textbook which was widely used at the University of Paris and elsewhere, and continued to be published and recommended until well into the sixteenth century. Holywood made the spherical shape of the earth explicit together with arguments to demonstrate this, and cited a figure for the earth's circumference which appears to have derived ultimately from Eratosthenes.

Among other examples of the absorption of new material, or of attempts to portray the world in a more accurate light, are Adam of Bremen's eleventh-century account of Iceland, Greenland, and Vinland; the use made in about 1250 by the French Dominican Vincent of Beauvais, in his *Speculum Mundi*, of information on the Mongols which had recently been brought to France by Carpini and Simon of St Quentin; and the mid-thirteenth-century map of Britain by the English chronicler Matthew Paris. In 1303 the Paduan astronomer and physician Petro de Abano interviewed Marco Polo, whom he described as 'the most extensive traveller and the most diligent enquirer whom I have ever known', and understood and recorded the significance of Polo's observations of the Pole Star close to the equator. This information was later passed on by another astronomer, Master Lemon of Genoa, to John of Marignolli. Boccaccio could refer quite casually to the land of Cathay as the setting for two of his tales in the *Decameron*, and both he and Petrarch possessed up-to-date information on the discovery of the Canary Islands; in 1333 Richard of Bury, the English scholar and bibliophile who was also bishop of Durham and keeper of the privy seal to Edward III, had a long conversation with Petrarch at Avignon about the true location of the island of Ultima Thule; in about

1340 the Florentine merchant Francesco Balducci di Pegolotti gave a detailed account of the route from Europe to China in his *La Pratica della Mercatura*; and in 1344 the participants at one of Edward III's tournaments all attended dressed as Tartars. In about 1375 recognizable drawings of such unfamiliar persons and objects as Mansa Musa the ruler of Mali in West Africa, a North African desert tribesman mounted on his camel, and a Chinese junk were included in the map ascribed to Abraham Cresques of Majorca and now known as the Catalan world atlas which was probably produced for presentation to Charles V of France: over a century before, in the 1250s, William of Rubruck had bemoaned his inability to draw any of the things he saw in Mongolia.

At the end of the fourteenth century Chaucer used the *Kalendarium*, composed in 1386 by the English Carmelite Nicholas of Lynn, to establish the chronological framework of his *Canterbury Tales*, and wrote a treatise on the astronomical and navigational instrument, the astrolabe. Chaucer's contemporary, the French crusading propagandist Philippe de Mézières, showed that scientific methods of navigation had become commonplace when he combined, in his *Letter to Richard II* of 1395, a reference to the compass needle with a long figurative comparison of the power of the loadstone with that of the king of England. In another of his works, *Le Songe du Vieil Pèlerin*, written in 1388–9, de Mézières made use of material on the Tartars and on Cathay as part of an allegorical travel narrative.

The examples just quoted (and no doubt many more could be found) are mainly random details of the European reaction to the discoveries of travellers in Asia, Africa, and the North Atlantic rather than evidence of any systematic attempt to assimilate and to come to terms with new information. There were, however, in the thirteenth century, at the time when Asian travel in particular was developing quickly in the wake of the Mongol conquests, men of great intellectual power and curiosity in western Europe, especially in the ranks of the newly founded orders of friars. The efforts of the Dominican Thomas Aquinas to absorb the newly regained works of Aristotle, and to make them consistent with Christian theology are, of course, the major example of this

intellectual activity. But there were others whose work had great
significance for the development of geographical speculation.
In about 1260 another Dominican, Albertus Magnus from Germany, wrote in his *De Natura Locorum* that the equatorial zone
was habitable and that the temperate zone to the south of the
equator must be inhabited, even though no man had ever been
there: both the existence of the antipodes and the peopling of
them which most earlier Christian writers had tried to avoid were
here clearly enunciated.

The best illustration of the level of achievement in the field
of geography of which thirteenth-century writers were capable is
the English contemporary of Albertus Magnus, the Franciscan
Roger Bacon, who was a product of the universities of Oxford
and Paris. His *Opus Maius*, composed soon after 1266, reveals a
very independent mind, and contains, for example, a clear statement of the importance of the experimental method in science.
Bacon's geographical ideas form part of the section of his treatise
devoted to mathematics, demonstrating that even in the work of
such an original scholar geography still had no independent status. None the less Bacon gave a very clear and reasoned account
of the spherical shape of the earth and its circumference. He also
discussed the size of the inhabited area of the world, the theory of
latitudes and longitudes, and, like Albertus Magnus, argued that
the antipodes existed and were inhabited.

The modern reader's attention is also drawn to the references
made by Bacon to very recent firsthand information about Asia
which he had gathered from the travel narratives of his fellow
Franciscans, Carpini and Rubruck. There is only one direct mention of Carpini, in connection with Tibet, but Bacon knew that he
had stayed with the Mongols in 1246, and it is also clear that he
had read his book. Quite possibly, like the Franciscan Salimbene
and many others, he had actually met Carpini when the latter
visited France after his return from Mongolia. Bacon had certainly met Rubruck as well as studying his book with care. He
knew that Rubruck had departed for the Mongol court in 1253;
he learned from him that the Caspian was land-locked, and
accepted this contradiction of classical authors; he recorded
that the Tatars were unable to pronounce the letter B (though

Rubruck was not named as the source for this, which Bacon may have learned in conversation); he followed Rubruck's scepticism about Prester John's existence; and he gave a description of the lands conquered by the Tatars. Bacon also referred to China which he called Great Cathay, and identified it correctly with the classical land of the Seres and of silk; he knew of Chinese paper money, of the peculiarities of Chinese written characters, and the fact that they were produced with a brush; he learned that the Tatars had obtained the written form of their language from the Uighurs (Ingeres in the text); and he even knew the Buddhist prayer *Om Mani padme hum*, which he rendered as *On man baccan*, 'that is "God thou knowest". '

Bacon emerges, even from such a cursory examination of his work, as a man of great curiosity, with a ready willingness to accept new information and ideas. Yet there are also serious defects in his work, which arise not so much from himself as from the very nature of the sources and ideas available to him. He was perfectly aware of the practical limitations placed upon any description of the world by the lack of precise information, and he remarked that he would use the accounts provided by earlier authors rather than proceeding 'by the true longitudes and latitudes of places with respect to the heavens, because the Latins do not have this knowledge as yet'. This conclusion was not entirely true, since as far back as 1178 Roger of Hereford had tried to adapt the *Toledo Tables* to the meridian of his home city, but the degree of accuracy was still very unsatisfactory. At the same time Bacon remarked explicitly that there were errors in the works of Pliny, Ptolemy, and other classical writers, and said that wherever possible he would draw on the firsthand experiences of men such as William of Rubruck, who had actually visited the places they described.

There were limits to the amount of recent knowledge that was readily available, and it is therefore not surprising to find extensive citations from classical authors like Aristotle, Pliny, and Ptolemy, from Christian writers such as Orosius, Jerome, Isidore, and Bede, and from Moslem sources such as al-Farghani, Averroes, Avicenna, and the *Toledo Tables*. It is also interesting to discover that on a number of occasions Bacon quoted from Ethicus, by whom he presumably meant the strange figure of Aethicus Ister, the supposed author of a treatise, probably written in the eighth century, which contained a large number of wondrous tales and other marvels. Ethicus was cited in support of the legend of Alexander the Great and the tribes of Gog and Magog; he was quoted as an authority equal with Rubruck for the geography of the lands of northern Asia since 'he travelled over all these regions and sailed the northern ocean with its islands'; Ethicus, together with Pliny, was also the source of a story about the Amazons.

Bacon's use of sources from the remote past could therefore lead to some strange conclusions, but in one case at least this practice had an important bearing on later events. He said nothing about the Atlantic as such, and his work exhibits no knowledge of Iceland or of any of the other Viking discoveries. However, on the basis of statements in classical authors such as Aristotle and Pliny, and in the Old Testament Book of Esdras, he contradicted the views of Ptolemy on the size of the habitable part of the earth, and concluded that it extended even further to the east than Ptolemy had believed. The size of the ocean was correspondingly reduced, with the consequence that the distance between Spain in the far west and India in the far east would be relatively short, and could in theory be navigated by a ship. Early in the fifteenth century Bacon's conclusion was quoted by Pierre D'Ailly in his *Imago Mundi*, which was in turn studied by Columbus, so that Roger Bacon contributed to the chain of geographical errors which led to the discovery of America in 1492.

The mixture of very recent accurate information, traditional theories, and imagination in the writings of a scholar of Bacon's calibre should be a warning not to expect too great a consistency or originality on the part of lesser lights. John of Marignolli, for example, may have disbelieved stories of the monstrous races, but he was fully prepared to accept others. His account of the island of Ceylon, which he visited on his return journey from China, is interspersed with references to Adam (whose footprint he was shown on the mountain known as Adam's Peak), and the Garden of Eden. He believed that Paradise was so close that it was possible to hear the sound of the waters falling from its fountain, and that the four rivers of Paradise, the Nile, Phison, Tigris, and Euphrates, flowed through Ceylon on the way to their respective parts of the world.

Marignolli was at least a genuine traveller whose narrative has considerable value, even though his experiences and his preconceptions could not be altogether separated. In a very different category is the work known as *The Book of Knowledge of all the World*, written in the late 1340s by an anonymous Spanish Franciscan. Told in the first person, it purports to be an account of a journey which took the author all over the world by land and sea, through Europe, Asia, and Africa. The *Book of Knowledge*, which badly needs a modern edition, has sometimes been taken at its face value, but it is far more likely to be a compilation drawing on other, as yet unidentified sources, and perhaps from the author's own imagination. His account of a region as close as Britain and Ireland is so garbled that it is clearly not the result of firsthand observation, while his claims to have visited parts of Africa hitherto unknown to Europeans have already been dismissed as highly improbable.

Any modern attempt to assess the extent and the quality of medieval geographical knowledge also has to come to terms with the manner in which writers as diverse in their abilities as Roger Bacon and the Spanish Franciscan described places and even whole regions of the earth's surface. Sometimes places which did not exist at all might be located with apparent precision: one example is the inclusion on maps of islands such as those of St Brendan, or Brasil; another is the statement by a thirteenth-century writer that Paradise could be reached from France by a journey of 1,425 days. It is clear enough now that none of these had any reality, but it was not at all clear in the thirteenth and fourteenth centuries, or even later. The practical impossibility of assigning an accurate latitude and longitude to remote parts of the world, and so establishing clear spatial relationships between the known and the unknown, led to further problems. Roger Bacon understood this difficulty, and admitted that in the current state of knowledge it was insoluble, but it is also well illustrated by the confusion which existed in Scandinavia and other parts of Europe over the relative positions of Iceland, Greenland,

and Vinland, and which probably contributed to the loss of contact with the Viking discoveries in North America.

The geographical names employed by medieval writers can also cause serious confusion, a confusion which is sometimes compounded by the twentieth-century habit of naming newly created states after long-disappeared predecessors. In some instances, such as Ghana and Mali, there is a very rough approximation between the medieval and the modern states, but other African names, such as Ethiopia , Sudan, and Guinea, which are all represented in the present century by states with well-defined boundaries, were anything but precise in medieval usage. Bacon, for example, gave an account of an African country situated on the shores of the Red Sea which he named 'Ethiopia', and which is clearly related to the modern state of the same name, but he also quoted Ptolemy's argument that nature required that there should be two races of Ethiopians, one on either side of the equator, and meaning simply 'black people'. This latter definition is very similar to that of the name 'Sudan', which is derived from the Arabic term, *Beled es-Sudan*, meaning 'the land of the blacks', and was applied as a generic description to all the lands to the south of the Sahara with which the Arabs had contact. Various forms of the name 'Guinea' appear in fourteenth-century European sources such as the *Book of Knowledge of all the World* and a number of the portolan maps which were then being drawn by Italian and Catalan cartographers, as if it were a well-defined location in West Africa which might actually have been visited. This is in fact another highly misleading expression which is thought to have originated with the word used for the Sudan by the Berber tribes of North Africa. Three languages, classical Greek, Arabic, and Berber, therefore provided three different words, each meaning roughly the same thing.

An even greater cause of confusion is the medieval use of the word 'India'. A distinction between 'India Major' and 'India Minor' has been traced back as far as the fourth century AD, but from the twelfth century a division into no less than three Indias became current, and was made familiar by the spurious *Letter of Prester John*. 'Nearer' or 'Lesser India' meant roughly the northern part of the subcontinent of India as it is understood today, while 'Further' or 'Greater India' referred to the southern part; 'Middle India' was used to describe Ethiopia, with all the additional imprecision associated with that word. It has, however, been suggested, using the modern analogy of 'Near', 'Middle', and 'Far East', that 'Middle India' should really be understood in the sense of 'Intermediate India', or half-way to India proper. This triple division of India is well represented in the narrative of Marco Polo's travels, and in the works of other thirteenth- and fourteenth-century writers. The groundwork was accordingly well laid in the medieval period for the multiplicity of Indies that were to appear in East and West as a result of the discoveries of Columbus and his successors.

Little is known in any systematic way about the audiences reached by medieval authors on geographical subjects. A scholar like Roger Bacon was by definition writing for a very specialized public, and his geographical material was in any case only part of a much larger scheme of knowledge; Giovanni di Piano Carpini's account of his mission to Mongolia was composed both for the special purposes of papal diplomacy, and for the interest of the people who flocked to meet and hear him on his return, and his work also became widely available through its incorporation into the encyclopaedia of Vincent of Beauvais; apart from the significant exception of Roger Bacon, and the preservation of several texts of his narrative in manuscripts of English provenance, there is little evidence that William of Rubruck's achievements were known; while John of Marignolli's description of his journey to China and India was buried in the history of Bohemia which he wrote in about 1354 at the court of the emperor Charles IV in Prague, and was not rediscovered until 1820.

The popularity of a work like Marco Polo's *Divisament dou Monde* can be seen in the number of surviving manuscripts, and in the speed with which they multiplied. Over 80 fourteenth- and fifteenth-century manuscripts are known, including 41 in Latin, 21 in Italian, 16 in French, 6 in German, and one in Irish. The Latin texts derived from a translation made in about 1320 by the Dominican Francesco Pipino, while some of the French texts descended from the translation of Rustichello of Pisa's rough-

and-ready French into Parisian French made in Venice in 1307. This was commissioned by the French knight Thibault de Chépoy, and was shortly recopied for Thibault's master Charles of Valois, the brother of Philip IV of France; in 1312 this copy was transcribed for countess Mahaut of Artois at Hesdin and then for her chancellor, Thierry d'Hirecon, a future bishop of Arras.

The wide circulation of manuscripts of Rustichello's account of Marco Polo's experiences did not necessarily imply an interest in the realities of the outer world on the part of its readers. Some degree of information was certainly imparted, but it is equally certain that entertainment was one of the author's main purposes, and this he achieved to great effect. The ambivalent quality of the work, and of its readers' reaction to it, is revealed in the fact that Marco Polo might be found in manuscript either with such works as *Mandeville's Travels*, *The Letter of Prester John*, the Alexander legend, and the narrative of Odoric of Pordenone's visit to the East, all of which contained a high proportion of fantasy material, or in company with the writings of Carpini, Hayton of Armenia, John of Cora, and Ricold of Montecroce, which were all basically accurate accounts of the East. The research of modern scholars such as Wittkower and Friedman suggests that the readers of travel literature either expected, or were assumed to expect, to be able to read about the marvels recounted in classical literature, with the result that manuscripts sometimes included illustrations of the monstrous races and wondrous animals when these were not mentioned, or were even disavowed, in the texts to which they were supposed to relate. This practice has been observed in several of the manuscripts of Marco Polo, and even to some extent in those of Mandeville where the amount of fantasy was in any case greater in the actual text. It is almost as if Marco Polo's narrative was somehow felt to be lacking in appeal. The famous report by Polo's contemporary, Jacopo of Acqui, that Polo had reported much less of his true experiences than he might have done for fear of being branded a liar, may reinforce this impression. So also does the fact that, despite the many translations of Marco Polo into a variety of European languages, there was apparently no English translation until as late as 1579. It is also noticeable that with certain exceptions, like the cartographer who used material from Marco Polo when preparing his world atlas in about 1375, and the scholar Petro de Abano, the number of written references to Polo by his near contemporaries seems to have been small.

This may well be an unfair verdict on Marco Polo's popularity among late medieval readers of travel literature, but it is very likely that his adventures were exceeded in popularity by another work, *The Travels of Sir John Mandeville*, which contained all the ingredients that a reader could possibly want. According to the text, Sir John Mandeville was an English knight from St Albans in Hertfordshire, who left England on 29 September 1322 or 1332 (depending on which variant of the text is followed). He then pursued his travels to Constantinople, Jerusalem and the Holy Land, Egypt, Ethiopia, India, Cathay, Persia, and Turkey, before returning to Europe and writing an account of his experiences in either 1356 or 1366. Nothing more about the author appears in the text, but in order to disarm any charges against his veracity he alleges that he visited the papal curia in Rome (*recte* 'the court of Rome', that is, at Avignon, if the work was actually composed when claimed), and showed the pope his book. The pope and his advisers had examined it, and the pope declared that it was all true: 'for he said that he had a book of Latin that contained all that and mickle more, after which book the *Mappa Mundi* is made; and that book he showed to me.'

About half of *The Travels of Sir John Mandeville* belongs to the familiar genre of narratives of pilgrim travel to the Holy Land, and needs no comment. But as Mandeville moved farther east so the wonders and the marvels in his story increased in number. On one of the islands of the east he found dog-headed men; on another giants with one eye in the middle of the forehead; he saw headless men whose face was on the chest, and men whose upper lip was large enough to shelter them from the sun; there were human beings with the genitals of both sexes, and others who lived off the smell of apples; and so on. He told of Gog and Magog enclosed behind a mountain barrier, and he identified them and their followers with the ten lost tribes of Israel; and inevitably he gave a detailed description of the land of Prester John, and of Paradise (though he did not claim to have been there) and the four rivers issuing from it.

So bald a summary of *Mandeville's Travels* does no justice to the skill with which the work was composed; nor does it explain the fascination which the book evidently held for medieval readers, and still holds even today. The plenitude of marvels pervading the narrative has naturally led many readers to the conclusion that the author was gifted with a vivid imagination, and was not to be trusted in anything he said. Even a cursory examination of the text is sufficient to show that it was meant to be read as a work of literature rather than as a literal description of a series of real journeys undertaken by one man during the first half of the fourteenth century: Mandeville's alleged appeal to the pope was no doubt intended as a hint that his book should not be taken too seriously.

It would, however, be very unwise to dismiss *Mandeville's Travels* out of hand as a serious source of evidence on European knowledge of the outer world. There are numerous other examples of fourteenth-century authors who used a real or an imaginary journey as a framework for their writing. The voyage of Ulysses in Dante's *Inferno*, Boccaccio's *Decameron* and his prose romance the *Filocolo*, Philippe de Mézières's *Songe du Vieil Pèlerin*, and Chaucer's *Canterbury Tales* are all cases in point. These works were all consciously fictional in character, but there are also examples to be found in other types of work. The Spanish Franciscan's *Book of Knowledge of all the World* was believed by its earliest editors to be an account of travels throughout the known world, but is now generally regarded as a compilation from a variety of sources rather than the product of much, if any, actual travel by its author. Even the records of genuine travel may not always be what they seem. Although there is no doubt that Marco Polo travelled through central Asia, China, and India, it has been suggested by Professor Jacques Heers that the real purpose of the *Divisament dou Monde* was to provide an encyclopaedic account of Asia, rather than a straightforward chronological narrative of travel. It has also been suggested that Marco Polo's original intention, before Rustichello transformed his reminiscences into the work we have today, was to write a practical handbook on Asia for use by other merchants. There is no evidence to support this idea, but such a work was composed in about 1340 by the Florentine Francesco Balducci di Pegolotti, and has been published under the title of *La Pratica della Mercatura*. Asia made up only a small part of this work, which surveyed the various places in Europe and the eastern Mediterranean in which Italian merchants carried on their affairs. Although Pegolotti had travelled extensively during his own business career, and is well known in English government records of the reign of Edward II under the name of 'Francis Balduch', he never made any claim that when he described the journey from the Black Sea to Peking he was doing so from firsthand knowledge. When viewed in this wider context the travels ascribed to Sir John Mandeville become rather less puzzling.

Mandeville's Travels reveals a number of other interesting features. It is noticeable, for example, that the author tended to locate the most extravagant of his wondrous and monstrous races on islands, where they would be safe from closer inspection: there is an echo here of the marvellous islands visited by St Brendan and his companions in the *Navigatio Brendani*. The realm of Prester John and Paradise were also placed in a corner of the world where they could not be reached, beyond the empire of Cathay in the remotest parts of eastern Asia. It has been noticed by modern scholars that as knowledge of the world increased, so the marvels that were believed to exist tended to be moved farther and farther away. The author of *Mandeville's Travels* clearly fits into this pattern, but once again he may have been hinting that some of the stories he told should not be taken too literally.

Whatever the truth of this, it is certain that, alongside all the traditional marvels, *Mandeville's Travels* does contain a considerable amount of sound geographical theory. In his account of the island of Sumatra the author made a lengthy digression to explain the differing appearances of the stars to the north and south of the equator; he gave clear evidence of his belief in an inhabited antipodes, and he argued that the earth might be circumnavigated 'if a man might find ready shipping and good company and thereto had his health'. To add spice to this idea he told the story of a man who had journeyed around the world until 'he found an isle where he heard men speak his own language'.

This portion of *Mandeville's Travels* is significant only in its lack of originality. The spherical shape of the world was common knowledge for anyone who had read John Holywood's *De Sphaera Mundi*. It also seems to have been a fairly common opinion that the world could, in theory at least, be circumnavigated: Roger Bacon, the fourteenth century English chronicler Ranulf Higden, and the fifteenth-century French writer Gilles le Bouvier all mentioned the possibility, while in the 1370s the French scholar Nicholas Oresme argued that a circumnavigation would take exactly four years, sixteen weeks, and two days! The geographical observations of Marco Polo, John of Monte Corvino, and other real travellers to the East have already been noted.

Careful study of the text of *Mandeville's Travels* during the past century has shown that much of the material in it was certainly, or very probably, derived from the works of earlier writers. Some of this, such as the stories of the marvellous races of men, was of the kind that had been in circulation in Europe since classical antiquity, but it is very significant that the author also had access to the writings of many of the European travellers in Asia in the thirteenth and early fourteenth centuries, and was using up-to-date and often accurate material. Among the sources which have been identified are the *Speculum Naturale* and the *Speculum Historiale* of Vincent of Beauvais, written in the mid-thirteenth century, which supplied material from Carpini's then recent account of his mission to Mongolia as well as many quotations from classical writers; the narrative of Odoric of Pordenone's travels in China and India which had been composed in 1330; the *Flor des estoires de la terre d'orient* written in 1307 by the Armenian prince Hayton; and the *Letter of Prester John*. Information on the Holy Land came from such sources as the early thirteenth-century *Historia Orientalis* by Jacques de Vitry, William of Tripoli's *De Statu Saracenorum* of 1270, and the account of the pilgrimage made in 1332-3 by the German knight William of Boldensele. A number of these works were conveniently brought together in a French translation under the title of *Le livre des merveilles* by Jean le Long of Ypres or St Bertin in 1351, and could have been used in this form by the author of *Mandeville's Travels*. Marco Polo's experiences may also have been drawn on in places, although there is no agreement among scholars as to the extent, if any, of the borrowing. A variety of purely literary sources, such as the romances of Alexander the Great and King Arthur, also made their contributions to a book which was a skilfully woven patchwork.

A so-far unsolved problem is the authorship of the *Travels*. One of the leading modern commentators on the work, M. C. Seymour, has remarked forthrightly: '*Mandeville's Travels* was written in French on the Continent, possibly at Liège and probably not by an Englishman, about 1357'; on the other hand Malcolm Letts, the editor of another important edition, is equally certain that the author was an Englishman, as the text itself alleges, and that he died and was buried at Liège in 1372; Josephine Waters Bennett, in her thorough but inconclusive study of Mandeville, has also argued that he was English, that the original language of the *Travels* was Norman-French, and that it was written in England and not on the Continent. The only common ground between these three scholars (who represent only the English-language research on the subject) is that the language used was French, even if there is no agreement as to which form was employed.

If we abandon the assumption that the author of Mandeville was definitely a man named Sir John Mandeville, and instead assume that this was a plausible sounding name adopted by the real author to cover his literary borrowings from a wide variety of different sources, then we may be nearer to understanding the nature of the *Travels*. One of the early commentators on Mandeville, George F. Warner, suggested in his 1889 edition that the name Mandeville was derived from a French romance named *Mandevie* by a certain Jean du Pin, completed in 1340, whose eponymous hero undertook an imaginary journey in a dream; and that the author of *Mandeville's Travels* might then have adapted both the title and the form to his own purposes.

It has also been suggested that a model for the *Travels* might have been found in those of the German pilgrim traveller William of Boldensele, whose narrative was certainly used by the author. Boldensele appears to have been a Dominican whose real name was Otto von Neuenhausen, and who adopted his mother's family name of Boldensele when he went to the Holy Land in 1332–3, as a penance imposed upon him by Pope John XXII for his earlier support of the emperor Ludwig of Bavaria. After his return he wrote an account of his travels in 1336 at the request of Cardinal Talleyrand of Périgord, and later seems to have resumed the habit of a Dominican. The idea of an alias may perhaps have appealed to the author of Mandeville while he was making use of Boldensele's narrative.

Whoever he was, and whatever the actual sources of his inspiration, the author of the *Travels of Sir John Mandeville* was certainly an artist of a high calibre whose work caught the imagination of readers all over Europe. Well over two hundred manuscripts are known, in the French of England, Paris, and the Low Countries, but also in a wide range of other languages: English, German, Latin, Spanish, Italian, Danish, Czech, and Irish. The *Travels* show both the extent of the real European knowledge of the world in the fourteenth century, and the bizarre fashion in which genuine information and soundly based theories could be intermingled with the purest fantasy, providing a good idea of what the growing number of literate persons of the time could know about the world at large, and of what they might hope to find if they were ever able to travel on their own account.

11

Geography in the fifteenth century

It might be expected that the century in which the Italian Renaissance was reaching new heights of achievement, in which America was discovered, and the sea route to India was opened, would also witness a revolution in geographical thought, and great advances in the assimilation of new information. In some respects this was the case, but the survival of traditional ideas and preconceptions, which was so marked a feature of the period down to the end of the fourteenth century, continued during the fifteenth, and was aided by the demands of the new breed of publishers for suitable material for their printing presses.

In the early 1480s, for example, William Caxton printed an English edition of Ranulf Higden's *Polychronicon*, which had been almost entirely unoriginal in its geographical content when it was first written in the early fourteenth century. At about the same time Caxton published *The Mirrour of the World*, a translation from a French original which had probably been written in Lorraine in about 1245. This referred to the spherical shape of the world, and even suggested that it might be circumnavigated, but gave no hint of the new geographical knowledge that was starting to be acquired when it was first composed. Caxton's version duly reproduced the tales of the terrestrial paradise and numerous wonders, as if nothing of moment had been discovered in the intervening two and a half centuries. The edition of *Mandeville's Travels* which Caxton had been planning when he died in 1491 was produced in 1496 by his successor Richard Pynson. Mandeville had already appeared in German, French, and Latin editions between 1478 and 1483, while the account of Marco Polo's travels entered print at about the same time.

If little seems to have changed at the level of popular travel literature, important developments in the ideas of theoretical geographers did take place during the fifteenth century. This did not, however, occur because scholars suddenly attempted to catch up with all the observations made by practical explorers in the preceding centuries, but was instead the result of another round of rediscovery of classical authors whose works for one reason or another had escaped the attentions of translators in the twelfth century.

The fifteenth-century rediscoveries were not of equal significance. One of the lesser lights among classical geographical writers was Pomponius Mela, whose treatise *De Chorographia* was produced in the mid-first century AD, and was extensively used by the Elder Pliny and later classical authors. Pomponius Mela would be of little concern to the present discussion if modern scholars had not generally assumed that his works were as widely known and quoted in the medieval period as those of Pliny or Solinus, and that they were also an important influence on the development of medieval cartography. It has recently been established that the *De Chorographia* was little known before 1400, other than to a group of fourteenth-century Italian humanists who included Petrarch and Boccaccio. In the early years of the fifteenth century copies of Pomponius Mela's text began to circulate among an influential group of French scholars, most notably Cardinal Pierre d'Ailly, one of the first western European scholars to make use of it, and his friend and contemporary Cardinal Guillaume Fillastre, who had the work transcribed while he was attending the Council of Constance, and added a long introduction of his own.

Pomponius Mela was of little significance compared with Claudius Ptolemy, whose treatise on astronomy, the *Syntaxis Mathematica*, better known by its Arabic title of *Almagest*, had been recovered and absorbed by western European scholars in the twelfth century. Ptolemy's other great work, the *Geography*, which contained the best of classical learning on its subject, remained the preserve of Greek and Moslem scholars until 1406 when the Florentine scholar Jacopo Angelo de Scarperia brought a Greek manuscript of it to Italy from Constantinople. Angelo finished his Latin translation in 1410, and fifteenth-century geographical scholarship was then dominated by the need to assimilate the new information and methods found in Ptolemy, and to come to terms with some of his ideas which contradicted traditional opinions.

The two French cardinals again played an important role. Guillaume Fillastre introduced the new translation of Ptolemy's *Geography* to northern Europe when in 1418 he commissioned a copy of it at Constance for presentation to the cathedral library at Rheims, and in 1427 he was responsible for adding maps of Scandinavia, Iceland, and Greenland, newly drawn by the Danish scholar Claudius Clavus, to another copy of the *Geography*. Fillastre also added a commentary on the maps, but it was Pierre d'Ailly who was primarily responsible for the study of Ptolemy.

D'Ailly's concern with Ptolemy is vividly shown by the two treatises he composed, the *Imago Mundi* of about 1410, and the *Compendium Cosmographiae* of about 1414, the first written when his only knowledge of Ptolemy was the *Almagest*, and the second after he had read the new translation of the *Geography*. The *Imago Mundi* was so closely based on classical and biblical sources that it might have been written in the thirteenth century. D'Ailly did not mention any of the travellers of the previous two centuries, although he was aware of the works of Roger Bacon which, as shown earlier, did contain important new information. The *Compendium Cosmographiae* also employed ancient sources, but for the first time a European scholar was faced with a classical Greek treatise which provided co-ordinates of latitude and longitude for a great many places on the earth's surface. Such information was not new, having been available from Arabic sources since the twelfth century, and Ptolemy's calculations were not necessarily an improvement on these, which were themselves often inaccurate. D'Ailly did not make use of more than a few hundred of the thousands of co-ordinates supplied by Ptolemy, but the principle was important, and geographical scholarship could not avoid being influenced by it in the future.

Ptolemy stimulated thought but he also presented problems. D'Ailly found that Ptolemy's belief that the Indian Ocean was land-locked contradicted the commonly held medieval idea that Africa was surrounded by sea. There is no evidence that anyone, apart from the Vivaldi brothers in 1291, had thought of attempting to circumnavigate Africa, and there was certainly no appreciation that Africa extended so far south of the equator. Despite the opinions of some of the thirteenth- and fourteenth-century European travellers in India, the orthodox theoretical view, to which d'Ailly also adhered, was that in any case the equatorial zone could not be crossed because of the intense heat. None the less d'Ailly rejected Ptolemy's statement, and continued to believe that Africa and India were separated by sea. Ptolemy had also argued that the land mass incorporating Europe and Asia extended over approximately 180 degrees of latitude, or roughly half the circumference of the earth. This estimate was considerably in excess of the correct figure of about 130 degrees. However, the commonly accepted view in the early fifteenth century was one that came originally from Marinus of Tyre, a writer of the early second century AD whose work was known to and used by Ptolemy. According to Marinus, the extent of the land mass was about 225 degrees, which implied that the distance by sea between the easternmost part of Asia and the most westerly parts of Africa and Europe was even shorter. This line of reasoning, which reached Pierre d'Ailly, with refinements of argument, via Bacon's *Opus Maius*, was also accepted by him in preference to Ptolemy's conclusion.

As manuscript copies of Ptolemy's *Geography* began to multiply and circulate more widely, his work became the subject of intense scholarly debate. It was discussed, for example, by some of the churchmen who had gathered for the Council of Florence in 1439, and when, a few years later, the humanist Aeneas Sylvius, the future Pope Pius II (1458–64), wrote his *Historia Rerum Ubique Gestarum*, he relied heavily on Ptolemy. When scholars disagreed with Ptolemy they followed the same procedure as d'Ailly, and fell back on classical and biblical authorities rather than applying any contemporary evidence: in 1439 Ptolemy's ideas were compared with those of Strabo who had written a century before him. None the less, Ptolemy's place as a major authority on geography was secure, and with the appearance of the first printed edition of the *Geography* at Vicenza in 1475 he began to reach a growing audience.

Ptolemy's contribution to fifteenth-century scholarship was

not restricted to the text of the *Geography*. Jacopo Angelo's translation contained Ptolemy's elaborate gazetteer of geographical co-ordinates, but did not include the set of maps, a world map and twenty-six regional maps, which were associated with the work. The relationship between Ptolemy and the maps is uncertain: it is likely that the world map was drawn by his contemporary Agathodaimon of Alexandria, but it has been suggested that the regional maps may have been drawn as late as the thirteenth century, by the Byzantine scholar Maximos Planudes. By 1427 the text of the *Geography* had been reunited with the maps, and altogether nearly fifty manuscripts of this version of the work are extant. In 1477, only two years after the *Geography* had been printed for the first time, an edition complete with maps was published at Bologna, and was destined to be the first of many. It was also inevitable that attempts should be made to improve on Ptolemy's maps. The earliest known additions are the maps of Scandinavia which Guillaume Fillastre incorporated in 1427, but from the 1460s increasing numbers of new maps were added by the editors of successive editions.

Ptolemy's maps gave a great impetus to cartography in a purely descriptive sense, but the fact that they had been drawn using the co-ordinates of latitude and longitude contained in his gazetteer also encouraged a more systematic and scientific approach to cartography. Many of his co-ordinates were incorrect in themselves, while a further complication was introduced because of his underestimate of the length of a geographical degree, arising from his acceptance of Marinus of Tyre's estimate of the circumference of the earth as 180,000 stadia (a figure which originated with Posidonius in the second century BC) in preference to the far more accurate calculation of 250,000 stadia made by Eratosthenes. Despite this, Ptolemy's example stimulated the search for a more satisfactory way of representing the curvature of the earth upon a plane surface, culminating in Mercator's world map of 1569 which employed the first practical system of projection.

Ptolemy would not, however, have exercised so great an influence if a long tradition of map-making had not already existed in Europe when his *Geography* was first translated. Cartography was perhaps the only area of intellectual activity in medieval Europe in which a serious attempt was made to adapt the current view of the world to the discoveries reported by travellers and sailors. Even the *mappae mundi* sometimes have to be taken seriously. The Ebstorf and Hereford *mappae*, for example, of about 1240 and 1290 respectively, contain elaborate details of monstrous races, and also show the sites of New Testament events as if these were meant to be contemporary. It has, however, been strongly argued that the Hereford, and possibly the Ebstorf map as well, had the serious purpose of providing intineraries for pilgrims travelling from those cities to the Holy Land. This information may in its turn have been derived from something akin to the itineraries of the Roman Empire which were used by its soldiers and civil servants, and which are now represented only in the twelfth- or early thirteenth-century copy now known as the Peutinger Tables.

There were, however, apart from the *mappae mundi*, two other types of map in late medieval Europe. These were charts designed for use as practical aids to navigation at sea, and world maps which shared some of the characteristics of *mappae mundi*, but also attempted to show the world in a more realistic light. The nautical chart was the product of a line of development whose details are not known, since it grew out of the accumulated knowledge and experience of sailors which for centuries was probably committed only to memory, and not permanently recorded. In classical antiquity sailing directions and coastal descriptions were sometimes set down in the form of a *periplus*, of which the *Periplus of the Erythraean Sea*, dating from the first century BC, and describing the Red Sea and the Indian Ocean, is the most famous. It is not known when the practice of writing down sailing directions was resumed in Europe, but sailors' notebooks or *portolani* were certainly being produced during the thirteenth century at the latest, at the time when international trade in the Mediterranean basin was reaching its peak. As with many other things to do with commerce, Italy seems to have played an important part in their development. Most of them wore out with constant use, but one example, which probably survives only because it was especially elaborate, is the late thirteenth-century

Lo Compasso da Navigare. This contains a detailed account of the coastlines and harbours of the Mediterranean and Black Sea, following the 'compass' or 'circuit' clockwise from Cape St Vincent in Spain to Safi on the Atlantic coast of Morocco, the place where the Vivaldi brothers of Genoa were last seen in 1291 before they departed into the unknown.

On its own the portolan was little different from the classical *periplus*. Its transformation into a chart which could be used as part of a system of navigation came about through its combination with a number of other devices which were also appearing, or at least are first recorded, during the thirteenth century. In conjunction with the rough measurement of time permitted by a sand-glass, a traverse board made it possible for a navigator to estimate the distance sailed in a given time on a particular course; by the end of the thirteenth century written traverse tables were already becoming available. But the key to the entire system, without which no course could have been followed accurately, and no chart drawn, was the mariner's compass. It is not known for certain when and where a magnetized pointer was first used for finding direction in Europe, although there is a traditional association with the Italian trading city of Amalfi. The principle was already known in eleventh-century China, but no clear connection between its use in China and in Europe has ever been established: the earliest references to the compass as a navigational instrument in the intervening Moslem world come from Iran in 1232 and Egypt in about 1282, one probably referring to the Indian Ocean and the other mentioning its use in the Mediterranean about forty years before. The late twelfth-century *De Natura Rerum* by the English scholar Alexander of Neckham, and a poem of about 1205 by the French writer Guyot de Provins, show, however, that the compass was known in Christian Europe even earlier. All these references are literary in character, and it is likely that the compass was employed by sailors for some time before it was recorded on shore. The earliest form of compass was nothing more than a magnetized needle supported by a small piece of wood floating in a bowl of water, and was useful only to find the general direction of travel when skies were overcast. With the introduction of a pivoted needle and of a card marked with the cardinal points of the compass, and later with further subdivisions, the mariner's compass became a very practical means of navigation. It was a short but intellectually very important step to transfer the written information contained in a portolan into a drawing of the coastline on a piece of parchment on which one or more compass roses could be superimposed to show the point of bearing from one important harbour to another. With this the portolan chart came into being. Some kind of chart was in use on board the ship which carried Louis IX of France across the Mediterranean to Tunis in 1270, and the Franciscan Raymond Lull was aware of them by 1286. The first surviving example is the *Carte Pisane*, preserved in Pisa but probably drawn in Genoa late in the thirteenth century.

Very few portolan charts have survived from the fourteenth century since, like the portolans before them, they were subject to the wear and tear of everyday use. Those that are extant are associated mainly with draughtsmen working in Venice, Genoa, and Majorca, all of which were major centres of maritime activity. It is not known how rapidly charts entered widespread use, but in the case of Majorca a considerable encouragement to their production must have been given by the king of Aragon's decree in 1354 that every Aragonese galley should carry at least two charts. The areas covered by portolan charts ranged roughly from the Black Sea to the Baltic, though not necessarily all on the one chart. The amount of information provided, and the accuracy with which a particular coastline was depicted bore a close relation to the areas with which merchants had regular contacts. The south coast of England and the south and east coasts of Ireland, for example, are much more clearly recognizable than other stretches of coast often quite close at hand. Portolan charts did not allow for the errors inherent in trying to represent a curved surface on a plane one in the absence of a system of projection, so that the directional lines which extended from the compass roses drawn on the charts were not in fact lines of constant bearing as they appeared to be. Neither was any allowance made for the distinction between magnetic north and true north, a difference of about ten degrees to the east in the Mediterranean in the fourteenth century. However, the portolan charts covered a relatively narrow range of latitude, and these sources of error did not accumulate sufficiently to become a major problem for navigators. Thirteenth- and fourteenth-century charts were above all practical tools of navigation whose users were familiar with the seas and the coastlines depicted, and whose draughtsmen were ready to incorporate new and more accurate information as this became available. The portolan charts reveal by their very existence that medieval Europeans could be much more open-minded in their view of the world than literary or scholarly sources would imply.

Some of this flexibility of outlook was also transferred to maps made for other purposes. The Genoese cartographer Petrus Vesconte, for example, who had drawn the first known dated portolan chart in 1311, was commissioned in about 1320 by the Venetian Marino Sanudo to draw a set of maps to illustrate the crusading scheme advanced in his *Liber Secretorum Fidelium Crucis*. Another Genoese, Giovanni da Carignano, may have drawn a map in about 1310 which included some new material about East Africa derived from the recent visit to his city of an embassy from the Christian kingdom of Ethiopia. Later in the fourteenth century other maps began to appear which attempted to cover a larger part of the world than the portolan charts. One of these was the so-called Laurentian portolan of about 1351 with its controversial outline of Africa, which was discussed earlier (see Chapter 8); another was produced in Majorca in 1339 by Angelino Dulcert, which is probably a Catalan form of the name of Angellino Dalorto of Genoa.

Dalorto's presence is an indication of the attraction held by Majorca even for well-established Italian mapmakers. The extensive Aragonese trade throughout the Mediterranean, and its close connections with North Africa meant that a great deal of information was available there. Full advantage of this opportunity was to be taken in about 1375 by the king of Aragon's Jewish cartographer Abraham Cresques, who was probably responsible for the world map which was later presented to Charles V of France, and which has become famous as the Catalan world atlas. The 1375 map retained some features of the traditional *mappa mundi*: the term itself appeared in the map's title;

Jerusalem was located, if not at the centre of the map, then quite close to it; and although the map concentrated on a wide band of territory from the Atlantic in the west to the far east of China, so forming a rectangle in shape, a circular framework was also lightly traced around it. In its outline of the Mediterranean, the Black Sea, and western Europe the Catalan atlas followed the by now standard pattern of the portolan chart. Lack of precise information made it impossible to treat the coasts of Africa and Asia in the same way, but the cartographer none the less incorporated details obtained from the firsthand observations of travellers or from reports of past events. He was aware, for example, of the voyage of Jaime Ferrer in search of the River of Gold in 1346, and he depicted Mansa Musa, the ruler of the West African kingdom of Mali, who had passed through Cairo in 1324 on his way to Mecca. In the case of Asia he included the names of many of the important cities of central Asia and China: Peking, Kinsai, Canton, and Zayton are all mentioned. It seems likely that he had access to the narrative of Marco Polo's journeys, and perhaps to the reports of other eastern travellers. The political divisions of Asia recorded on the map were those governed by the Great Khan and his subordinate khans, a structure which had already passed from the scene when the map was drawn. There are many errors and ambiguities in the Catalan world atlas, but as a serious attempt to show the extent of fourteenth-century European knowledge of the world in pictorial form it is outstanding, and may be taken as a symbol of the medieval expansion of Europe as a whole. It is also a visual counterpart of the literary description of the world which was being presented in *Mandeville's Travels* at about the same time.

By comparison with the Catalan atlas some of the world maps of the fifteenth century appear to be very inferior products, but there were attempts to adapt medieval conceptions of the world to recent developments in theory and practical knowledge. The world map of the Venetian navigator Andrea Bianco was drawn in 1436 in conjunction with a set of conventional portolan charts, but in itself differed little from the one made by Petrus Vesconte in about 1320. Its main claim to fame now is that it may have been used much later as a basis for the production of the Vinland Map.

Bianco did, however, make up for this archaic production in 1448 when he drew a portolan chart while he was in London depicting recent Portuguese discoveries in the Azores and along the coast of West Africa. In that same year a German Benedictine, Andreas Walsperger, drew what amounts to a traditional *mappa mundi* with some modern features. Having claimed that 'this mappa mundi or geometrical description of the globe is made from the cosmography of Ptolemy proportionally according to longitude, latitude, and the divisions of climate', he included a representation of the terrestrial paradise and a number of the monstrous races. But in deference to newly found knowledge he located the apple-smellers, cyclopes, blemmyae, troglodytes, and others in the vicinity of the South Pole instead of their customary homelands in Africa and Asia.

The Genoese world map of 1457 is notable for recording details of the recently completed travels by the Venetian Nicolo Conti in India, Java, Sumatra, and the neighbouring islands, including the spice islands of the Moluccas. Conti's information was also made use of by the Venetian cartographer Fra Mauro for the world map which he was drawing when he died in 1459, and which was completed by another hand in the following year. Fra Mauro's captions emphasized the great wealth of the spice islands, and in one very significant comment he claimed that it was possible to sail into the Indian Ocean. His conclusion was based on a statement by Solinus rather than on any current evidence that Africa might be circumnavigated, but it showed a readiness to reject the authority of Ptolemy whose works were circulating freely by this time. Fra Mauro was also conscious from his reading of Marco Polo, the source of his information on China, that Ptolemy's framework did not allow adequate space for the proper representation of Asia.

Fifteenth-century cartography was in a limbo between the traditional schematic view of the world provided by the *mappae mundi*, the compass bearings and carefully drawn coastlines of the portolan charts, the attempts by Italian and Catalan cartographers to incorporate new information into their world maps, and the pervasive but also confusing influence of Claudius Ptolemy. Map-makers were doing their best under very trying circumstances: they were well aware that old ideas would have to be modified or discarded but could not yet decide on how they should be replaced. Meanwhile the navigators of Portugal and other European nations were undertaking voyages which would soon put the theories of scholars and the imaginings of literature severely to the test. With or without the discovery of the unsuspected American continent, Europe in the middle of the fifteenth century was rapidly entering upon, if not a new world, then certainly a radically altered perception of the old one.

V

The fifteenth-century expansion of Europe

12

Fresh start or new phase?

The standard treatment of the fifteenth-century expansion of Europe begins with the capture by the Portuguese in 1415 of the city of Ceuta on the Moroccan side of the Straits of Gibraltar, and proceeds with a description of the Portuguese progress by regular stages down the west coast of Africa until in 1498 Vasco da Gama sailed around the Cape of Good Hope, and reached the port of Calicut in India. Equally standard and equally familiar is the voyage of Christopher Columbus in 1492 which led to his discovery of the Bahamas, and so to that of the American continent. Sometimes, by way of introduction, a brief reference will be made to the exploits of an earlier generation of European travellers, such as Giovanni di Piano Carpini and Marco Polo. There may be a passing mention of the crusades, or of the quest for Prester John; or an account of the strange tales about the East contained in such works as *The Travels of Sir John Mandeville*.

There is no denying that great and stirring events did occur in and after 1415. It is equally true that the voyages of 1492 and 1498 set in train a series of developments of profound significance both for Europeans and for the peoples they encountered in America and in Asia: the circumnavigation of the globe by one of Magellan's captains, Sebastian del Cano, in the appropriately named *Victoria*, barely thirty years after the first voyage of Columbus, is suggestive of something dramatically new and original, as is the possible first sighting by the Portuguese in the early 1520s of the coastline of what later turned out to be Australia. The implication of these facts and of the way in which they are treated is that the overseas expansion which began in the fifteenth century was essentially a self-contained movement, to be explained by such contemporary factors as the Renaissance which inspired scholars and explorers to seek new intellectual and geographical horizons; a movement that was assisted by revolutionary new techniques in navigation, and by new designs of shipping; that was led by heroic men of vision such as Prince Henry of Portugal and Christopher Columbus; that was stimulated by the advance of the Ottoman Turks into Europe, and their interruption of the valuable trade in eastern spices. Seen in this light the fifteenth-century expansion is curiously lacking in antecedents. Vasco da Gama's voyage was at least a consequence of all that had happened since 1415, but the discoveries made by Columbus appear to have no antecedents at all, other than his careful annotation of the works of scholars whose arguments supported his case, and his persistence between 1484 and 1492 in trying to convince the rulers of Portugal, Castile, England, and France in turn that his scheme to reach Japan and Cathay by an ocean voyage to the west was soundly based.

Such a simplified account does no justice to the many eminent scholars who have studied the fifteenth-century expansion of Europe, and who are well aware both of the complexity of the events of the fifteenth century itself, and of the fact that these did not occur suddenly or in a vacuum. However, their work has not usually probed back very far before this period, while conversely, specialists in the earlier history of European expansion have not in general carried their studies much beyond 1400. In consequence the primary event of the capture of Ceuta in 1415 has lost little of its attraction as a historical turning-point.

The earlier chapters of this book have been written first of all to establish the extent of medieval Europe's external contacts. The second purpose has been to attempt to discover whether the new knowledge acquired by European travellers in Asia, Africa, and the North Atlantic was absorbed into the picture of the world presented in works of scholarship and literature. The results are necessarily impressionistic because of the enormous amount of potential evidence, and the complexity of the problem, but they strongly suggest that in the fifteenth century the 'European world-view', if such it can be called, was a mixture of theories and marvellous tales dating back to classical antiquity, together with recently rediscovered classical material such as the *Geography* of Ptolemy, and some, but by no means all, of the reports composed by thirteenth- and fourteenth-century travellers. The one remaining task is to examine the fifteenth-century expansion of Europe in the light of these conclusions, in order to decide whether it was, in fact, a new beginning in European relations with the outside world, as it usually appears, or whether it may legitimately be regarded as a new phase, with perhaps a fresh cast of actors drawn mainly from Portugal and Castile, but with its roots deeply embedded in previous European experience and conceptions. There is no simple answer, but it should already be apparent that some kind of connection between the two periods of European expansion did exist.

For the sake of clarity it is convenient for the moment to take the fifteenth-century expansion at its face value, and begin in traditional fashion with the capture of Ceuta in 1415. Ceuta was strategically sited at the entrance to the Mediterranean, which made it a natural starting-point for the systematic exploration of the Atlantic coastline of Africa in the years that followed. This movement was led in great part by Prince Henry of Portugal, who had earlier been at the siege of Ceuta. In 1419–20 the island of Madeira was colonized; in the mid-1420s the Portuguese attempted to occupy those islands in the Canary archipelago which had not already been claimed by Castile since the Bethencourt expedition of 1402; and the Azores were explored and occupied between 1427 and 1439. Progress down the African coast began in earnest in 1434 when one of Prince Henry's followers, Gil Eannes, succeeded in passing Cape Bojador, which hitherto had been a psychological as well as a physical barrier to navigation, and returned home to Portugal to report on his achievement. In 1444 the Portuguese navigators Nuno Tristão and Dinis Diaz, reached respectively the mouth of the Senegal river, and the Cape Verde islands, and at about the same time the first cargoes of gold and slaves were shipped back to Portugal, so turning exploration into a profitable venture. After the discovery of Sierra Leone in or shortly before 1460, the year of Prince Henry's death, progress slowed down until 1470–5 when the Gulf of Guinea was explored in a series of voyages which ended at a point four degrees to the south of the equator. The coastline, whose easterly direction in the Gulf had given the Portuguese hope that they were about to pass the southern tip of Africa, and enter the Indian Ocean, then turned southwards again at apparently interminable length which strained Portuguese patience almost to the limit. However, in 1483 Diogo Cão reached the mouth of the Congo river; in 1488 Bartholomew Diaz finally demonstrated that it was after all possible to circumnavigate Africa by his discovery of the Cape of Good Hope; and in July 1497, after careful preparations, Vasco da Gama left Lisbon on the voyage which took him to Calicut in India on 20 May 1498, and then back to Lisbon in the summer of 1499.

From 1441 the Portuguese voyages had been assisted, and indeed made feasible, by the widespread use of a new type of vessel known as the *caravel*, of about 50 tons in displacement, and with two masts, each bearing a triangular lateen sail, which allowed for great manœuvrability, making it ideal for the exploration of unfamiliar and often dangerous coastlines and river estuaries. The caravel was also able to sail against the wind, which permitted it to make return voyages between Portugal and the west coast of Africa despite the unfavourable winds and currents. As a design the caravel was a great improvement on earlier types of vessel, such as the galley which, although manœuvrable, needed a large crew to work it, and was therefore not suitable for long voyages away from a home port; or the single-masted sailing vessel with one large square sail which could not sail against the wind. The caravel was also capable of development. Towards the end of the fifteenth century larger versions of up to 200 tons, and with a third mast, were being constructed, allowing a longer range of operation when they were used for voyages of discovery, and also the carrying of profitable cargoes. When convenient it was also possible to change the caravel's sailing characteristics by altering its rig. The most famous example of this is Columbus's *Niña* which set out from Palos in August 1492 as a *caravela latina* with three masts, each carrying a lateen sail, and was converted in the Canaries to a *caravela redonda*, two of its masts probably being repositioned and equipped with square sails, retaining the lateen rig only on the mizen-mast. All of this was done with the aid of local shipwrights in the space of a week, and made the *Niña* more suitable for sailing across the Atlantic with a following wind.

There were also significant improvements in the techniques of navigation during the fifteenth century. A navigator's need to know his position, both for the present and to enable himself or others to return to it in the future, was partially met by the calculation of latitude. This was especially important for the Portuguese exploration of the coastline of Africa which, with the exception of the Gulf of Guinea, ran in roughly a north–south direction. North of the equator, and at night, latitude could be calculated by observing the height of the Pole Star above the horizon using a relatively simple instrument, the quadrant. The surviving evidence suggests that this method was in use by the mid-1450s when it was described by the Venetian, Alvise Cadamosto, who accompanied a number of Portuguese voyages at this period. But by this time the Portuguese were approaching the equator, and the Pole Star was too low in the sky to be used effectively in navigation. Unlike many of the thirteenth- and fourteenth-century European travellers to India, who had noted the disappearance of the Pole Star merely in passing, the Portuguese had to do something practical to replace it as a navigational aid, and this was achieved by making observations of the height of the sun by means of a more complicated instrument, the astrolabe. In 1484 King John II of Portugal appointed a commission of mathematicians to study and perfect this method, and then to draw up written tables of declination which could be used at sea. Such tables probably circulated in manuscript for some time before the appearance in 1509 of a printed version under the title of the *Regimento do astrolabio e do quadrante*. In the kingdom of Castile the foundation in 1502 of the *Casa de la Contratacion* had among its objects the training of navigators, the manufacture of instruments, and the making and frequent revision of a map, the *padron real*, to record the progress of discovery. The need for accurate methods of measuring time to allow the calculation of longitude while at sea was also understood by the end of the fifteenth century, while the phenomenon of magnetic variation, which made it dangerous to rely too heavily on a compass reading in unfamiliar waters, was also recognized and allowed for.

There is also evidence that the fifteenth-century voyages

undertaken by the Portuguese did owe something at least to contemporary scholarship. In 1428, for example, Prince Pedro of Portugal, the elder brother of Henry the Navigator, visited Florence to collect maps and other information which might be of value to the Portuguese enterprises; while in Venice he was also presented with a manuscript of Marco Polo. By the middle years of the century the Portuguese authorities were seeking guidance on the next stage in their quest for India, and in 1457 commissioned the Venetian monk and cartographer Fra Mauro to draw them a world map which embodied the results of their own discoveries, and those of other travellers. The map he sent to Lisbon in 1459 has been lost but another, probably very similar map, he was working on at the time of his death, shows that he made use of material drawn both from Marco Polo, and also from Nicolo Conti's report on India and the east which the latter had given to the humanist scholar and papal secretary Poggio Bracciolini after he returned home to Venice in 1444. At about the same time the Portuguese were also consulting the Florentine geographer Paolo Toscanelli on the best way to reach the east. His advice on the subject is known only from a copy of a letter dated 1474 which he wrote to Fernão Martins, one of the advisers of the King of Portugal. By the mid-1480s the Portuguese had accumulated enough expertise to dispense with external advisers, but the young Genoese navigator Christopher Columbus acquired a copy of Toscanelli's letter in 1483 or 1484, and added it to the material he was gathering from literary works such as Marco Polo, and from scholarly treatises such as those of Pierre d'Ailly and Aeneas Sylvius. It is also possible, though not provable, that the ideas of Columbus were influenced by Martin Behaim of Nürnberg, who produced the first known terrestrial globe in 1492.

However, this apparently straightforward picture of heroic leadership, technical advances, and intellectual stimulation is open to a number of important qualifications. The role of Prince Henry of Portugal, for example, while still seen as important, has been subjected to considerable reassessment. The traditional view that he gathered scholars, navigators, and cartographers around him at Sagres on the peninsula of St Vincent overlooking the Atlantic, that he was himself a man of profound learning, that he supervised the design of improved ships and instruments, and that his position as Protector of the university of Lisbon allowed him to encourage scientific learning there have been examined and found to have very little substance. There is no evidence that he had read any of the major classical or Arabic works on geography; it is not certain whether Ptolemy's *Geography* was available in Portugal during his lifetime, and it is not known whether he ever read the text of Marco Polo acquired by his brother Pedro; even the apparently close connection between Henry and the Majorcan school of cartography which was created by the migration to Portugal of Jafuda Cresques, the son of the probable maker of the Catalan world atlas, is uncertain. It has also been calculated that, of the thirty-five known voyages to the west coast of Africa between 1419 and 1460, the period of Henry's supposedly close supervision of all the details of exploration, only eight were certainly inspired directly by him; and of the total length of African coastline which was explored during these years, more than half was achieved between 1440 and 1449 when Henry's brother Pedro was regent of Portugal, and took charge of exploration. It is also significant that a greater distance was covered between 1469 and 1475, when the west African trade was leased to Fernão Lopes by Alfonso V of Portugal, on condition that he should explore a hundred leagues of coast a year, than in the entire forty years of Henry's activity.

There is also ample evidence of a flourishing maritime tradition in Portugal long before the time of Prince Henry. Portuguese ships and merchants were a familiar sight in many of the ports of northern Europe in the thirteenth century, while Lisbon was a natural stopping-place for Italian vessels *en route* from Genoa or Venice to London or Bruges; the creation in 1317 of a royal fleet, and of the office of admiral, were a recognition of Portugal's development as a state, and of the monarchy's desire to assert itself; from as early as 1377 the crown also offered a subsidy towards the construction of ships. This policy was, however, designed to encourage trade rather than to sponsor the building of any particular type of vessel, whether of novel or traditional design.

The ships used in the early stages of Portuguese expansion in the fifteenth century were single-masted vessels, which were also small enough to be rowed when necessary: these, the *bark* of about 25 tons, and the slightly larger *barinel*, had been sufficient to allow Gil Eannes to make his historic passage of Cape Bojador in 1434. The caravels which replaced them from 1441 were ordinary ships taken out of their existing service, and were not specially designed for the purpose at the behest of Prince Henry or anyone else. The first caravels had been fishing vessels in use off the Atlantic coasts of Spain and Portugal from as early as the thirteenth century.

Exactly how this early caravel developed into its fifteenth-century successor is unknown, but it is significant that between about 1250 and 1400 there was a great deal of experimentation in ship design both in the Mediterranean and on the Atlantic coasts of Europe, with the result that a multiplicity of designs came into being within the limits of a few basic types. The lateen sail, for example, which gave the caravel its manœuvrability, was a familiar feature of Arab shipping but had probably been in use in the Mediterranean in classical times; so had the galley powered by oars and sails, and the single-masted round ship with one big sail which was used for carrying cargo. In the thirteenth century new and larger versions of the galley were constructed in Genoa and Venice to meet the stresses of Atlantic sailing on voyages to England and the Low Countries, and with sufficient space to carry bulky cargoes of wool and cloth back to their home ports. In northern Europe the most common form of cargo vessel was the *cog*, which had been developed in the Baltic in the eleventh and twelfth centuries, and by the end of the thirteenth century had superseded the traditional Viking ship, the *knarr*, as a cargo carrier. In many respects the cog was like the Mediterranean round ship, but it embodied very significant improvements both in the handling of its single square sail, and also in its steering: the stern-post rudder was far more efficient than the older steering oar or board, and had probably been invented as early as the twelfth century. The cog is thought to have been introduced into the Mediterranean in about 1300, and added to the ingredients available to shipbuilders and shipowners trying to devise ships which would bring the greatest economic return or would be most suitable for particular sailing conditions.

A similar pattern of trial and error can be found in the case of navigation. Despite the undoubted intellectual and practical advances in navigation achieved in Portugal and Castile by the end of the fifteenth century, the new techniques were subject to severe limitations. Not all navigators were equally able to afford the expense of the new methods or, assuming that they could acquire an astrolabe and a book of tables, equally capable of using them. The use at sea of a complicated instrument such as the astrolabe was difficult even for a literate and highly trained navigator. In other cases new techniques developed on land for other purposes were slow in being applied at sea: although mariners' charts had existed in manuscript form since the thirteenth century, the first known printed chart for use at sea did not appear until as late as 1539; similarly, Mercator's projection of 1569, which had important implications for chart-making, was used only for world maps until 1599, when the English mathematician Edward Wright published his *Certaine Errors In Navigation*. The problem of calculating longitude was not solved at all until the invention of the marine chronometer by John Harrison in the eighteenth century. The second voyage of Captain Cook between 1772 and 1775 was the first occasion on which longitude could be calculated consistently and accurately over a long period of time.

With the exception of the Portuguese voyages from the 1480s onwards, most fifteenth-century exploration was based on methods and instruments, such as the compass, traverse board, lead, and portolan chart, which had been in use since at least the thirteenth century. Even the sophisticated astrolabe was not new, having existed since classical antiquity as a specialized instrument for use by land-based scholars and astronomers. One of the sources of theoretical information recommended for the training of navigators by the Portuguese royal commission in the 1480s was John Holywood's *De Sphaera Mundi*, which had been in circulation since the thirteenth century; a translation for use by seamen was printed in Lisbon in 1537; and it was still recommended as the best introduction to its subject by the English scholar John Dee as late as 1570.

Just as important as instruments were the accumulated experience and instinct of individual navigators who brought navigation by dead reckoning to a fine art. One way of transmitting such knowledge was through books of sailing directions and coastal descriptions, known according to country as *rutters*, *routiers*, or *roteiros*, which began to appear in northern Europe and along the Atlantic coastline in the fifteenth century at a time when charts were still little used in these areas. They were the northern equivalent of the portolans which had long been used in the Mediterranean. One of the best known examples is *Le routier de la mer*, composed by Pierre Garcie in France in 1483–4, which gave instructions for sailing around the coasts of England and Wales, France, Portugal, and Spain, as far as Gibraltar. This was printed in 1502, and a translation of a later enlarged version of 1520 was published in England in 1528 as *The Rutter of the Sea*. Because of their geographical location Spanish and Portuguese sailors were ideally placed to gain the benefits of the new and traditional methods of navigation used in both the Mediterranean and along the Atlantic coastline, but for many sailors the old rough-and-ready methods remained the rule.

Even a navigator of the fame and achievement of Columbus can be included in the latter category. Although he carried a quadrant with him on his first crossing of the Atlantic in 1492, he does not appear to have used it to obtain his latitude. Since he had no means of calculating longitude, and also little prior knowledge of the winds and currents that he would meet on the journey, he had no choice but to use all the skill at dead-reckoning navigation he had acquired during his career. It is little wonder that Columbus's estimates of his position were often little more than inspired guesses. Nor is it surprising that, although modern scholars are certain that his first landfall, at the island which he named San Salvador, in October 1492, was somewhere in the Bahamas, there is still no agreement as to which island it was. The recent revival of an argument first stated in the nineteenth century that San Salvador should be identified with the modern Samana Cay rather than the usual Watling Island has provoked a heated debate.

By contrast the fifteenth-century Portuguese navigators, the main thrust of whose voyaging was from north to south rather than from east to west, were greatly assisted by the technique of latitude sailing which they developed during the century; for them knowledge of longitude was of less immediate importance until they reached the Indian Ocean. Even when they did so, they were able to draw, as did Vasco da Gama in 1498, on the fruits of the long experience of Arab navigators in these waters. The Portuguese also accumulated a considerable knowledge of winds and currents during their exploration of the coast of West Africa. This led to the classic manœuvre known as the *volta da Guiné*, involving a wide sweep out to sea when returning to Portugal from the African coast, so that the final approach to Lisbon was made from the west rather than from the south. In 1487 and in 1498 both Diaz and da Gama employed a similar technique in the southern hemisphere by sailing far west into the Atlantic (in da Gama's case almost as far as Brazil) before turning eastwards towards the Cape of Good Hope. In some respects the confidence engendered by such mastery of ocean sailing was a more important and original contribution to fifteenth-century navigation than the more obvious scientific techniques, which were difficult to master, and often slow to be adopted.

The influence of Renaissance scholarship on the fifteenth-century discoveries also requires some qualification. As a fundamental explanation of the discoveries the Renaissance may safely be ruled out. Scholarly support seems only to have been called into play in pursuit of objectives and ambitions that had already been established for quite different reasons, and when it did have an influence this was often as confusing as it was enlightening. When, for example, the Portuguese were told by Fra Mauro that it should be possible to circumnavigate Africa in order to reach the east, they had to set this opinion alongside both the knowledge that they had themselves already gained about Africa, and the powerful authority of Ptolemy's *Geography* according to which such a voyage was impossible. There was the additional problem that Fra Mauro was unable to express a clear opinion on the size of the globe because of the conflicting statements he had found on the matter.

The Portuguese were faced with the further confusion caused by the contradictory opinion of Toscanelli that the best way to reach the East would be to sail westwards. He calculated that the distance from Lisbon to Kinsai on the coast of Cathay, which was known from Marco Polo's account of it, would be no more than 5,000 nautical miles. Even this distance would be easier to cover because ships could stop *en route* at the island of Antilia, which was thought to exist in the Atlantic, and also at Cipangu or Japan, which was known to exist from Marco Polo's account of it, but which neither he nor any other European traveller had actually visited. Toscanelli's estimate was less than half the true distance, and unbeknown to him or anyone else an entirely new and unexpected continent lay in the way. Toscanelli's opinion was rejected in Lisbon, where enough information had probably been gathered from other sources to suggest that he was underestimating the difficulty of a westwards voyage. Having made a difficult but perfectly reasonable decision to dismiss Toscanelli's ideas, the Portuguese were then succeeded by Columbus for whom Toscanelli was exactly the inspiration he was seeking. In his reading of Ptolemy's *Geography*, and Pierre d'Ailly's *Compendium Cosmographiae* Columbus found estimates that the world's land mass extended over either 180 or 225 degrees of the earth's circumference. Both estimates were greatly in excess of the true figure, but Columbus then proceeded on the basis of his reading of Marco Polo to reduce the width of the ocean still further, until by a series of ingenious calculations he was able to convince himself that even Toscanelli's estimate of distance was excessive. Columbus's ideas were accordingly a mixture of both fifteenth-century and classical ideas which he proceeded to treat in a highly individual fashion, compounding the errors of his sources with his own private obsession. It is little wonder that the Portuguese scholars to whom he submitted his plans in 1484 recognized them as a new version of Toscanelli's earlier scheme, and rejected them out of hand.

By 1484 the Portuguese were almost certain that a little more effort would bring them around Africa, and into the Indian Ocean, and so to the wealth of the east. From our knowledge that they did in fact succeed in doing this in 1498, it is easy to assume that India was the destination at which Portuguese expansion was directed from the very beginning in 1415. There is a sense in which this was true, and to which it will be necessary to return later in the chapter, but it is altogether too simple to see the capture of Ceuta in this light alone. At one level the events of 1415 were no more than yet another of the many military expeditions which various European powers had undertaken since the early eleventh century against strong points on the coast of North Africa, and especially against those which influenced control of the straits of Gibraltar. As far back as the 1340s Portugal appears to have harboured ambitions against Morocco.

Just why the Portuguese chose to attack Ceuta when they did is more difficult to answer. The desire of James I of Portugal to give his three sons, Edward, Pedro, and Henry, the chance to prove their worthiness for knighthood on the battlefield is one reason given later by Prince Henry's biographer Azurara. Although it is unlikely that such a large expedition would have been mounted for this reason alone, there is probably more to commend it than many historians will allow. It is also likely that Portugal, which had confirmed its political independence from Castile at the battle of Aljubarrota as recently as 1385, wished to share in the spoils of Moslem North Africa before these fell to their rivals, Aragon and Castile. In some respects the king of Portugal was in 1415 in the same position as his cousin Henry V of England, as the leader of a newly established dynasty, with energy to spare and ambitions to fulfil. As a wealthy city, and with access to the grain-growing areas of Morocco, Ceuta was an ideal target. The city was to be held by the Portuguese, if only with difficulty, even after the failure of their attempt in 1437 to capture the nearby port of Tangier. Expansion in North Africa of the traditional kind was to remain an object of Portuguese policy throughout the fifteenth century, coexisting with, and sometimes competing for resources with, the exploration of the west coast of Africa. Portuguese interest in North Africa did not cease until the destruction of the army of King Sebastian at Alcazar in Morocco in 1578.

Ceuta was certainly a wealthy city in 1415, and gold was no doubt found among its plunder, but the suggestion that the

Portuguese took Ceuta in order to gain control of the Saharan gold trade, or that they first heard of the trade after capturing the city, and so were motivated to track the gold to its source in West Africa by means of maritime exploration is seriously misleading. Portugal was indeed short of gold bullion to finance its international trade, and the quest for gold was certainly one of the major reasons for the fifteenth-century Portuguese voyages, but the existence of the gold had been known for centuries through the commercial contacts between the Iberian peninsula and Morocco, and it was equally well known that the gold came from somewhere beyond the Sahara whose trade routes no Christian merchant could hope to follow. Merely capturing a Moroccan port would have no significance in getting to the source of the gold, while its role as a Mediterranean outlet for the Saharan caravans would at once be taken over by other Moslem-controlled centres. Rumours about a gold-rich kingdom to the south of the Sahara, to which the Berber-derived name of 'Guinea' was given, had been current in the Iberian peninsula since at least the early fourteenth century. No European is known to have penetrated to Guinea to test the truth of the rumours, but the voyage of Jaime Ferrer in search of the 'River of Gold' had been one attempt to do so, and was recorded on the Catalan world atlas. The Portuguese probably knew well before 1415 that the only hope of reaching the source of the gold was to go by sea, and this policy was duly vindicated in the 1440s when the first cargoes of West African gold began to be shipped back to Portugal. Neither the Portuguese nor any of their later European rivals ever discovered the actual source of the gold, any more than the Moslems of North Africa had, but they were at least able to tap their share of the trade without having to go through Moslem middlemen.

The Portuguese navigation of the waters of the Atlantic off the west coast of Africa and the western shores of Europe, which appears to be such an original feature of the fifteenth-century expansion, was not based just on the existence of a long maritime tradition, but also upon the extensive experience which they or their agents had accumulated in these same waters during the fourteenth century. The earlier discoveries of the Canaries, and probably of both Madeira and the Azores were not exploited during the fourteenth century, and particularly in the case of the Azores, which may have been discovered by accident, the locations of the islands were probably not known with any great accuracy. None the less it is likely that some memory of them remained in the early fifteenth century, so that the Portuguese expeditions to Madeira in 1419–20, and the occupation of the Azores after 1427 were really rediscoveries. The one significant difference was that they now began to be settled and exploited. Madeira, for example, was to be planted with sugar cane for which there was a ready market in Europe, and for which the nearby African coast supplied the labour, in the form of slaves, which would not have been available in Portugal itself.

In all the cases so far cited, their conquest of Ceuta, their quest for West African gold, and their exploitation of the Atlantic islands, the Portuguese were pursuing policies whose origins can be found well before the fifteenth century; each policy was perfectly comprehensible in itself, and in no case is it necessary to assume that an ambition to open a new sea route to India played any part. There is, however, another important dimension of Portuguese activity which also seems to have little or nothing to do with India. Given that the Portuguese gained considerable experience of Atlantic navigation in the fourteenth century, it is reasonable to ask whether they extended their knowledge of the Atlantic in the fifteenth century, and whether in particular they may have anticipated the rediscovery of America by Columbus. Some Portuguese historians have argued very strongly that they did so, but their conclusions have sometimes gone further than the limited evidence will allow. In some cases their insistence that the Portuguese monarchy imposed a strict policy of silence upon its navigators, and an embargo upon passing information to those of other nations has almost led to the conclusion that the less evidence there is for fifteenth-century Portuguese voyaging in the Atlantic, the more likely it is to have taken place. Seen in this light, modern Portuguese claims have often been dismissed as preposterous, but it is fair to say that there is at least a genuine problem.

The European perception of the Atlantic at the end of the

fourteenth century was not necessarily one of a vast and hostile desolation, a 'green sea of darkness', but rather of the existence of numerous islands. Many of these, such as Iceland and the Faeroes in the North Atlantic, and the Canaries further south, were known to exist; others, such as the islands of Brasil, St Brendan, and Antilia, were commonly thought to exist. Of the latter three, the first two arose from legends of Irish origin, while Antilia was associated with a tale about Christians who had allegedly fled there from the Arab invaders of the Iberian peninsula. When nautical charts began to be drawn during the fourteenth century all of these islands, both real and imaginary, duly appeared also.

The discovery of an Atlantic chart dated 1424, and drawn by the Italian cartographer Zuana Pizzigano, prompted its editor, Professor Armando Cortesão, to argue that the appearance on it of the island of Antilia could best be explained on the assumption that the Portuguese had made a recent, and otherwise unknown, discovery of land in the western Atlantic. There is no way of proving this argument, and it is more likely that Antilia is yet another example of the marking of an island on a map in the hope that time would show whether it really existed. On the other hand, there is a real problem to be answered, since the Portuguese did know the Azores which lay out in the Atlantic about 1,000 miles west of Portugal; and since the full extent of the Azores was not immediately apparent when the Portuguese began to explore them in 1427, there was a strong incentive for further Atlantic exploration. The last two islands in the group, Flores and Corvo, were discovered by Diego de Teive as late as 1452. There are several other known voyages in the waters around the Azores, culminating in 1487 in the voyage planned by Ferdinand van Olmen, a Flemish settler on the island of Terceira who is better known as Fernão Dulmo, the Portuguese form of his name. The Portuguese crown authorised van Olmen to sail to the west of the Azores for a period of forty days, but nothing is known of the fate of the expedition, or even whether it set out. None of this evidence proves that the Portuguese actually did find land in the Atlantic beyond the Azores, but there is no doubt that their previous experience of the Atlantic, and their own and other peoples' belief in additional islands only awaiting discovery were strong incentives to further exploration: both de Teive in 1452 and van Olmen in 1487, the latter only five years before the voyage of Columbus, gave the island of Antilia as the object of their search.

However, another line of approach has been to suggest that the Portuguese may have learnt of the existence of new lands in the Atlantic from contacts with Scandinavia. It has, for example, been argued that in the early 1470s João Vas Corte Real, another settler from Terceira in the Azores, visited Denmark, and from there made a voyage to Greenland and Newfoundland, in the company of Didrick Pining and Hans Pothorst, two Germans in Danish service. Two of Corte Real's sons, Gaspar and Miguel, were later to be involved in voyages to Newfoundland in 1501 and 1502, but the evidence for a voyage in the 1470s is based only on sixteenth-century sources, and has not stood up to scrutiny.

Quite apart from the question of Portuguese navigation in the North Atlantic, the Corte Real story also assumes that one at least of the former Viking homelands was still active in Atlantic exploration in the fifteenth century, whereas the Danish interest seems to have been restricted to a tenuous relationship with its dependency of Iceland. Contact with Greenland cannot be demonstrated after the very early fifteenth century, and if it took place at all, was probably very haphazard. Even the splendidly seaworthy Viking ships which had been the indispensable instrument of the Vikings' discoveries in the tenth and eleventh centuries had passed out of use for deep sea work by the end of the thirteenth century, in favour of less exciting but more profitable cargo-carrying vessels like the cog.

While Scandinavia appears to have contributed nothing directly to the fifteenth-century expansion of Europe, it is still possible that sailors from other European nations may have picked up surviving traditions about Greenland, and even about Markland and Vinland during visits to Iceland. It is well established that from about 1408 fishermen and traders from ports in eastern England, and from Bristol and South Wales, were visiting Iceland, despite repeated prohibitions issued by both the Danish and the English governments. Dutch and German vessels were also involved in the Icelandic trade. It has also been suggested that English and other ships might occasionally have been to Greenland in search of trading opportunities.

By about 1480 conflict between the English and Danish authorities in Iceland had led to the exclusion of English sailors from those waters, and it is possible that this led some of them to look for alternative sources of profit in the North Atlantic. Professor D. B. Quinn's discovery of the record of an official inquiry held at Bristol in 1481 into the recent voyage of two Bristol vessels, the *Trynite* and the *George*, for the purpose 'of examining and finding a certain island called the Isle of Brasil' somewhere to the west of Ireland, opened a fruitful but so far inconclusive line of research. The problem was further complicated when Dr L. A. Vigneras discovered in the archives of the kingdom of Castile a letter from a certain John Day to the Lord Grand Admiral of Castile. Intensive research on this document has shown that John Day was a London merchant named Hugh Say, that his correspondent was almost certainly Christopher Columbus himself, and that it was written in 1497 after the return of Columbus from his second voyage, and shortly after the return of John Cabot from his first voyage of discovery to Newfoundland on behalf of the English crown. The significant part of the letter is the statement that: 'It is considered certain that the cape of the said land was found and discovered in the past by the men from Bristol who found "Brasil" as your Lordship well knows. It was called the Island of Brasil and it is assumed and believed to be the mainland that the men from Bristol found.' The implications are clear that sailors from Bristol really had discovered something in the Atlantic at an unspecified date before 1497, and that Columbus already knew of this. Whether this event had occurred at the time of the 1481 voyage or shortly thereafter, and whether Columbus had already heard about it before he sailed in 1492 cannot be proved. It has, however, been suggested by Professor Quinn that the Bristol voyages in the 1480s may themselves have owed something to information picked up in the course of trade with Portugal, as well as to the voyages to Iceland.

It is clear, then, that in the fifteenth century there was intense interest in the waters of the Atlantic, and that one of the most powerful incentives for Atlantic exploration was the quest for islands, of which there seemed to be no end. The best conclusion that one can reach is that, although there is no convincing evidence of a European crossing of the Atlantic between the last recorded Viking visit to Markland in 1347 and the first voyage of Columbus in 1492, it is none the less possible that someone had preceded Columbus in the fifteenth century. Even if Columbus himself had not discovered the New World in 1492, it seems that someone was going to do so, and sooner rather than later.

Columbus too had been influenced by rumours about the islands of the Atlantic, but the main thrust of his ambition was to reach the mainland of Asia, using the islands as convenient stopping places *en route*. In itself his plan to reach Asia by a westerly route was not as revolutionary as it is usually made to appear. As we saw in chapter 10, it had long been a commonplace of thought that the world was a sphere, and that it might therefore be possible to circumnavigate it. To the opinions cited earlier we may add the fictional account of a voyage around the encircling world ocean by the highly imaginative author of the eighth-century *Cosmography* ascribed to Aethicus Ister; and behind all these views there lay much older authorities such as Aristotle, or the Old Testament author of the Book of Esdras. By the fifteenth century a circumnavigation of the earth or a direct voyage from Europe to Asia seems to have become as much a literary topos as it was a scientific theory. The real question was whether or not it was a practical proposition, and on this there was room for widely differing opinions.

Although they rejected Columbus's plan, the Portuguese were also seeking a sea route to the riches of Asia. While Portuguese involvement in North Africa, their exploration of the coast of West Africa, and their voyaging in the Atlantic can all be explained without reference to any quest for India and for the East in general, there was nonetheless a profound underlying interest in the East from the very beginning, which took an increasingly precise form as the Portuguese learnt more about the African coastline, and it began to seem that a sea route around Africa to India was a real possibility. The discovery of the New World at the end of the century helps to obscure the fact that

Asia, whether it be defined as India or as the empire of the Great Khan in Cathay, was the main objective of the fifteenth-century expansion of Europe. It was in this area of activity that there was the greatest degree of continuity between the experiences of the European land travellers of the thirteenth and fourteenth centuries, and the sea travellers of the fifteenth. The surviving evidence on the activities of European missionaries shows that they were present in China and in Central Asia until very nearly the end of the fourteenth century and in some areas in the vicinity of the Black Sea until well into the fifteenth century. A similar pattern is observable in the operations of European merchants in the Far East, India, Iran and around the Black Sea. It was in Asia that the legendary Prester John, the hoped for saviour of the Holy Places, had been sought for until the early decades of the fourteenth century, and it was there too that the Mongol rulers of Iran and the Great Khan himself in Cathay, whom it had been hoped would be real military allies against Islam, were located. Asia and its wonders figured largely in the commonly available literature of the later middle ages, in works such as Marco Polo's *Divisament dou Monde* or *The Travels of Sir John Mandeville*, which played a large part in influencing fifteenth-century European expectations of the outer world.

These conclusions are apparently contradicted by the fact that in the early fifteenth century, when the Portuguese voyages of discovery were getting under way, the continent of Asia was in some respects less accessible to Europeans and to Christians than it had been for several centuries. The European colonial states in the eastern Mediterranean, which had been one of the major consequences of the crusading movement at the end of the eleventh century, had finally been extinguished in 1291, leaving the island of Cyprus ruled over by the titular kings of Jerusalem, as one of their few tangible relics. The kingdom of Cilician Armenia, which had been a bulwark of Christianity at the junction between Asia Minor and Syria, and a point of entry into western Asia for European merchants and missionaries, was overrun by Egypt in 1375. The Mongol empire, whose control of most of Asia had made possible the extraordinary extension of European horizons in the thirteenth and fourteenth centuries, had passed into oblivion well before 1400. At the same time the Ottoman Turks were profiting by the weakness of the Mongols and the Byzantine empire to expand their dominions in Asia Minor, and to pose a threat both to Constantinople, which they took in 1453, and to Europe itself. At the end of the fourteenth century there was a new wave of Mongol conquest under the command of Tamerlane, which chiefly affected central Asia and Syria, making travel in these regions even more precarious and difficult. There was also the fact that from the middle of the fourteenth century Europe had undergone the effects of a prolonged economic crisis and the devastations of plague. Christendom, whose boundaries had once seemed about to embrace all Christian communities throughout the known world, was now thoroughly fragmented and driven in upon itself, becoming virtually synonymous with Europe. Nothing might seem more unlikely than a continued European involvement with Asia, but there is no doubt that this occurred, to some extent in the realm of ideas, impressions, and memories of what was still a recent past, but also in the form of actual material contacts with the fringes of Asia in the eastern Mediterranean, with central Asia and India, and even with areas farther afield.

Modern scholarship beginning with the work of A. S. Atiya in 1938 and now supported by a steadily increasing amount of published research, has shown for example that the crusade survived the débâcle of the loss of Acre in 1291 both as an ideal, and as an actual military movement. The crusading projects that were advanced in the early decades of the fourteenth century by such men as Marino Sanudo and Raymond Lull were by no means the last of their kind. Philippe de Mézières, the French-born chancellor of Peter I of Cyprus, spent much of his long career in trying to persuade the rulers of western Europe to make peace, so that they could undertake a new crusade. His Order of the Passion, to which he succeeded in recruiting a number of the leading nobles of France and England by 1395, was designed to aid the Holy Land, and it occupied his energies until his death in 1405. The visit to the Holy Land and Egypt in 1421–3 by the Burgundian knight Ghillebert de Lannoy, was devoted to collecting information which might assist a future crusade. Between 1433 and 1439 another Burgundian, Bertrand de la Broquière, visited both the Holy Land and the Turkish dominions in Asia Minor and the Balkans with the same purpose. His opinion was a negative one, but as late as 1452 his master, Duke Philip the Good of Burgundy, appointed one of his bishops to co-ordinate the crusade, and the latter also wrote a treatise on how to undertake it. Aeneas Sylvius, who became Pope Pius II, in 1458, was another crusading propagandist, but by his time the retaking of the Holy Land had to be abandoned in the face of the more immediate danger from the Turks in Europe.

In the fourteenth century one of the major objectives of the Avignon papacy had been the organization of a new crusade, a policy which was made all the more difficult after England and France went to war in 1337, forcing the abandonment of the crusade that Philip VI of France had been planning since 1331. No crusading expedition actually went to the Holy Land, but crusading was conducted on a number of other fronts. Participation in the Baltic crusade was a summer-time sport for members of the western European nobility, such as Earl Henry of Derby, the future Henry IV, who went to Prussia in 1390 and 1392; there were major expeditions against the Turks in Smyrna in 1344, against Alexandria in 1365, and Tunis in 1390. In 1396 an army of French and Burgundian knights, together with contingents from many other parts of Europe, met and was disastrously defeated by the Turks at Nicopolis on the Danube; and in the Iberian peninsula there was the continuing war of the *Reconquista*, which was conducted in the fifteenth century against the kingdom of Granada, the one remaining Moslem stronghold. Granada eventually fell in 1492 to the combined forces of Castile and Aragon, but in 1433 it had been an open question whether Portugal should attack Granada, either in addition to its existing policy of conquest and exploration in Africa, or as an alternative to it.

The crusade was then an idea which was still very familiar to late medieval Europe as a whole, despite the growing impracticability of reconquering the Holy Land, but it had a particular appeal in the Iberian peninsula where the Holy War had a continuous existence dating back to well before the beginning of the crusades in the eleventh century. The military religious orders which had grown up in the kingdom of Castile to prosecute the war against Islam had their Portuguese counterpart in the Order of Christ, founded in 1319, of which Prince Henry the Navigator was later to be the governor. The depiction of Henry as a crusader by his biographer Azurara, which may seem anachronistic and contrary to his image as a 'Renaissance man', accordingly has a good deal to commend it. It is also arguable that when the Portuguese fleet used its superior fire-power at the battle of Diu in 1509 to establish naval control in the Indian Ocean, its commander was unconsciously fulfilling some of the crusading schemes put forward between 1290 and 1330 for the destruction of Moslem commerce.

Just as the practice of pilgrimage to the Holy Land and the development of international trade in the eastern Mediterranean had anticipated the beginning of the crusades in the eleventh century, so too they continued long after the loss of Acre in 1291. The Holy Places were visited throughout the fourteenth and fifteenth centuries by numerous Christian pilgrims, such as the Irish Franciscan Symeon Semeonis in 1323–4, the German William of Boldensele in 1333, and the Florentine Lionardo Frescobaldi in 1384. For a time, in the late thirteenth and early fourteenth centuries, European trade with Moslem Egypt declined, partly because of the papal embargo on commerce, but also because of the existence of alternative routes through the Mongol dominions. As the Mongol empire collapsed, European trade with the Moslem-held ports of the eastern Mediterranean resumed, and was to continue on a large scale during the fourteenth and fifteenth centuries. In the 1440s, for example, the great French merchant and financier Jacques Coeur, whose money helped to pay for the reconquest of Normandy from England, was doing business directly with Alexandria in Egypt, and also with Syria. But he was exceptional, and for the most part trade with the Moslem world was carried out, as it always had been, by Italian merchants, especially those of Venice. The coming of the Turks seems to have had little effect on the eastern trade even after the fall of Constantinople in 1453, since Egypt was and remained the focal point of the commerce in spices and other luxury goods from farther Asia. Ironically it was not the Turks but the Portuguese who disrupted the spice trade, both by their opening of the direct sea route to India in 1498, and by the extension of their naval power over the carrying trade of the Indian Ocean in the following years.

Although the collapse of the Mongol empire and the conquests by the Ottoman Turks and Tamerlane created barriers to European penetration of Asia, there were none the less contacts during the fifteenth century with both central Asia and India which helped to preserve recollections of the earlier much closer relations, and so prepared the way for the resumption of European involvement with Asia from the end of the century. The Bavarian Johann Schiltberger, who was captured by the Turks at Nicopolis in 1396, and then captured again by Tamerlane at Ankara in 1402, spent the next twenty-five years in the service of his captors in various parts of central Asia, and in Siberia, Egypt, and Arabia, before making his escape in 1427. After his return he wrote an account of his experiences which appears to have circulated widely in manuscript, and was printed as early as about 1473: the owner of one fifteenth-century manuscript had it bound up with other important works on travel, including Marco Polo, Mandeville, and St Brendan. Another early fifteenth-century visitor to central Asia was Ruy Gonzales de Clavijo, who was sent as an envoy to the court of Tamerlane in Samarkand in 1403 by Henry III of Castile, and returned to Spain in 1406. While at the city of Sultaniyeh, the former capital of the Il-khans of Iran, Clavijo became aware of the trade which came by sea from China to Ormuz on the Persian Gulf, and he noted the presence even at this date of Genoese and Venetians, and of the continuing trade with Christian-held ports such as Caffa in the Crimea and Trebizond on the Black Sea. As a source of information on central Asia at a time of turmoil Clavijo's account has something in common with those written at the time of the Mongol conquests in the thirteenth century, and also shows its author as a man of considerable powers of observation.

One of the most remarkable and most important of the fifteenth-century travellers in Asia was the Venetian, Nicolo Conti, who left home in 1419 on a journey to Syria which then extended into an extraordinary series of wanderings which took him to India, Ceylon, Sumatra, Java, Burma, Malaya, and finally back to the Holy Land via the Indian Ocean and the Red Sea, arriving back in Venice in 1444. In the account he gave of his travels to Poggio Bracciolini, Conti spoke of the wealth of the spice islands of the East, perpetuated the traditional but very confusing description of the three Indias, and claimed that Cathay, or China, which he had not visited, was still ruled by the Great Khan from his capital at Peking. Since Conti's information passed into the general knowledge and the cartography of the time, it is likely that he was responsible, along with the much earlier work of Marco Polo, for some of the erroneous conceptions of the Far East which were held by Columbus and other explorers at the end of the fifteenth century.

The quest for an eastern alliance, which had been an important feature of European relations with Asia, and especially with the Mongol rulers of Iran, in the thirteenth and early fourteenth centuries, also had a fifteenth-century sequel. One form in which it was expressed was in the Venetian attempt to enlist the aid of the new rulers of Iran against the Turks. Caterino Zeno was sent to Tabriz for this purpose in 1471, and was followed in 1474 by Josafat Barbaro and Ambrogio Contarini. None of these embassies had any success. On the other hand there is ample evidence of a continuing interest in the long-established legend of the Christian ruler Prester John, whose kingdom was now thought to lie in Africa. The search for Prester John had much to do with the attempted reunion of the Latin and Coptic churches at the Council of Florence in 1442; it lay behind the tour of Europe which was undertaken by Prince Pedro of Portugal between 1428 and 1437, and also behind the fictional visit he made to the land of Prester John in the Indies, described in the literary work of Gomez de Santisteban published in 1515.

These considerations help to explain the hope of Henry the Navigator, as described by his biographer Azurara, that his explorations of the west coast of Africa would reveal the presence of potential Christian allies, and also offer an indication of the place that India held in the fifteenth-century Portuguese ambitions. The key is to be found in the vagueness, discussed in an earlier chapter, with which commonly used geographical expressions were defined, and in particular the terms 'Ethiopia' and 'India'. Given the almost complete ignorance in Europe of the internal geography and political organization of the African continent, it was perfectly reasonable to assume that the Christian kingdom of Ethiopia, which was known to exist somewhere in the eastern part of Africa, might be found to extend right across the continent from east to west. To add to the confusion, Ethiopia was also often referred to as Middle India, as part of the long-standing concept of the three Indias which covered a geographical range from Africa to the Far East. In this sense India, as a distant and ill-defined destination, was probably a factor in Portuguese plans from the very beginning of the fifteenth century.

The bull of Pope Nicholas V in 1454, which granted the Portuguese rights over all their discoveries *usque ad Indos*, is consistent with this traditional view of India. However, it was also from the 1450s that the Portuguese were beginning to think of India as a real destination which might be reached by sea, since this was the time when they began to consult foreign experts such as Fra Mauro and Toscanelli on the best route to the east. The Portuguese were already aware of the voyages which had been made down the west coast of Africa in the fourteenth century, and may have suspected that Cape Bojador itself had been passed long before 1434, while the highly implausible claim by the Genoese business man Antonio Usodimare that he had met a descendant of one of the Vivaldi brothers when he visited West Africa with a Portuguese expedition in the 1450s, does at least suggest that their attempt to reach India by circumnavigating Africa in 1291 was still remembered.

By the 1480s there was no question but that Portugal was determined to open a practicable sea route to India, and it was in 1487 that three separate but closely connected expeditions were sent out: that of Ferdinand van Olmen into the Atlantic west of the Azores, which was ostensibly intended to look for the island of Antilia, but may also have been an attempt to gather evidence on a possible western route to Asia; that of Bartholomew Diaz which actually succeeded in proving that Africa could be circumnavigated; and finally the mission of Pero da Covilhã to the east.

Covilhã and his companion Afonso de Paiva were assigned the
dual task of trying to reach the kingdom of Prester John in
Ethiopia, and of finding out details of the routes by which spices
reached Egypt from the East. The history of their mission is
controversial, but it is likely that Paiva died in Cairo, possibly
after visiting Ethiopia. Covilhã visited Calicut and Goa in India,
and probably also Sofala in East Africa, before going back to
Cairo, and then to Mecca, which was thought in Europe to be a
great commercial centre as well as a place of pilgrimage. He
finally went to Ethiopia where he remained for the rest of his life,
and where he was met in 1520 by Francisco Alvares, a member of
the first Portuguese embassy to go directly there, and to return to
Europe. Although Covilhã himself never returned to Portugal, it
is likely that news of his discoveries about the patterns of Indian
Ocean trade, and about the sources of the spices to be obtained in
the ports of India did reach Portugal, via two other Portuguese
envoys, the Jews Joseph of Lamego and Rabbi Abraham of Beja.
The latter had left Portugal after Covilhã, possibly with the news
of the success of Bartholemew Diaz, and Covilhã probably met
them in Cairo before going to Ethiopia to attempt to solve the
mystery of Prester John. In this way the traditional knowledge of
the existence of the spice trade of India, and the legend of Prester
John both contributed in a very direct fashion to the Portuguese
investigation of the sea route to India, and to the voyage of Vasco
da Gama in 1498.

13
Conclusion

When viewed with the advantages of hindsight, it seems evident that the expansion of Europe in the fifteenth century marked the beginning of an entirely new phase in the relations of Europe with the outer world. The discovery, exploration, conquest, and settlement of North and South America were in themselves dramatically different from anything that had gone before. The earlier discoveries made in North America by the Vikings had only, so far as is now known, touched the fringes of the continent; their achievements were almost certainly unknown to the fifteenth-century navigators of the Atlantic, and even if they had been, would not have prepared anyone for the immense and complex reality of America, or for the equally profound intellectual adjustment to the idea of a new world. The sixteenth- and seventeenth-century phases of European expansion involved large-scale conquests of territory in the Americas, and also saw the beginning of large-scale and continuing transfers of population from Europe. Here was something substantially new. The overseas expansion of Europe between about 900 and 1400 had not generally been accompanied by conquest and settlement, with the significant exceptions of Iceland and Greenland in the North Atlantic, and the crusader states created in the eastern Mediterranean and Cyprus. To these might be added the lordships established in Greece at the time of the Latin Empire of Constantinople in the thirteenth century, and by the exploits of the Catalan Grand Company in the early fourteenth century. But of these territories only Iceland and Cyprus were still in European hands at the end of the fifteenth century. Because of the shortage of suitable land Iceland and Greenland had absorbed only limited numbers of people, while the lands of Syria and Palestine were already densely populated when the first crusaders arrived: large numbers of Europeans visited them as soldiers, pilgrims, or merchants, but few stayed to put down permanent roots. The closest medieval parallel with the conquest and settlement of North and South America comes from within Europe itself, in the colonization of the Slav lands of central and eastern Europe and the Baltic, and in the settlement of areas such as Wales and Ireland on the western fringes of the continent.

European expansion in the East during the sixteenth and seventeenth centuries did not, except for the Spanish conquest of the Philippines, lead to the acquisition of large areas of territory, but was marked by the creation of commercial empires held together by naval supremacy at sea, and by the holding of strategic points such as Goa, Malacca, and Macao. None the less the scale of European activities and the amount of wealth they generated were far in excess of anything achieved by European merchants in Asia in the thirteenth and fourteenth centuries.

When these points are allowed, it is still arguable that the contrast between the medieval expansion of Europe and the expansion which occurred during the fifteenth and later centuries should not be too sharply drawn. Although the post-1500 achievements were very impressive, they were, in J.H. Parry's expressive phrase, a 'discovery of the sea'. The world may have been circumnavigated, and voyages across the Atlantic and in the Pacific became routine, if often very hazardous undertakings, but exploration of the land lagged far behind. Even though, for example, the Grand Canyon of Arizona was seen by one of Coronado's officers as early as 1540, the exploration of North America was not really completed until the early nineteenth century. Similarly, the Portuguese exploration of the coasts of West and East Africa was not followed immediately by the occupation of territory on a large scale: that too was a feature of the nineteenth century. As late as the mid-nineteenth century basic features of Africa, such as the true sources of the Nile and the geography of much of the continent to the north and south of the equator, were quite unknown. In Asia the island empire of Japan, whose description by Marco Polo had aroused the interest of Christopher Columbus, remained substantially unknown to outsiders until it was forcibly opened by United States naval power in the 1850s; while the journeys of Sir Marc Aurel Stein in

China and central Asia at the beginning of the present century were a deliberate attempt to retrace the steps of Marco Polo in a way that no European had been able to do since the fourteenth century.

The slow pace of intellectual adjustment in sixteenth-century Europe to the implications of the new discoveries has been remarked upon by many scholars; there was even a surprising lack of interest among the literate public in reading about the new world. The result was the preservation of traditional ideas, whether in the form of the continued use of scientific writings like the thirteenth-century *De Sphaera Mundi*, or in the repetition of tales of the wonders and monstrous races of the east. The world map drawn in about 1500 by Juan de la Cosa, who had accompanied Columbus on his second voyage in 1493, included such customary details as Gog and Magog, and the *blemmyae* of the deserts of Libya, men with faces on their chests like the anthropophagi of *Othello*. Juan de la Cosa probably did this partly out of deference to custom and to fill up blank spaces, but a more thoroughgoing example of the preservation of old ideas can be found in the *Margarita Philosophica* by George Reisch, the confessor of the emperor Maximilian, which was written in about 1496, and published in the first of a number of sixteenth-century editions in 1503. This contained many of the long-familiar legends and fantasies, while at the same time contriving to omit any mention of the Portuguese voyages of the fifteenth century. There were also examples in the sixteenth century of the wonders of the East being transferred to the new world, where they were supplemented by new ones, such as the Fountain of Youth, El Dorado, and the Seven Cities of Cibola. The mixture of fact and fiction, and the reluctance to adjust existing ideas in the light of new information are very reminiscent of the way in which medieval Europe had viewed the world.

The medieval expansion of Europe is a phenomenon deserving of study in its own right, and the evidence that has been presented is sufficient to show that it was a complex and persistent movement involving a surprisingly large part of the land masses of the world over a very long period of time. Even if there were no observable connection between this and the overseas expansion of the fifteenth and later centuries, it would still be significant. But as we have seen, there were in fact close connections between the two periods at many levels. The revival of international commerce in the eleventh century was a powerful incentive for overseas expansion then, and remained so despite the economic slump of the fourteenth and early fifteenth centuries, and the barriers placed in the way of European merchants after the collapse of the Mongol dominions in Asia. The rise of Turkish power may have complicated these ambitions, but it did not prevent their fulfilment so long as trade with the ports of Syria and Egypt remained possible. A few individuals from Europe also continued to overcome all the difficulties, and to penetrate a considerable distance into Asia. The Venetian traveller Nicolo Conti was one example, while the Genoese merchants, Hieronimo di Santo Stefano and Hieronimo Adorno, were in Calicut in India only a year or two before the arrival there of Vasco da Gama in 1498. The Portuguese desire to trade directly with India was the ambition of a poor country to seek new sources of wealth and to do so at the expense both of Moslem and Christian middlemen: in this sense the Venetians were as much the rivals of Portugal as were the Moslems who controlled Egypt and the Indian Ocean trade routes. The opening of a sea route to India may not have been an immediate priority for Henry the Navigator, and for other Portuguese leaders at the beginning of the fifteenth century, but it is likely that India was in their minds both because of the vague way in which it was defined, and because they were not put off by any knowledge of the great distance to be travelled by sea in order to get there.

The Portuguese interest in Africa was initially the product of the traditional trading links between the Iberian peninsula and North Africa, of the many previous attempts to conquer Moslem-held territory there, and of the knowledge that gold existed somewhere in a part of West Africa which was not accessible to Europeans by the Saharan trade routes. There was really no fundamental inconsistency in Portuguese policy towards North and West Africa in the fifteenth century. The Portuguese exploration of the coast of Africa, and indeed the whole of their expansion towards India can also be seen in terms of the crusading ideal which had flourished in varying forms since the eleventh century. So too can the voyages of Columbus who was also driven by the desire to extend the bounds of Christianity. Both he and the Portuguese were concerned to search for allies against the world of Islam, preferably Christian ones such as Prester John, who was still being actively sought at the end of the fifteenth century, but others if necessary: the letter of credence that Columbus bore to the Great Khan is an example of a policy which had its roots in the diplomatic missions of the thirteenth century.

The techniques of navigation and the types of ship available to the fifteenth-century explorers were in many respects little better than those of their thirteenth- and fourteenth-century predecessors. Individual courage and length of experience counted for as much as new methods. The voyages in the Atlantic during the fifteenth century had no close relation to those of the Vikings in earlier centuries, but they certainly were related both to the four-teenth-century discoveries of island groups such as the Canaries and the Azores, and also to the persistent belief in the existence of other islands like Brasil and Antilia. The pre-1492 rumours of the existence of land across the Atlantic which were recorded in the sixteenth century by Las Casas may owe something to hindsight, but there is no doubt that in the fifteenth century there was an intense interest in the Atlantic which long preceded the first voyage of Columbus. Columbus may have been the first navigator since the Vikings actually to cross the Atlantic, but it is unlikely that he was the first to make the attempt.

Above all it was in the realm of ideas that a close link existed between the fifteenth-century expansion of Europe and that of the earlier centuries. Without such ideas as the legend of Prester John, or previous knowledge of both the real and imaginary characteristics of India, or the information about the Far East gained during the rule of the Great Khans, or continuance of the crusading ideal, the fifteenth-century expansion of Europe would have been quite literally inconceivable. Seen against this background, the motives ascribed to Henry the Navigator by his biographer Azurara, who depicts him as a latter-day crusader, seem comprehensible, and probably not far from the truth. The contribution made to the expansion of Europe by the intellectual movement of the Italian Renaissance is tenuous and hard to define, but Italy did make a very important contribution to the fifteenth-century discoveries through the long experience of its navigators, shipbuilders, cartographers, and instrument makers, and through the financial resources and business acumen of its merchants and bankers. It was entirely appropriate that the New World should have been discovered by a Genoese, and named after a Florentine.

For all the future importance of the New World, it might be argued that the medieval expansion of Europe ended as it had begun, with the continent of Asia. It had started in the eleventh and twelfth centuries with the penetration by European merchants and crusaders of the western fringes of Asia in Syria and Palestine, and had continued in the thirteenth and fourteenth centuries with the travels to distant Mongolia, India and China by merchants, missionaries and envoys. Many of the fifteenth-century voyages of discovery, whether westwards across the Atlantic, or to the south around Africa and into the Indian Ocean, had Asia as their ultimate destination. Both Columbus and Cabot hoped to find the land of the Great Khan, and after them came others seeking a shorter passage to the East either around or through the Americas. When, in 1535, Jacques Cartier found his path westwards barred by rapids on the St Lawrence river above the site of the future city of Montreal, he named them *Sault La Chine*, the Chinese Rapids. A hundred years later, in 1634, a French *coureur des bois*, Jean Nicolet, was sent west to investigate rumours of a great inland sea from which a waterway led to Asia, and reports of a yellow-skinned people, who could only be Chinese, living on its shores. When Nicolet reached Green Bay on Lake Michigan he thought the cliffs ahead of him must be the coastline of China, landed, and donned a robe of Chinese silk. No Chinese dignitary came to greet him, only the local tribe of Indians. Had he but known it, Jean Nicolet was in a sense the last of the European envoys to the Great Khans, whose paths had criss-crossed Asia in the thirteenth and fourteenth centuries, and whose successors had helped to open the sea routes to the East and to the New World in the fifteenth.

Bibliography

There are many general studies of the history of European expansion. The three volumes of C. R. Beazley's *The Dawn of Modern Geography* (London, 1897–1906) are now out of date in many respects, but as a summary of European geographical knowledge and writings during the period from the fifth to the fifteenth century they are unsurpassed, and are still of value for reference. The volume of public lectures edited by A. P. Newton as *Travel and Travellers of the Middle Ages* (London, 1926) is still entertaining but now largely outmoded. *A History of Discovery and Exploration* published by Aldus and Jupiter Books in five volumes (London, 1973) is generally well written, and is exceptional for the quality of its illustrations, and the clarity of its maps. On the history of geographical ideas G. H. T. Kimble's *Geography in the Middle Ages* (London, 1938; repr. New York, 1968) was a pioneering work which remains of great value, as does the older work of J. Kirtland Wright, *The Geographical Lore of the Crusades: A Study in the History of Medieval Science and Tradition in Western Europe* (New York, 1925; new edn. New York, 1965). The most recent attempt to examine European relations with the outer world over a long period of time is G. V. Scammell's *The World Encompassed: The First Maritime Empires, c.800–1650* (London, 1981), which studies the growth of commercial empires from the Vikings and the Hanse at the beginning, via the Venetians, Genoese, and Portuguese, to the overseas trade of Spain, Holland, France, and England. Among the many books on shorter periods are C. Cipolla, *European Culture and Overseas Expansion* (London, 1970); P. Chaunu, *L'expansion européenne du XIIIᵉ au XVᵉ siècle* (Paris, 1969)—an English edition under the title *European Expansion in the Later Middle Ages* was published in Amsterdam in 1979, but without revision of the bibliography which is the central feature of this volume, no. 26 in the *Nouvelle Clio* series, and with some serious errors of translation; B. Penrose, *Travel and Discovery in the Renaissance, 1420–1620* (Cambridge, Mass., 1967); M. Mollat, *Les explorateurs du XIIIᵉ au XVIᵉ siècle: premiers regards sur des mondes nouveaux* (Paris, 1984); J. Meyer, *Les européens et les autres de Cortés à Washington* (Paris, 1975); J. R. Hale, *Renaissance Exploration* (London, 1968); E. P. Cheyney, *European Background of American History, 1300–1600* (repr. New York, 1961)—although first published in 1904, this is still a very stimulating book. The classic introductions to the history of European expansion are the various works of J. H. Parry, *Europe and a Wider World, 1415–1715* (London, 1949; published in the U.S.A. under the title *The Establishment of the European Hegemony, 1415–1715)*; *The Age of Reconnaissance, 1450–1650* (London, 1963); *The European Reconnaissance: Selected Documents* (New York, 1968); and *The Discovery of the Sea* (Berkeley, Los Angeles, and London, 1981).

Among articles on the nature of European expansion and discovery the following are of particular interest: L. Weckman, 'The middle ages in the discovery of America', *Speculum*, xxvi (1951); W. E. Washburn, 'The meaning of "discovery" in the fifteenth and sixteenth centuries'. *American Historical Review*, lxviii (1962–3); J. L. Allen, 'Imagination and geographical exploration', in *Geographies of the Mind*, ed. D. Lowenthal and M. J. Bowden (New York, 1976); 'The place of the imagination in geography', in J. Kirtland Wright, *Human Nature in Geography* (Cambridge, Mass., 1966); P. M. Watts, 'Prophecy and discovery: on the spiritual origins of Christopher Columbus's "Enterprise of the Indies" ', *American Historical Review*, xc (1985); G. V. Scammell, 'The new world and Europe in the sixteenth century', *The Historical Journal*, xii (1969); G. V. Scammel, 'The great age of discovery, 1400–1650', Hakluyt Society Presidential Address, 1981.

The relationship between Europe and the civilizations of Islam and of China is extremely difficult to assess, but some clues may be found in such works as N. Daniel, *The Arabs and Mediaeval Europe* (London and Beirut, 1975); H. A. R. Gibb (ed.), *Ibn Battuta: Travels in Asia and Africa* (London, 1929); D. F. Lach, *Asia in the Making of Europe*, i, *The Century of Discovery* (Chicago and London, 1965); J. Needham, *The Grand Titration: Science and Society in East and West* (London, 1969); L. White, Jr., *Medieval Religion and Technology: Collected Essays* (Berkeley, 1978). For modern attempts to retrace the steps of some of the medieval European explorers of Asia see, for example, Sir Aurel Stein, *On Ancient Central-Asian Tracks*, ed. J. Mirsky (Chicago and London, 1964); O. Lattimore, *Mongol Journeys* (London, 1941).

Editions of original sources bearing on the history of travel and discovery may be found in many places, but the publications of the Hakluyt Society which have been in progress since 1847 are the most important single collection. Similarly, many journals publish articles containing details of the latest research and interpretations, but those with a particular relevance to the history of European expansion include *Terrae Incognitae*, published in Amsterdam by the Society for the History of Discoveries, *Imago Mundi*, published in London by the International

Society for the History of Cartography, and *The Mariner's Mirror*, produced in London by the Society for Nautical Research. There is also a great deal of valuable material in the published *Actes* of the *Colloques internationaux d'histoire maritime*, which have been held at intervals since 1956.

I
The Beginnings of the Medieval Expansion of Europe

Chapter 1: Classical discoveries and Dark Age transformations

On classical geographical theories E. H. Bunbury's *A History of Ancient Geography* (2 vols., London, 1883; repr. New York, 1959) is still useful, but should be supplemented by more recent works such as J. O. Thomson, *A History of Ancient Geography* (Cambridge, 1948); G. Kish (ed.), *A Source Book in Geography* (Cambridge, Mass., and London, 1978); and C. Ronan, *The Cambridge Illustrated History of the World's Science* (Cambridge, 1985). On the extent of travel in the ancient world see, for example, M. Cary and E. H. Warmington, *The Ancient Explorers* (London, 1929; revised edn. London, 1963); J. Boardman, *The Greeks Overseas* (London, 1964); R. E.M. Wheeler, *Rome beyond the Imperial Frontiers* (London, 1954); C. F. C. Hawkes, *Pytheas: Europe and the Greek Explorers* (Oxford, 1977); R. Hennig (ed.), *Terrae Incognitae*, i (Leiden, 1944), *Notices of travel from c.1493 BC to AD 166*; H. N. Chittick, 'Observations on pre-Portuguese accounts of the East African coast', in M. Mollat (ed.), *Sociétés et compagnies de commerce en Orient et dans l'océan Indien* (Paris, 1970); J. J. Tierney, 'The Greek geographic tradition and Ptolemy's evidence for Irish geography', in *Colloquium on Hiberno–Roman Relations and Material Remains*, Sept. 1974, *Proceedings of the Royal Irish Academy*, lxxvi Sect. C, nos. 6–15 (Dublin, 1976).

There is no single volume which covers adequately the geographical ideas and the extent of European geographical knowledge in the period between the collapse of the western Roman empire and the eleventh century. The best introductions are the works of G. H.T. Kimble, J. Kirtland Wright, and C. R. Beazley (vols. i and ii). There are valuable indications of intellectual attitudes in M. L.W. Laistner, *Christianity and Pagan Culture in the Later Roman Empire* (Ithaca, 1963), in id., *Thought and Letters in Western Europe, AD 500–900* (London, 1957), and in J. O. Thomson, op. cit. See also the very valuable essay by W. Oakeshott, 'Some classical and medieval ideas in Renaissance cosmography', in D. J. Gordon (ed.), *Fritz Saxl Essays* (London, 1957).

The persistent belief in marvels and wonders is very thoroughly treated in the excellent study of J. B. Friedman, *The Monstrous Races in Medieval Art and Thought* (Harvard, 1981). For details of Martianus Capella see *Martianus Capella and the Seven Liberal Arts*, (tr.) W. H. Stahl and R. Johnson, 2 vols. (New York, 1977); L. W. Jones, *An Introduction to Divine and Human Readings by Cassiodorus Senator* (New York, 1946); L. Bréhaut, *Isidore of Seville: An Encyclopaedist of the Dark Ages* (New York, 1912); C. W. Jones, 'Bede's place in medieval schools', in G. Bonner (ed.), *Famulus Christi* (London, 1976); T. R. Eckenrode, 'Venerable Bede's theory of ocean tides', *The American Benedictine Review*, xxv (1974); C. W. Jones (ed.), *Bedae Opera de Temporibus* (Cambridge, Mass., 1943); F. S. Betten, 'The knowledge of the sphericity of the earth during the earlier middle ages', *Catholic Historical Review*, NS, iii (1923-4); C. W. Jones, 'The flat earth', *Thought*, ix (1934); F. S. Betten, 'St Boniface and the doctrine of the antipodes', *American Catholic Quarterly Review*, xliii (1918); H. Van der Linden, 'Virgile de Salzbourg et les théories cosmographiques au VIIIᵉ siécle', Académie royale de Belgique, *Bulletin de la Classe des Lettres* (Brussels, 1914); H. Löwe, *Ein literarischer Widersacher des Bonifatius: Virgil von Salzburg und die Kosmographie des Aethicus Ister* (Mainz, 1951); *Virgil von Salzburg: Missionar und Gelehrter*, ed. H. Dopsch and R. Juffinger (Salzburg, 1985); W. Wolska (ed.), *La topographie chrétienne de Cosmas Indicopleustes: théologie et science au VIᵉ siécle* (Paris, 1962); Dicuil, *Liber de Mensura Terrae*, ed. J. J. Tierney (Dublin, 1967).

On travel see, for example: Adamnan, *De Locis Sanctis*, ed. D. Meehan (Dublin, 1958); J. Wilkinson, *Jerusalem Pilgrims before the Crusades* (Warminster, 1977); J. J. O'Meara (ed.), *The Voyage of Saint Brendan* (Dublin, 1976); H. P. A. Oskamp, *The Voyage of Mael Duin: a Study in Early Irish Voyage Literature* (Groningen, 1970); R. Hennig (ed.), *Terrae Incognitae*, ii (Leiden, 1951), *Notices of travel, c. A D 340-1200*; C. R. Beazley, *The Dawn of Modern Geography*, i (London, 1897).

Chapter 2: Europe in the eleventh century

There are many books dealing with the development of Europe in this period but see, for example, D. Hay, *Europe: the Emergence of an Idea* (Edinburgh, 1957); H. Focillon, *L'an mil* (Paris, 1970); R. S. Lopez, *The Commercial Revolution of the Middle Ages, 950-1350* (Englewood Cliffs, 1971); D. C. Douglas, *The Norman Achievement* (London, 1969); D. W. Lomax, *The Reconquest of Spain* (London, 1978); K. M. Setton (ed.), *A History of the Crusades*, i (Philadelphia, 1955);

M. Clagett, G. Post, and R. Reynolds (eds.), *Twelfth-century Europe and the Foundations of Modern Society* (Madison and London, 1966).

Chapter 3: Commerce and the crusades

On the development of international commerce see R. S. Lopez, op. cit.; R. H. Bautier, *The Economic Development of Medieval Europe* (London, 1971); Y. Renouard, *Les hommes d'affaires italiens du moyen âge* (second edn., Paris, 1968); J. and F. Gies, *Merchants and Moneymen: the Commercial Revolution, 1000–1500*; G. V. Scammell, *The World Encompassed: the First Maritime Empires, c. 800–1650* (London, 1981); D. Herlihy, R. S. Lopez, and V. Slessarev (eds.), *Economy, Society and Government in Medieval Italy: Essays in Memory of Robert L. Reynolds* (Kent, Ohio, 1969); R. S. Lopez, 'Les influences orientales et l'éveil économique de l'Occident, *Journal of World History*, i (1954)—this is a seminal article; R. S. Lopez and I. W. Raymond (eds.), *Medieval Trade in the Mediterranean World* (New York and London, 1955); R. S. Lopez, *Byzantium and the World around it* (London, 1978).

The literature on the crusades is enormous. The best short account is H. E. Mayer, *The Crusades* (Stuttgart, 1965, English translation by J. Gillingham, Oxford, 1972); the classic detailed narrative is in the three volumes of S. Runciman, *A History of the Crusades* (Cambridge, 1951–4). The multi-volume *A History of the Crusades*, edited by K. M. Setton, and covering most aspects of the crusades from their origins to their consequences, has now reached five volumes. (Philadelphia and Madison, 1955–85). On the origins of the crusades, and on the Holy War in Spain and the Baltic lands see T. P. Murphy (ed.), *The Holy War* (Columbus, 1976); I. S. Robinson, 'Gregory VII and the soldiers of Christ', *History*, lviii (1973); J. Riley-Smith, *What were the Crusades?* (London, 1977); D. W. Lomax, *The Reconquest of Spain* (London, 1978); A. MacKay, *Spain in the Middle Ages: from Frontier to Empire, 1000–1500* (London, 1977); E. Christiansen, *The Northern Crusades: the Baltic and the Catholic Frontier, 1100–1500* (London, 1980). On the political situation in the eastern Mediterranean at the time of the crusades and on the Moslem reaction to the crusades see P. M. Holt (ed.), *The Eastern Mediterranean Lands in the Period of the Crusades* (Warminster, 1977); id., *The Age of the Crusades: The Near East from the Eleventh Century to 1517*) London, 1986); A. Maalouf, *The Crusades through Arab Eyes* (London, 1984); F. Gabrieli, *Arab Historians of the Crusades* (London, 1969 and 1984). On the colonial society established in the crusader states see, for example, R.C. Smail, *The Crusaders in Syria and the Holy Land* (London, 1973); id., *Crusading Warfare, 1097-1193* (Cambridge, 1956); J. Prawer, *The Latin Kingdom of Jerusalem: European Colonialism in the Middle Ages* (London, 1972); M. Benvenisti, *The Crusaders in the Holy Land* (Jerusalem, 1970, New York, 1972); J. Richard, *The Latin Kingdom of Jerusalem* (Amsterdam, 1979); D. Baker (ed.), *Relations between East and West in the Middle Ages* (Edinburgh, 1973); R.W. Southern, *Western Views of Islam in the Middle Ages* (Harvard, 1961).

The work of many of the most eminent scholars of the crusades is widely scattered through specialized journals. However, the publication of volumes of collected papers has brought together much of the most important work in convenient form. Some examples are: C. Cahen, *Turcobyzantina et Oriens Christianus* (London, 1974); B. Hamilton, *Monastic Reform, Catharism and the Crusades (900-1300)* (London, 1979); J. Richard, *Croisés, missionaires et voyageurs: les perspectives orientales du monde latin médiéval* (London, 1983); J. Richard, *Orient et Occident au moyen âge: contacts et relations (XIIᵉ-XVᵉ siècle)* (London, 1976); J. Richard, *Les relations entre l'Orient et l'Occident au moyen âge: études et documents* (London, 1977). Two recent Festschrift volumes in honour of distinguished scholars contain a large number of valuable articles: B.Z. Kedar, H.E. Mayer, and R.C. Smail (eds.), *Outremer: Studies in the History of the Crusading Kingdom of Jerusalem presented to Joshua Prawer* (Jerusalem, 1982); P.W. Edbury (ed.), *Crusade and Settlement: Proceedings of the First Conference of the Society for the History of the Crusades* (Cardiff, 1985)—this volume was dedicated to R.C. Smail.

On contemporary attitudes to the crusades in Europe and criticisms of them see P.A. Throop, *Criticism of the Crusades: A Study of Public Opinion and Crusade Propaganda* (Amsterdam, 1940), and the recent work of E. Siberry, *Criticism of Crusading, 1095-1274* (Oxford, 1985).

Many of the books cited above include some assessment of the significance and impact of the crusades, but particular note should be taken of K.M. Setton (ed.), *A History of the Crusades*, iv and v (Madison, 1977 and 1985); C. Cahen, *Orient et Occident au temps des Croisades* (Paris, 1983); N. Daniel, *The Arabs and Mediaeval Europe* (London and Beirut, 1975).

The most important collection of source material on the history of the crusades is to be found in *Recueil des historiens des croisades: Historiens occidentaux*, 5 vols. (Paris, 1844-95; repr. 1967). Material can, however, be found in more convenient form in such books as L. and

J. Riley-Smith (eds.), *The Crusades: Idea and Reality, 1095–1274* (London, 1981); E. Peters (ed.), *The First Crusade* (Philadelphia, 1971); id. (ed.), *Christian Society and the Crusades, 1198–1229* (Philadelphia, 1971).

II
Europe and Asia

Chapter 4: Europe and the Mongol invasions

The most recent study of the history and conquests of the Mongols is D. Morgan, *The Mongols* (Oxford, 1986). This is an excellent book which also has an up-to-date account of the extensive bibliography on the Mongols. It does not, however, supersede the earlier book by J. J. Saunders, *The History of the Mongol Conquests* (London, 1971), which is particularly good on the Mongol impact on Europe. Another study of the Mongols, with a large number of illustrations, is E. D. Phillips, *The Mongols* (London, 1969). For more detailed accounts of the Mongol way of life, and of the career of Genghis Khan see R. Grousset, *L'empire des steppes: Attila, Gengis Khan, Tamerlan* (Paris, 1969); R. Grousset, *Conqueror of the World: the Life of Chingis Khan* (Edinburgh and London, 1967; translation of the French edition, Paris, 1944). The publication of the collected papers of eminent scholars of the Mongols and European relations with them has brought together a great deal of important material. See, for example, J. A. Boyle, *The Mongol World Empire, 1206–1370* (London, 1977); D. Sinor, *Inner Asia and its Contacts with Medieval Europe* (London, 1977); J. Richard, *Orient et Occident au moyen âge: contacts et relations (XIIe–XVe siècle)* (London, 1976); J. Richard, *Les relations entre l'Orient et l'Occident au moyen âge: études et documents* (London, 1977); J. J. Saunders, *Muslims and Mongols* (University of Canterbury, Christchurch, New Zealand, 1977). The history of the Mongol impact on Iran, a region with which western Europe was to have especially close contacts, is treated in J. A. Boyle (ed.), *The Cambridge History of Iran*, vol. v, *The Saljuq and Mongol Periods* (Cambridge, 1968).

For discussions of the Mongol impact upon Europe at the time of the invasions of the 1230s and 1240s see many of the works already cited but especially: D. Sinor, 'The Mongols and Western Europe', in K. M. Setton (ed.), *A History of the Crusades*, iii (Madison, 1975), and in Sinor, *Inner Asia and its Contacts with Medieval Europe*; J. A. Boyle, 'The last barbarian invaders: the impact of the Mongol conquest upon East and West', in Boyle, *The Mongol World Empire*; J. J. Saunders, 'Matthew

Paris and the Mongols', in T. A. Sandquist and M. R. Powicke (eds.), *Essays in Medieval History presented to Bertie Wilkinson* (Toronto, 1969); C. W. Connell, 'Western views of the origin of the Tartars', *Journal of Medieval and Renaissance Studies* iii (1973); C. J. Halperin, *Russia and the Golden Horde: The Mongol impact on Medieval Russia*, (Bloomington, 1985); J. Fennell, *The Crisis of Medieval Russia, 1200–1304* (London, 1983). For a suggestive account of the Mongol role in spreading another form of devastation see W. H. McNeill, 'The impact of the Mongol empire on shifting disease balances, 1200–1500', in McNeill, *Plagues and Peoples* (Oxford, 1977).

Source material on the history of the Mongols and their way of life may be found in, for example, B. Spuler (ed.), *History of the Mongols based on Eastern and Western Accounts of the Thirteenth and Fourteenth Centuries* (London, 1972; translation of the German edition, Zurich, 1968); J. A. Boyle (ed.), *The History of the World Conqueror by Ata Malik Juvaini*, 2 vols. (Manchester, 1958); A. Waley (tr.), *The Secret History of the Mongols and Other Pieces* (London, 1963); C. Dawson (ed.), *The Mongol Mission* (New York and London, 1955)—this invaluable translation of the narratives of Carpini and Rubruck, and of the letters of a number of the western missionaries in China has been reprinted under the title *The Mission to Asia* (London, 1980), and reprinted again under the same title by the University of Toronto Press on behalf of the Mediaeval Academy of America (Toronto, 1986).

Many of the books and articles cited above deal with the attempts by the papacy and other western European powers to learn more about the Mongols by diplomatic means. See especially J. J. Saunders, *op. cit.*; J. A. Boyle, *The Mongol World Empire*; D. Sinor, op. cit. But see also the very important work by I. de Rachewiltz, *Papal Envoys to the Great Khans* (London, 1971); and the articles by G. G. Guzman, 'Simon of Saint-Quentin and the Dominican mission to the Mongol Baiju: a reappraisal', *Speculum*, xlvi (1971), and 'The encyclopaedist Vincent of Beauvais and his Mongol extracts from John of Piano Carpino and Simon of Saint-Quentin', ibid., xlix (1974). The attitudes of Carpini and Rubruck towards the Mongols may usefully be compared with those of Giraldus Cambrensis towards the Welsh and the Irish: cf. R. Bartlett, *Gerald of Wales, 1146–1223* (Oxford, 1982).

For source material see B. Spuler, op. cit.; C. Dawson, op. cit.; and also H. Yule (ed.), *Cathay and the Way Thither*, 4 vols., Hakluyt Society (London, 1913–16); A. Van Den Wyngaert (ed.), *Sinica Franciscana*, i (Florence, 1929).

Chapter 5: The eastern missions

The work of western missionaries in Asia could until recently be studied only in the highly specialized and widely scattered writings of many eminent scholars. The standard work on the subject is now, however, J. Richard's *La papauté et les missions d'Orient au moyen âge (XIIIᵉ– XVᵉ siècle)*, Collection de l'Ecole Française de Rome, xxxiii (Rome, 1977). There is also a recent summary of the missions in western Asia and the eastern Mediterranean lands in volume v of *A History of the Crusades*, ed. K. M. Setton (Madison, 1985). See also I. de Rachewiltz, op. cit.; J. J. Saunders, 'The decline and fall of Christianity in medieval Asia', in Saunders, *Muslims and Mongols*; D. Sinor, op. cit.; J. Richard, *Orient et Occident au moyen âge: contacts et relations (XIIᵉ– XVᵉ siècle)* (London, 1976); J. Richard, *Les relations entre l'Orient et l'Occident au moyen âge: études et documents* (London, 1977); P. W. Brown, *The Indian Christians of St Thomas* (Cambridge, 1956), A. C. Moule, *Christians in China before the year 1550* (London, 1930); P. Pelliot, 'Les Mongols et la papauté', *Revue de l'Orient chrétien*, xxiii (1923), xxiv (1924), xxviii (1931–2). For discussions of thirteenth-century European attitudes towards missionary activity see R. I. Burns, 'Christian–Islamic confrontation in the west: the thirteenth-century dream of conversion', *American Historical Review*, lxxvi (1971); B. Z. Kedar, *Crusade and Mission: European Approaches towards the Muslims* (Princeton, 1984); E. Christiansen, *The Northern Crusades: the Baltic and the Catholic Frontier, 1100–1500* (London, 1980).

For source material on the eastern missions see, for example, C. Dawson, op. cit.; A. Van den Wyngaert, op. cit.; H. Yule, op. cit.; G. Golubovich (ed.), *Biblioteca Bio-bibliografica della Terra Santa e dell'Oriente francescano*, 5 vols. (Florence, 1906–27); R. Hennig (ed.), *Terrae Incognitae*, vol. iii, *1200–1415* (Leiden, 1953).

Chapter 6: European merchants and the East

On the development of European international commerce see R. S. Lopez, *The Commercial Revolution of the Middle Ages, 950–1350* (Englewood Cliffs, 1971); R. H. Bautier, *The Economic Development of Medieval Europe* (London, 1971); R. S. Lopez and I. W. Raymond (eds.), *Medieval Trade in the Mediterranean World* (New York and London, 1955); G. V. Scammell, *The World Encompassed* (London, 1981). There is a considerable amount of material about European trade with Asia, and its relationship with trade in the Mediterranean in E. Ashtor, *The Levant Trade in the Later Middle Ages*, chap. 1 (Princeton,

1983), and also in J. Heers, *Marco Polo* (Paris, 1983). However, much of the research on the subject is still to be found in the form of specialized articles and monographs such as the following: J. Heers, *Gênes au XVe siècle: activité économique et problèmes sociaux* (Paris, 1961); B. Z. Kedar, *Merchants in Crisis: Genoese and Venetian Men of Affairs and the Fourteenth-century Depression* (New Haven and London, 1976); I. Origo, 'The domestic enemy: eastern slaves in Tuscany in the thirteenth and fourteenth centuries', *Speculum*, xxx (1955); L. Petech, 'Les marchands italiens dans l'empire mongol', *Journal asiatique*, ccl (1962); M. Lombard, 'Caffa et la fin de la route mongole', *Annales E.S.C.*, (1950); R. S. Lopez, 'China silk in Europe in the Yuan period', *Journal of the American Oriental Society*, lxxii (1952); id., 'European merchants in the medieval Indies: the evidence of commercial documents', *Journal of Economic History*, iii, part 2 (1943); id. 'L'extrême frontière du commerce de l'Europe médiévale', *Le Moyen Âge*, lxix (1963); E. Baratier, 'Les Genois en Asie centrale et en extrême-Orient au XIVe siècle: un cas exceptionnel?', in *Economies et Sociétés au moyen âge: Mélanges offerts à Edouard Perroy* (Paris, 1973). See the article by J. Aubin in M. Mollat (ed.) *Océan Indien et Méditerranée: travaux du sixième colloque international d'histoire maritime* (Paris, 1964), and those by C. Cahen, R. H. Bautier, E. Baratier, R. S. Lopez, J. Richard, and M. Balard in M. Mollat (ed.), *Sociétés et compagnies de commerce en Orient et dans l'océan Indien*, *Actes du huitième colloque international d'histoire maritime* (Paris, 1970). There are also several relevant articles in J. Richard, *Les relations entre l'Orient et Occident au moyen âge* (London, 1977), and id., *Orient et Occident au moyen âge (XIIe–XVe siècle)* (London, 1976).

For source material see, for example, R. S. Lopez and I. W. Raymond, op. cit.; Francesco Balducci Pegolotti, *La Pratica della Mercatura*, ed. A. Evans (Cambridge, Mass., 1936; reprinted New York, 1970); R. Hennig (ed.), *Terrae Incognitae*, iii (Leiden, 1953); H. Yule, op. cit.

Despite the extensive literature on Marco Polo, there is no readily available recent scholarly study in English. See, however, J. Heers, *Marco Polo* (Paris, 1983) and id., 'De Marco Polo à Christophe Colomb: comment lire le *Divisement dou Monde*', *Journal of Medieval History*, x (1984). See also L. Olschki, *Marco Polo's Asia* (Berkeley, Los Angeles, and London, 1970). For older scholarly work see especially H. Yule (ed.), *The Book of Ser Marco Polo*, 2 vols. revised by H. Cordier (third edn., London, 1903); H. Cordier, *Ser Marco Polo: Notes and Addenda to Sir Henry Yule's Edition* (London, 1920); P. Pelliot, *Notes on Marco Polo: Ouvrage posthume*, 2 vols. (Paris, 1959 and 1963). There are important articles on Marco Polo in *Oriente Poliano: Studi e Conferenze tenute all'Is. M. E. O. in Occasione del VII Centenario della Nascita di Marco Polo* (Rome, 1957); see also H. Franke, 'Sino-western contacts under the Mongol empire', *Journal of the Hong Kong Branch of the Royal Asiatic Society*, vi (1966). An easily available and scholarly translation of the narrative of Marco Polo's experiences is *The Travels of Marco Polo*, trans. R. E. Latham (London, 1958). For the problems of manuscript tradition and authorship see L. F. Benedetto, *La Tradizione Manoscritta del 'Milione' di Marco Polo* (Turin, 1962); G. del Guerra, *Rustichello da Pisa* (Pisa, 1955).

Chapter 7: The lost alliance: European monarchs and Mongol 'crusaders'

The extraordinary history of this phase of relations between Europe and the Mongols is recorded in a very extensive specialized literature. There are, however, several works through which it can be approached. See especially I. de Rachewiltz, *Papal Envoys to the Great Khans* (London, 1971); D. Morgan, *The Mongols* (Oxford, 1986); D. Sinor, 'Les relations entre les Mongols et l'Europe jusquà la mort d'Arghoun et de Bela IV', *Journal of World History*, iii (1956–7); id., 'The Mongols and Western Europe', in K. M. Setton (ed.), *A History of the Crusades*, iii (both these papers are reprinted in D. Sinor, *Inner Asia and its Contacts with Medieval Europe* (London, 1977)). There are several important articles in J. A. Boyle, *The Mongol World Empire, 1206–1370* (London, 1977), and in J. Richard, *Orient et Occident au moyen âge* (London, 1976). See also J. A. Boyle (ed.), *The Cambridge History of Iran*, v (Cambridge, 1968); L. Lockhart, 'The relations between Edward I and Edward II of England and the Mongol Il-khans of Persia', *Iran*, vi (1968); C. Brunel, 'David d'Ashby auteur méconnu des *Faits des Tartares*', *Romania*, lxxix (1958); P. Meyvaert, 'An unknown letter of Hulagu, Il-khan of Persia, to King Louis IX of France', *Viator*, xi (1980); S. Schein, '*Gesta Dei per Mongolos*, 1300: the genesis of a non-event', *English Historical Review*, xciv (1979); T. S. R. Boase (ed.), *The Cilician Kingdom of Armenia* (Edinburgh and London, 1978); P. M. Holt, *The Age of the Crusades: the Near East from the Eleventh Century to 1517* (London, 1986); J. F. Verbruggen, *The Art of Warfare in Western Europe during the Middle Ages* (Amsterdam, 1977); J. R. S. Phillips, 'Edward II and the prophets', in W. M. Ormrod (ed.), *England in the Fourteenth Century* (Woodbridge, 1986).

For source material see, for example, B. Spuler (ed.), *History of the Mongols* (London, 1972); J. Mirsky (ed.), *The Great Chinese Travellers* (London, 1965)—this includes the account of the mission of Rabban

Sauma to Europe in 1287; J. A. Montgomery (ed.), *The History of Yaballaha III and his Vicar, Bar-Sauna* (New York, 1927 and 1966); C. Desimoni, 'I conti dell'ambasciata al Chan de Persia nel MCCXCII', *Atti della Societa Ligure di Storia Patria*, xiii (1877–84)—edited from Public Record Office, E, 101/308/13,14,15; K. Jahn, (tr.), *Histoire universelle de Rašīd al-Dīn*, vol. i, *Histoire des Francs* (Leiden, 1951).

III
Two continents and an ocean

Chapter 8: Medieval Europe and Africa

Although there are considerable numbers of scholarly works on various aspects of medieval European contacts with Africa, this subject poses many problems of interpretation. On the history of Africa itself the standard work is now J. D. Fage and R. Oliver (ed.), *Cambridge History of Africa*, vols ii and iii (Cambridge, 1977 and 1978); see also J. D. Fage, *A History of Africa* (London, 1978). These books can be used alongside the excellent *Atlas of African History* by J. D. Fage (second edn. London, 1978). The three volumes of Ch. de la Roncière's *La découverte de l'Afrique au moyen âge* (Cairo, 1924–7) remain the most substantial attempt to establish the extent of European knowledge, although they are now outdated in many respects. See also the very readable and scholarly book by E. W. Bovill, *The Golden Trade of the Moors* (second edn. Oxford, 1970); there is an important chapter in G. H. T. Kimble, *Geography in the Middle Ages* (London, 1938).

On European relations with North Africa see especially W. H. C. Frend, 'North Africa and Europe in the early middle ages', *Transactions of Royal Historical Society*, fifth series, v (1955); C. Courtois, 'Grégoire VII et l'Afrique du nord', *Revue Historique*, cxcv (1945); H. C. Kreuger, 'The routine of commerce between Genoa and Northwest Africa during the late twelfth century', *Mariner's Mirror*, xix (1932); K. M. Setton (ed.), *A History of the Crusades*, iii; Ch.-E. Dufourcq, *L'Espagne catalane et le Maghrib aux XIIIᵉ et XIVᵉ siècles* (Paris, 1965); E. Ashtor: *The Levant Trade in the Later Middle Ages* (Princeton, 1983); V. Magalhães-Godinho, *L'économie de l'empire Portugais aux XVᵉ et XVIᵉ siècles* (Paris, 1969)—on the subject of the African gold trade; F. Braudel, *The Mediterranean and the Mediterranean World in the Age of Philip II*, vol. i, part 2, 'The Mediterranean and the gold of the Sudan' (Paris, 1966 and London, 1972); B. W. Diffie, *Prelude to Empire: Portugal Overseas before Henry the Navigator* (Lincoln, Nebraska, 1960); B. W. Diffie and G. D. Winius, *The Founda-*

Bibliography

tions of the Portuguese Empire, 1415–1580 (Minneapolis, 1977); A. R. Lewis, 'Northern European sea power and the straits of Gibraltar, 1031–1350 A. D', in W. C. Jordan, B. McNab, and T. Ruiz (eds.), *Order and Innovation in the Middle Ages: Essays in Honour of Joseph R. Strayer* (Princeton, 1976).

European knowledge of East Africa and the Indian Ocean is subject to many problems of definition and interpretation. See especially O. G. S. Crawford (ed.), *Ethiopian Itineraries, circa 1400–1524*, Hakluyt Society, second series, cix, 1955 (Cambridge, 1958), Introduction and Appendix III; id., 'Some Medieval theories about the Nile', *Geographical Journal*, cxiv (1949); C. F. Beckingham, *Between Islam and Christendom* (London, 1983), especially i, 'The achievements of Prester John', and ii, 'The quest for Prester John'; J. Richard, *La papauté et les missions d'Orient au moyen âge* (Rome, 1977); id., *Orient et Occident au moyen âge contacts et relations* (London, 1976), especially xxiv, 'Les premiers missionaires latins en Ethiopie', and xxvi, 'L'Extrême-Orient legendaire au moyen âge: Roi David et Prêtre Jean'; id., 'Les navigations des occidentaux sur l'océan Indien et la mer Caspienne', in M. Mollat (ed.), *Sociétés et compagnies de commerce en Orient et dans l'océan Indien* (Paris, 1970); R. S. Lopez, 'European merchants in the medieval Indies: the evidence of commercial documents', *Journal of Economic History* vol. III., part 2 (1943); J. Le Goff, 'The medieval West and the Indian Ocean', in id., *Time, Work and Culture in the Middle Ages* (Chicago, 1980).

On European knowledge of West Africa and the waters of the Atlantic adjoining it see especially the two important studies by R. Mauny, *Tableau géographique de l'Ouest africain au moyen âge* (Dakar, 1961), and *Les navigations médiévales sur les côtes sahariennes antérieures à la découverte portugaise* (Lisbon, 1960). See also B. W. Diffie, op. cit.; B. W. Diffie and G. D. Winius, op. cit.; Chaunu, *European Expansion in the Later Middle Ages* (Amsterdam, 1979, translation of *L'expansion européenne du XIIIᵉ au XVᵉ siècle*, Paris, 1969); C. Verlinden, *Les origines de la civilisation atlantique* (Paris, 1966); id., 'Les italiens et l'ouverture des routes de l'Atlantique', in M. Mollat (ed.), *Les Routes de l'Atlantique: Travaux du neuvieme colloque international d'histoire maritime* (Paris, 1969); id., *The Beginnings of Modern Colonization* (Ithaca and London, 1970); id., 'Lanzarotto Malcello et la découverte portugaise des Canaries', *Revue Belge de Philologie et d'Histoire*, xxxvi (1958); R. W. Unger, *The Ship in the Medieval Economy, 600–1600* (London and Montreal, 1980); L. T. Belgrano, 'Nota sulla spedizione dei Fratelli Vivaldi nel MCCLXXXXI', *Atti della Societa Ligure di Storia Patria*, xv (1881); F.M. Rogers, 'The Vivaldi expedition', *Seventy-third Annual Report of the Dante Society* (Cambridge, Mass., 1955).

For source materials see O.G.S. Crawford, op. cit., C. Markham (ed.), *Book of the Knowledge of all the Kingdoms, Lands and Lordships that are in the World . . . written by a Spanish Fransciscan*, Hakluyt Society, second series, xxix, 1912 (London, 1912); R. Hennig (ed.), *Terrae Incognitae*, iii (Leiden, 1953); H.A.R. Gibb (ed.), *Ibn Battuta: Travels in Asia and Africa* (London, 1929); N. Levtzion and J. Hopkins (eds.), *Corpus of Early Arabic Sources for West African History* (Cambridge, 1981).

Chapter 9: Medieval Europe and North America

There are several books which examine medieval European knowledge of the Atlantic, and the evidence for the discovery of North America, although they are by no means always in agreement on their conclusions. See, for example, V.H. Cassidy, *The Sea Around them: the Atlantic, A.D. 1250* (Baton Rouge, 1968); G.J. Marcus, *The Conquest of the North Atlantic* (Woodbridge, 1980); C.O. Sauer, *Northern Mists* (Berkeley, Los Angeles, and London, 1968); T.J. Olesen, *Early Voyages and Northern Approaches* (Toronto, 1963); D.B. Quinn, *North America from Earliest Discovery to First Settlements* (New York, 1977); S.E. Morison, *The European Discovery of America: the Northern Voyages* (New York, 1971). Several of the above discuss the extent of early Irish voyaging in the Atlantic, but for one attempt (among many) to demonstrate that Irish monks had reached North America long before the Vikings see T. Severin, *The Brendan Voyage* (London, 1978), and the review article by J.J. O'Meara in *The Times Literary Supplement*, 14 July 1978. There are many excellent books about the exploits of the Vikings. The most up to date are G. Jones, *A History of the Vikings* (second edn. Oxford, 1984) and id., *The Norse Atlantic Saga* (second edn. Oxford, 1986), which contain the results of the most recent research on the Vikings and North America. Another valuable book, which is particularly good on the evidence, both real and imaginary, for a Viking presence in North America, is F.D. Logan, *The Vikings in History* (London, 1983). On the history of Iceland see B.E. Gelsinger, *Icelandic Enterprise: Commerce and Economy in the Middle Ages* (Columbia, 1981); the development of Greenland under the Vikings is excellently treated in F. Gad, *The History of Greenland*, vol. i, *Earliest Times to 1700* (London, 1970). The problem of the Vikings and Vinland is examined in most of the books already mentioned, but there are several important works on specific aspects of the question. On the saga evidence about Vinland see Per Jon Johanesson, 'The date of the composition of the Saga of the Greenlanders', *Saga Book of the Viking Society for Northern Research*, xvi (1962-5); for the development of Viking shipping see R. W. Unger, *The Ship in the Medieval Economy, 600-1600* (London and Montreal, 1980). The archaeological evidence was presented in an initial report by H. Ingstad in *Westward to Vinland* (London, 1969); the final reports on the Ingstads' excavations have now been published as *The Discovery of America*, vol. i, *Excavations at L'Anse aux Meadows, Newfoundland, 1961-1968*, by Anne Stine Ingstad (this is a revised edition of the work first published in Oslo in 1977), and *The Discovery of America*, vol. ii, *Historical Aspects and other Background Matter*, by Helge Ingstad (both Oxford, 1986). The most up-to-date discussion of the Vikings and North America, apart from the above two volumes, is in the papers contained in E. Guralnick (ed.), *Vikings in the West* (Chicago, 1982)—the conclusions of this volume are included in the appendices of G. Jones, *The Norse Atlantic Saga* (1986 edn.). See also P. Schledermann, 'Ellesmere island: Eskimo and Viking finds in the high Arctic', *National Geographic*, clix (May, 1981); M. L. Colker, 'America rediscovered in the thirteenth century?', *Speculum*, liv (1979).

For source material see, for example, J. J. O'Meara (ed.), *The Voyage of St Brendan* (Dublin, 1978); M. Magnusson and H. Pálsson (tr.), *The Vinland Sagas: the Norse Discovery of America* (London, 1965); L. M. Larsen (ed.), *The King's Mirror* (New York, 1917); G. Jones, *The Norse Atlantic Saga*; D. B. Quinn (ed.), *North American Discovery, circa 1000-1612* (New York, 1971).

There is an enormous literature on the innumerable claims that one nation or another got to America before its rivals. These problems are discussed in many of the books already mentioned but see also the following: R. A. Skelton, T. E. Marston, and G. D. Painter (eds.), *The Vinland Map and the Tartar Relation* (New Haven, 1965); W. E. Washburn (ed.), *Proceedings of the Vinland Map Conference* (Chicago, 1971); the proceedings of the Royal Geographical Society symposium published as 'The strange case of the Vinland Map', *Geographical Journal*, (1974) (see also the preface of this book); on the Madoc legend see T. Stephens, *Madoc* (London, 1893) and G. A. Williams, *Madoc: the Making of a Myth* (London, 1979); the Kensington Rune-Stone evidence is presented in H. R. Holand, *Norse Discoveries and Explorations in America, 982-1362* (New York, 1969), and criticized in many other works; Nicholas of Lynn is discussed in S. Eisner (ed.), *The*

Kalendarium of Nicholas of Lynn (Athens, Georgia, 1980); for the legend of the Zeno brothers see R. H. Major (ed.), *The Voyage of the Venetian Brothers, Nicolo and Antonio Zeno to the Northern Seas in the XIVth Century*, Hakluyt Society, first series, 1 (London, 1873); W. H. Hobbs, 'The fourteenth-century discovery of America by Antonio Zeno', *The Scientific Monthly*, lxxii (1951); F. J. Pohl, *Prince Henry Sinclair and his Expedition to the New World in 1398* (London, 1974); on mythical islands in the Atlantic see T. J. Westropp, 'Brasil and the legendary islands of the North Atlantic: their history and fable', *Proceedings of the Royal Irish Academy*, xxx, section C (1912–13).

IV
Europe and the world, *c.* 1100–1450

Chapter 10: Scholarship and the imagination

There is no really satisfactory guide to geographical ideas and perceptions in medieval Europe, and the following bibliography is intended only as a general indication of the kind of material which has been consulted for writing this chapter. The sources used were very miscellaneous in character and included, for example, a very stimulating lecture on *mappae mundi* and their interpretation which was delivered to the postgraduate seminar in medieval studies at University College, Dublin in 1981 by Professor J. H. Andrews of Trinity College, Dublin.

The best introductions to geographical ideas are still G. H. T. Kimble, *Geography in the Middle Ages* (London, 1938 repr. New York, 1968), and J. Kirtland Wright, *The Geographical Lore of the Time of the Crusades* (New York, 1925; new edn. New York, 1965). But see also W. Oakeshott, 'Some classical and medieval ideas in Renaissance cosmography', in *Fritz Saxl Essays*, ed. D. J. Gordon (London, 1957); the very important essay by the late J. K. Hyde, 'Real and imaginary journeys in the later Middle Ages', *Bulletin of the John Rylands Library*, lxv (1982–3); E. G. R. Taylor, 'The cosmographical ideas of Mandeville's day', in M. Letts (ed.), *Mandeville's Travels*, Hakluyt Society, second series, ci, 1950 (London, 1953); J. K. Wright, 'Notes on the knowledge of latitude and longitude in the middle ages', *Isis*, v (1922); J. Richard, 'Les récits de voyages et de pèlerinages', *Typologie des sources du moyen âge*, ed. L. Genicot, fascicle xxxviii (Turnhout, 1981); K. H. Krüger, 'Die Universalchroniken', ibid., fascicle vi (Turnhout, 1976); E. Moore, 'The geography of Dante', in Moore, *Studies in Dante*, third series, *Miscellaneous Essays* (Oxford, 1903; repr. Oxford, 1968); J. C. Russell, 'Hereford and Arabic science in England, about 1175–1200', in Russell,

Twelfth-Century Studies (New York, 1978); 'The cosmography of John Holywood', in J.J. Bayly and P.B. Rowley, (eds.), *A Documentary History of England*, vol. i (*1066–1540*) (London, 1966); J. Le Goff, 'The medieval West and the Indian Ocean', in Le Goff, *Time, Work and Culture in the Middle Ages* (Chicago, 1980, translation of French edition, Paris, 1977); R. Wittkower, 'Marvels of the East', *Journal of Warburg and Courtauld Institutes*, v (1942); id., 'Marco Polo and the pictorial tradition of the marvels of the East', in *Oriente Poliano* (Rome, 1957) (these two papers are also reprinted in Wittkower, *Allegory and Migration of Symbols* (London, 1977); J. Richard, 'Voyages réels et voyages imaginaires, instruments de la connaissance géographique au moyen âge', in G. Hasenohr and J. Longère (eds.), *Culture et travail intellectuel dans l'Occident médiéval* (Paris, 1981); F. Borlandi, 'Alle origini del libro di Marco Polo', in *Studi in Onore di Amintore Fanfani*, i (Milan, 1962); G.G. Guzman, 'The encyclopaedist Vincent of Beauvais and his Mongol extracts from John of Piano Carpini and Simon of Saint-Quentin', *Speculum*, xlix (1974); M.C. Andrews, 'The classification of medieval *mappae mundi*', *Archaeologia*, lxxv (1924–5); A.L. Moir and M. Letts, *The World Map in Hereford Cathedral* (Hereford, 1979); N. Denholm-Young, 'The *Mappa Mundi* of Richard of Haldingham at Hereford', in Denholm-Young, *Collected Papers* (Cardiff, 1969); J. Heers, 'De Marco Polo à Christophe Colomb: Comment lire le *Divisement dou Monde?*', *Journal of Medieval History*, x (1984); H.M. Smyser, 'A view of Chaucer's astronomy', *Speculum*, xlv (1970).

Monographs which contain material of value for the study of medieval geographical ideas and perceptions include J.B. Friedman, *The Monstrous Races in Medieval Art and Thought* (Cambridge, Mass., 1981); C.K. Zacher, *Curiosity and Pilgrimage: the Literature of Discovery in Fourteenth-century England* (Baltimore and London, 1976); V. Cassidy, *The Sea Around Them: the Atlantic Ocean, A.D. 1250* (Bâton Rouge, 1968); L. Bagrow, *History of Cartography*, revised by R.A. Skelton (London, 1964); M.W. Labarge, *Medieval Travellers: the Rich and Restless* (London, 1982); A. Mieli, *La science arabe et son role dans l'évolution scientifique mondiale* (Leiden, 1966); C.H. Haskins, *Studies in the History of Medieval Science* (Cambridge, Mass., 1927); N. Daniel, *The Arabs and Mediaeval Europe* (Beirut and London, 1975); L. Olschki, *Marco Polo's Asia* (Berkeley and Los Angeles, 1960); G. Cary, *The Medieval Alexander* (Cambridge, Mass., 1956); P. Noble, L. Polak, and C. Isoz (eds.), *The Medieval Alexander Legend and Romance Epic* (London, 1982); J. Taylor, *The Universal Chronicle of*

Ranulf Higden (Oxford, 1966); D. F. Lach, *Asia in the Making of Europe* (Chicago and London, 1965).

On the complex question of the Prester John letter see the two articles by C. F. Beckingham, 'The achievements of Prester John' and 'The quest for Prester John', in Beckingham, *Between Islam and Christendom: Travellers, Facts, Legends in the Middle Ages and the Renaissance* (London, 1983); V. Slessarev, *Prester John, the Letter and the Legend* (Minneapolis, 1959). The possibility that the *Letter* might have originated in twelfth-century Germany as an item in the propaganda battle between empire and papacy is argued in the important new paper by B. Hamilton, 'Prester John and the Three Kings of Cologne', in H. Mayr-Harting and R. I. Moore (eds.), *Studies in Medieval History presented to R. H. C. Davis* (London, 1985).

Among the many editions of and writings on *Mandeville's Travels* see, for example, G. F. Warner (ed.), *The Buke of John Maundevill*, Roxburghe Club (London, 1889); M. Letts (ed.), *Mandeville's Travels*, Hakluyt Society, second series, ci, 1950 (London, 1953); M. C. Seymour (ed.), *Mandeville's Travels* (Oxford, 1967); C. W. R. D. Moseley (ed.), *The Travels of Sir John Mandeville* (London, 1983); J . W. Bennett, *The Rediscovery of Sir John Mandeville* (New York, 1954).

Apart from obvious works such as those recounting the travels of Marco Polo, and the alleged travels of Mandeville, there are many original sources which have a bearing, in part or in whole, on the subject of geographical ideas. The following are just a few of those that might be consulted: S. Rypin (ed.)., *Three Old English Prose Texts*, Early English Text Society, clxi (London, 1924: for 1921)—this includes the *Letter of Alexander the Great to Aristotle*, and *The Wonders of the East*); C. C. Mierow (ed.), *The Two Cities: a Chronicle of World History to the Year 1146 A. D.*, by Otto Bishop of Freising (New York, 1928; reprinted New York, 1966); Roger Bacon, *The Opus Maius*, tr. R. B. Burke, 2 vols. (New York, 1928; repr. New York, 1962); C. Dawson (ed.), *The Mission to Asia* (also published as *The Mongol Mission*) (London, 1955 and 1980; Toronto, 1986); H. Yule (ed.), *Friar Jordanus, Mirabilia Descripta: the Wonders of the East*, Hakluyt Society, xxxi, 1863 (London, 1863); H. Yule (ed.), *Cathay and the Way Thither*, 4 vols., Hakluyt Society (London, 1913–16); C. Markham (ed.), *The Book of the Knowledge of all the Kingdoms, etc., by a Spanish Franciscan*, Hakluyt Society, second series, xxix, 1912 (London, 1912); *Polychronicon of Ranulph Higden*, i, ed. C. Babington and J. R. Lumby, Rolls Series (London, 1865); G. W. Coopland (ed.), *Philippe de Mézières, Letter to King Richard II* (Liverpool, 1975); id. (ed.), *Philippe de Mézières, Songe d'un Vieil Pèlerin*, 2 vols. (Cambridge, 1969); N. Levtzion and J.P. Hopkins (eds.), *Corpus of Early Arabic Sources for West African History* (Cambridge, 1981); O.H. Prior (ed.), *Caxton's Mirrour of the World*, Early English Text Society, cx, 1912 (London, 1913); E.T. Hamy (ed.), *Gilles le Bouvier, dit Berry, Le livre de la description des pays* (Paris, 1908).

Chapter 11: Geography in the fifteenth century
There is no sharp and sudden division between the ideas of the fifteenth and earlier centuries, so that many of the works already cited are still relevant. See especially G.H.T. Kimble, *Geography in the Middle Ages*, and the very stimulating essay by W. Oakeshott, 'Some classical and medieval ideas in Renaissance cosmography'. Also important are D. Hay, *Europe: the Emergence of an Idea* (Edinburgh, 1957; repr. New York, 1966); N. Broc, *La géographie de la Renaissance, 1420–1520* (Paris, 1980). A valuable guide to the stages by which earlier scientific learning in general, not simply on geography, was made available is M.B. Stillwell, *The Awakening Interest in Science during the First Century of Printing, 1450–1550: an Annotated Checklist of First Editions* (New York, 1970). There is also a very lucid treatment of scientific ideas in C.A. Ronan, *The Cambridge Illustrated History of the World's Science* (Cambridge, 1983). Important articles include C.M. Gormley, M.A. Rouse, and R.H. Rouse, 'The medieval circulation of the *De Chorographia* of Pomponius Mela', *Mediaeval Studies*, xlvi (1984); Th. Goldstein, 'Geography in fifteenth-century Florence', in J. Parker (ed.), *Merchants and Scholars: Essays in the History of Exploration and Trade* (Minneapolis, 1965).

On the history of navigation, and in particular on that of the mariner's compass see especially E.G.R. Taylor, *The Haven-Finding Art* (London, 1958); R.W. Unger, *The Ship in the Medieval Economy, 600–1600* (London and Montreal, 1980); D.W. Waters, 'Science and the techniques of navigation in the Renaissance', in C.S. Singleton (ed.), *Art, Science and History in the Renaissance* (Baltimore, 1967), also published by the National Maritime Museum, Greenwich, as *Maritime Monographs and Reports*, no. 19 (London, 1974); F.C. Lane, 'The economic meaning of the invention of the compass', in id., *Venice in History* (Baltimore and London, 1966); B.M. Kreutz, 'The Mediterranean contribution to the medieval mariner's compass', *Technology and Culture*, xiv (1973).

On the history of cartography the best short introduction is G.R. Crone, *Maps and their Makers* (London, 1953, and later editions). See also L. Bagrow, *History of Cartography*, revised by R. A. Skelton (London, 1964); there is also a large amount of valuable material on the development of world maps in the introduction to the otherwise discredited *The Vinland Map and the Tartar Relation*, ed. R. A. Skelton, T. E. Marston, and G. D. Painter (New Haven, 1965); for a study which illuminates the development of portolan charts see T. J. Westropp, 'Early Italian maps of Ireland from 1300 to 1600', *Proceedings of the Royal Irish Academy*, xxx, Section C (Dublin, 1912–13). Catalogues and reproductions of medieval *mappae mundi*, portolan charts, and world maps are to be found in such works as M. Destombes (ed.), *Mappemondes, A. D. 1200–1500* (Amsterdam, 1964); A. E. Nordenskiöld, *Facsimile-Atlas to the Early History of Cartography* (Stockholm, 1889; reprinted New York, 1973); A. Z. Cortesão and A. Teixeira da Mota (ed.), *Portugaliae Monumenta Cartographica*, 4 vols. (Lisbon, 1960); D. B. Durand, *The Vienna-Klosterneuburg Map Corpus of the Fifteenth Century* (Leiden, 1952); and the very important volume of colour reproductions of marine charts from the *Carte Pisane* onwards, edited with valuable descriptive notes by M. de la Roncière and M. Mollat du Jourdin, *Les portulans: cartes marines du XIIIe au XVIIe siècle* (Fribourg, 1984).

V

The fifteenth-century expansion of Europe

Chapter 12: Fresh start or new phase?

For a guide to the most important of the many books on the fifteenth-century expansion of Europe see the bibliography to the Introduction of this book. Special attention may be drawn to the works of J. H. Parry, particularly his last major study in the field, *The Discovery of the Sea* (Berkeley, Los Angeles, and London, 1981). The evidence for a possible sighting of the shores of Australia by the Portuguese is discussed by O. H. K. Spate in his book *Let Me Enjoy: Essays partly Geographical* (Canberra, 1965). In addition to the books given in the Introduction, material on the Portuguese exploration of the coast of West Africa and the opening of the route to India may be found in C. R. Boxer, *The Portuguese Seaborne Empire, 1415–1825* (London, 1969); G. R. Crone, *The Discovery of the East* (London, 1972); B. W. Diffie and G. D. Winius, *The Foundations of the Portuguese Empire, 1415–1580* (Minneapolis, 1977). Prince Henry of Portugal is discussed in all of these, but among older studies of his career see, for example, R. H. Major, *The Life of Prince Henry of Portugal* (London, 1868; repr.

London, 1967); C. R. Beazley, *Prince Henry the Navigator* (London, 1901; repr. London, 1968). A reassessment of his activities may be found in B. W. Diffie and G. D. Winius, op. cit.; E. Axelson, 'Prince Henry the Navigator and the discovery of the sea route to India', *Geographical Journal*, cxxvii (1961); P. E. Russell, 'Prince Henry the Navigator', Canning House Seventh Annual Lecture 1960, published by the Hispanic and Luso-Brazilian Councils, London, in *Diamante*, xi (1960). An enormous amount of material on Prince Henry, and on Portuguese overseas expansion in general, was published in Lisbon in and around 1960 as part of the celebrations of the fifth centenary of Henry's death. Unfortunately most of this is available only in specialized libraries and cannot be obtained either by library purchase or through inter-library loan. One important Portuguese work that is readily available, however, is V. Magalhães-Godinho, *L'économie de l'empire Portugais aux XVe et XVIe siècles* (Paris, 1969).

The medieval precedents for Portuguese involvement in Africa, and the development of shipping resources, are well studied in B. W. Diffie and G. D. Winius, op. cit., and in B. W. Diffie, *Prelude to Empire: Portugal Overseas before Henry the Navigator* (Lincoln, Nebraska, 1960). On the analogies between medieval European colonial activities and those of the fifteenth century and later see especially C. Verlinden, *The Beginnings of Modern Colonization* (Ithaca and London, 1970) and id., *Précédents médiévaux de la colonie en Amérique* (Mexico City, 1954).

On shipping and navigation see the items listed under Chapter 11, especially E. G. R. Taylor, *The Haven-Finding Art*; R. W. Unger's very important book, *The Ship in the Medieval Economy*; and D. W. Waters, 'Science and the techniques of navigation in the Renaissance' in Singleton, *Art, Science and History*. See also J. H. Parry, *The Discovery of the Sea*; A. R. Lewis and T. J. Runyan, *European Naval and Maritime History, 300–1500* (Bloomington, 1985); M. E. Mallett, *The Florentine Galleys in the Fifteenth Century* (Oxford, 1967); B. Landström, *Sailing Ships* (London, 1969); G. F. Bass (ed.), *A History of Seafaring* (London, 1972); B. M. Kreutz, 'Ships and shipping and the implications of change in the early medieval Mediterranean', *Viator*, viii (1976); D. W. Waters, *The Rutters of the Sea: The Sailing Directions of Pierre Garcie* (New Haven and London, 1967); E. Poulle, 'Les sources astronomiques (textes, tables, instruments), *Typologie des sources du moyen âge occidental*, fascicle xxxix (Turnhout, 1981); M. Mollat (ed.), *Le Navire et l'Economie Maritime du XVe au XVIIIe siècles* (Paris, 1957); id., *Le Navire et l'Economie Maritime du moyen âge au XVIIIe siècle principal-*

ement en Méditerranée (Paris, 1958)—these contain the proceedings of the first and second *Colloque International d'histoire maritime*; *The Planispheric Astrolabe*, by members of the staff of the National Maritime Museum (Greenwich, 1976); R.T. Gould, *John Harrison and his Timekeepers*, National Maritime Museum (Greenwich, 1958); G.R. Tibbetts, *Arab Navigation in the Indian Ocean before the Coming of the Portuguese*, Royal Asiatic Society (London, 1971); M. Mollat and P. Adam (eds.), *Les Aspects Internationaux de la Découverte Océanique*, Proccedings of the fifth *Colloque International d'histoire maritime* (Paris, 1966).

On Portuguese voyaging and discoveries in the Atlantic before the fifteenth century see the bibliography to Chapter 8. On the controversies surrounding Portuguese Atlantic voyaging in the fifteenth century itself, and on the 'policy of silence' see, for example, J. Cortesão, 'The pre-Columbian discovery of America', *Geographical Journal*, lxxxix (1937); G.R. Crone, 'The alleged pre-Columbian discovery of America', loc. cit.; A. Cortesão, 'The North Atlantic nautical chart of 1424', *Imago Mundi*, x (1953). The mythical islands of the Atlantic are discussed in a number of the books on European knowledge of the Atlantic which are cited in the bibliography to Chapter 9, but see also: T.J. Westropp, 'Brasil and the legendary islands of the North Atlantic', *Proceedings of the Royal Irish Academy*, xxx, section C (1912–13); G.E. Buker, 'The seven cities: the role of a myth on the exploration of the Atlantic', *The American Neptune*, xxx (1970).

There are many studies of the background to, and the history of, the discovery of America in the fifteenth century, dealing with the familiar story of Columbus, and also with less familiar aspects such as the Bristol voyages in search of the island of Brasil. See especially G.R. Crone, *The Discovery of America* (London, 1969); J.H. Parry, *The Discovery of the Sea*; S.E. Morison, *The European Discovery of America: The Northern Voyages* (New York, 1971), and id., *The European Discovery of America; The Southern Voyages* (New York, 1974); D.B. Quinn, *North America from Earliest Discovery to First Settlements: the Norse Voyages to 1612* (New York, 1977); id., *England and the Discovery of America, 1481–1620* (London, 1973); K.R. Andrews, *Trade, Plunder and Settlement: Maritime Enterprise and the Genesis of the British Empire, 1481–1630* (London, 1984); C. Verlinden, *The Beginnings of Modern Colonization* (Ithaca and London, 1970); M. Mollat (ed.), *Les Routes de l'Atlantique*, Proceedings of the ninth *Colloque International d'histoire maritime* (Paris, 1969); *La Découverte de l'Amérique, De Petrarque à Descartes*, xviii, directeur P. Mesnard (Paris, 1968).

The works listed above contain a great deal of material on the career of Columbus. Despite the immense amount of research that has been undertaken, many of the details still remain controversial, but see, for example, S. E. Morison, *Admiral of the Ocean Sea: A Life of Christopher Columbus* (Boston, 1942). A recent study of Columbus's motivations is P. M. Watts, 'Prophecy and discovery: on the spiritual origins of Christopher Columbus's "Enterprise of the Indies" ', *American Historical Review*, xc (1985). The continuing debate over where Columbus first landed in 1492 is well illustrated in J. Judge, 'Our search for the true Columbus landfall', *National Geographic*, clxx (1986), and in the counter-arguments which this swiftly produced: see *1992: A Columbus Newsletter*, no. 6, Spring 1987, John Carter Brown Library (Providence, Rhode Island). This news-letter is an invaluable guide to the many conferences, publications, and other celebrations which are being planned for 1992.

On the relations of English and other sailors with Iceland and possibly with Greenland in the fifteenth century, and on the controversial subject of the Bristol voyages in the Atlantic *circa* 1480 see, for example, E. M. Carus-Wilson, *Medieval Merchant Ventures* (London, 1954), D. B. Quinn, *England and the Discovery of America, 1481–1620* (London, 1974), which also has references to the extensive literature on the subject, and J. A. Williamson (ed.), *The Cabot Voyages and Bristol Discovery under Henry VII*, Hakluyt Society, second series, cxx (Cambridge, 1962).

On the history of the crusades and crusading projects in the fourteenth and fifteenth centuries see A. S. Atiya, *The Crusades in the Later Middle Ages* (London, 1938; second edn. New York, 1970) and J. F. Verbruggen, *The Art of Warfare in Western Europe during the Middle Ages* (Amsterdam, 1977). More recent work on the subject may be found in N. Housley, *The Avignon Papacy and the Crusade, 1305–1378* (Oxford, 1986); S. Schein, 'The future *regnum Hierusalem*. A chapter in medieval state planning', *Journal of Medieval History*, x (1984); C. J. Tyerman, 'Marino Sanudo Torsello and the lost crusade: lobbying in the fourteenth century', *Transactions of the Royal Historical Society*, fifth series, xxxii (1982); id., 'Sed nihil fecit? The last Capetians and the recovery of the Holy Land', in J. Gillingham and J. C. Holt (eds.), *War and Government in the Middle Ages*, (Woodbridge and Totowa, 1984). The standard work on Mediterranean trade in this period is now E. Ashtor, *The Levant Trade in the Later Middle Ages* (Princeton, 1983).

The interest in the East on the part of European states which was provoked by the legend of Prester John and the hope of an alliance with eastern Christians is well illustrated in F.M. Rogers, *The Quest for Eastern Christians: Travels and Rumour in the Age of Discovery* (Minneapolis, 1962), and id., *The Travels of the Infante Dom Pedro of Portugal* (Cambridge, Mass., 1961). On the 1487 mission of Pero da Covilhã see especially C.F. Beckingham, *Between Islam and Christendom* (London, 1983).

Among the many original sources for the fifteenth-century expansion of Europe see, for example, the following, all publications of the Hakluyt Society: O.G.S. Crawford (ed.), *Ethiopian Itineraries, circa 1400–1524*, second series, cix 1955 (Cambridge, 1958); C.R. Markham (ed.), *Narrative of the Embassy of Ruy Gonzalez de Clavijo to the Court of Timour at Samarcand, A.D. 1403–6*, first series, xc (London, 1894; repr. New York, n.d.); J.B. Telfer (ed.), *The Bondage and Travels of Johann Schiltberger, a Native of Bavaria, in Europe, Asia and Africa, 1396–1427*, first series, lviii (London, 1879; repr. New York, 1970); Lord Stanley of Alderley (ed.), *Travels to Tana and Persia by Josafa Barbaro and Ambrogio Contarini*, first series, xlix (London, 1873; repr. New York, n.d.); C.R. Beazley and E. Prestage (eds.), *The Chronicle of the Discovery and Conquest of Guinea written by Gomes Eannes de Azurara*, first series, c (London, 1899; repr. New York, n.d.); J.W. Blake (ed.), *Europeans in West Africa, 1450–1560*, second series, lxxxvi, 1941 (London, 1942; repr. Nendeln, 1967); G.H.T. Kimble (ed.), *Esmeraldo de Situ Orbis by Duarte Pacheco Pereira*, second series, lxxix (London, 1937; repr. Nendeln, 1967); C.R. Markham (ed.), *The Journal of Christopher Columbus during his First Voyage, 1492–93, and Documents relating to the Voyages of John Cabot and Gaspar Corte Real*, first series, lxxxvi (London, 1893; repr. New York, 1971); H.E.J. Stanley (ed.), *The Three Voyages of Vasco da Gama and his Viceroyalty*, first series, xlii (London, 1869; repr. New York, n.d.); C.R. Markham (ed.), *The Letters of Amerigo Vespucci*, first series, xc (London, 1894; repr. New York, n.d.); R.H. Major (ed.), *India in the Fifteenth Century*, first series, xxii (London, 1857; repr. New York, 1970).

Chapter 13: Conclusion

The impact of the fifteenth- and sixteenth-century discoveries both upon Europe itself and the regions with which Europeans had contact is largely outside the scope of this book, and is in any case a massive topic which is still very much under debate by specialists in the field. There are, however, several publications which give a good impression of the problems. See especially J.H. Elliott's important study, *The Old World and* the New, 1492–1650 (Cambridge, 1970); D. Hay, *Europe: the Emergence of an Idea* (Edinburgh, 1957); F. Chiappelli (ed.), *First Images of America: the Impact of the New World on the Old*, 2 vols. (Berkeley, Los Angeles, and London, 1976); W. E. Washburn, 'The meaning of "discovery" in the fifteenth and sixteenth centuries', *American Historical Review*, lxviii (1962–3); G. V. Scammell, 'The new worlds and Europe in the sixteenth century', *The Historical Journal*, xii (1969); id., 'The great age of discovery, 1400–1650', Hakluyt Society Presidential Address, 1981. See also V. Magalhães-Godinho, *L'économie de l'empire portugais aux XVe et XVIe siècles* (Paris, 1969); A. A. B. de Andrade, *Mundos Novos do Mundo* (Lisbon, 1972). On the survival of many of the monstrous races and other wonders see, for example, J. B. Friedman, *The Monstrous Races in Medieval Art and Thought* (Cambridge, Mass., 1981); V. I. J. Flint, 'Monsters and the antipodes in the early middle ages and enlightenment', *Viator*, xv (1984). Many of the general works cited in the bibliography to the Introduction of this book are also relevant.

Index